D1564538

Kuo Mo-jo

HARVARD EAST ASIAN SERIES 55

The East Asian Research Center at Harvard University administers research projects designed to further scholarly understanding of China, Japan, Korea, Vietnam, and adjacent areas.

Kuo Mo-jo

The Early Years

DAVID TOD ROY

HARVARD UNIVERSITY PRESS

Cambridge, Massachusetts

1971

0496904

98108

© Copyright 1971 by the
President and Fellows of Harvard College

All rights reserved

Distributed in Great Britain
by Oxford University Press, London

Preparation of this volume has been aided by
a grant from the Ford Foundation.

Library of Congress Catalog Card Number 77–123569
SBN 674–50570–0

Printed in the United States of America

To my father and mother,
Andrew Tod Roy and Margaret Crutchfield Roy,
to whom I owe, in addition to everything else,
my interest in China.

Acknowledgments

The topic of this book first suggested itself to me in the spring of 1956 when I chanced upon a volume of Kuo Mo-jo's autobiography in the home of Joan Hsü, a Chinese friend in New York. That summer I returned to Harvard after a three-year absence and resumed my undergraduate studies in the Department of History. In the spring of 1957 Professor John K. Fairbank approved this subject as a suitable topic for my undergraduate dissertation and made it possible for me to pursue research during my senior year under the tutorial direction of Professor Benjamin I. Schwartz. Thus from its very inception this book has owed its existence to the encouragement and continuing interest of these two scholars and teachers nonpareil.

I owe a special debt of gratitude to the former Librarian of the Chinese-Japanese Library of the Harvard-Yenching Institute, Alfred Kaiming Chiu, and to his successor, Eugene Wu, both of whom have rendered me invaluable assistance which was invariably not only gracious but enthusiastic. I am also indebted for much scarce source material to the indefatigable efforts of my book dealer in Hong Kong, Mr. Lau Siew-Sing.

Among those too numerous to mention who have helped me in one way or another I am especially grateful for the assistance of the following persons: Chan Hok-lam, Cheng Ch'ing-mao, Lloyd Eastman, James J. Freeman, James

Robert Hightower, Roy Hofheinz, Akira Iriye, Harold L. Kahn, Kao Yu-kung, Cornelius J. Kiley, Donald Klein, Philip Kuhn, James T. C. Liu, Sidney Liu, Edwin O. Reischauer, Barbara Chew Roy, Ezra Vogel, Lili Wang, C. Martin Wilbur, and Yang Lien-sheng.

At various stages of the research and writing of this book I have received financial support from the Ford Foundation, the Society of Fellows, and the East Asian Research Center at Harvard University, to all of which I tender my sincere thanks.

Though this book could not have come into being without the assistance and encouragement of the above people and institutions, the author alone is responsible for its inadequacies.

David T. Roy

Chicago, June 23, 1970

Contents

0496904

98108

Introduction

Kuo Mo-jo is possibly the most versatile Chinese intellectual of our day. There is hardly an area of twentieth-century Chinese cultural life in which his influence has not been felt. He is one of the most prolific writers and scholars of modern times, and, although the quality of his work is uneven, he has made substantial contributions in such diverse fields as poetry, drama, fiction, autobiography, translation, intellectual and cultural history, archeology, paleography, and cultural and political propaganda. So wide-ranging have his interests been that it is not as paradoxical as it might at first seem that the man who did more than any other to introduce Western romanticism and modern poetry to China should end his career as president of the Chinese Academy of Sciences.

Throughout the many vicissitudes and various interests of his long career his preoccupation with himself has remained a constant factor. His entire literary output is little more than an autobiography in a variety of modes, and even in his scholarly work his personal prejudices and private obsessions obtrude themselves at every turn. Unpleasant as this trait in his character often is, it is to it that we owe the fact that we have a more complete autobiographical record for Kuo Mo-jo than for any other Chinese figure who has ever lived. Taken together, these autobiographical writings of his constitute one of the most illuminating documents available to the student of modern China.

1

It is sometimes alleged that for a Chinese, especially one with any knowledge or understanding of his traditional culture, to become a communist is a contradiction in terms. Kuo Mo-jo was one of the first of the leading Chinese intellectuals to embrace Marxism-Leninism in the 1920's, and it was why he chose to do so that first interested me in the study of his career. I have come to the conclusion that this apparent alteration in his intellectual allegiance did not mark a sharp break, or even a significant discontinuity, in his development. Not only were there factors in his background and elements among his predilections which facilitated such a transition, but once the step was taken he continued to carry much of the intellectual baggage with which he started out.

It is, perhaps, too early to say to what extent Kuo Mo-jo's reactions to Western culture, China's problems, and Marxism-Leninism are representative. But even if the story of the formative years in his life is read as an isolated case history, I believe that it is not only interesting in itself, but throws light on many aspects of the transitional period through which he lived.

Kuo Mo-jo was born, in 1892, into a nouveau riche family which had achieved a dominant position in its own village and was trying to attain gentry status through the education of its sons. The lack of a long family tradition of office-holding in the framework of the traditional Confucian ideology may have made it easier for him to adjust to the new forces which were breaking down the old Chinese society than it was for many of his contemporaries. The changes in the examination system in the wake of the Boxer Rebellion, which began to take effect after he had undergone only four years of the traditional education, were the most potent factors in reorienting his outlook as a child. The brevity of his experience with the rigid old-

2

fashioned education and his early exposure to alien traditions in the new school system help to explain the comparative ease with which he assimilated new ideas, but until he went to Japan in 1914 he remained traditionally oriented.

The particular elements in the tradition to which Kuo Mo-jo was attracted proved significant. The unorthodox reformist and progressive theories of the New Text school, particularly those of Liao P'ing, and the pantheism, nature worship, and iconoclasm of *Chuang-tzu* were important factors in determining the Western writers to whom he felt attracted in his later career.

During his first four years in Japan his loneliness and depression led him to take an interest in mysticism and religion. He studied Buddhism and Christianity, steeped himself in the ideas of Wang Yang-ming, and began to take a greater interest in the philosophical content of *Chuang-tzu*. At the same time, as his command of English and German improved, he fell under the influence of Tagore and Goethe, in whose philosophical assumptions he found many affinities with *Chuang-tzu* and Wang Yang-ming.

As early as the summer of 1918 Kuo Mo-jo had visions of starting a magazine devoted entirely to literature. These dreams came to fruition with the founding of the Creation Society in 1921. During the intervening period he established himself as one of the most promising young writers in the new literary movement which had just begun to make its influence felt in the Chinese intellectual world. The chief impetus to this development was supplied by the works of Walt Whitman, which Kuo Mo-jo discovered in the autumn of 1919. It was the element of Whitmanism in his poetry which made it as successful as it was, and the influence of Whitman's ideas and attitudes was both profound and lasting. It seems to have been in emulation of

Whitman that he first turned his attention to the internal situation in China, calling for iconoclasm and revolution, and identifying himself with the common man. He later repudiated both Tagore and Goethe, but his general attitudes remain not unlike those of Whitman to the present day.

The period from 1921 to 1924 saw the rise and fall of the early Creation Society and Kuo Mo-jo's gradual transition from romanticism to Marxism-Leninism. His initial admiration for the figures of Marx and Lenin was a romantic one and there were elements in his romanticism which may have tended to facilitate his approach to Marxism-Leninism. It can, in fact, be demonstrated that there were certain strands of continuity between the Chinese tradition to which he was exposed in his youth, the romanticism which he espoused between 1918 and 1923, and the Marxism-Leninism of his post-1924 period.

In the autumn of 1923 the Creation Society began to show signs of an internal collapse which resulted in its temporary dissolution in the spring of 1924. Kuo Mo-jo felt himself, to some extent, personally responsible for this development and his feelings of anxiety were aggravated by serious domestic difficulties. His Japanese common-law wife finally left him and returned to Japan with his children in February 1924. This event reduced him to a state of mental and physical prostration, and during the next two months he narrowly escaped a nervous breakdown. By April, when he rejoined his family in Japan, he was ripe for a religious conversion.

In the summer of 1924 Kuo Mo-jo announced himself a convert to Marxism-Leninism, but his letters at the time and his subsequent conduct indicate that this did not mean an effective repudiation of his romantic ideals, which he had merely projected into the future. It was not the relative

4

validity of Marxism-Leninism as an economic theory that appealed to Kuo Mo-jo, who had little knowledge of economics in any case, but rather the apocalyptic vision of the world which it afforded. He felt that by becoming an adherent of this doctrine he could join forces with history and regain his sense of pride and responsibility as a participating member of an ancient culture with a badly bruised sense of self-esteem.

The development of Kuo Mo-jo's ideas and attitudes during the thirty-odd years of his life sketched above cannot be understood or explained solely in intellectual terms. There was no inevitable progression from one set of ideas to another determined by any internal logic, but rather a dialectical relationship between his ideas and the vicissitudes of his personal life and his larger social and political environment. Without reference to these elements in the picture, his intellectual development would remain incomprehensible.

Kuo Mo-jo's response to the events of this crucial transitional period in modern Chinese history does not represent an inevitable reaction. It is probably unsafe to generalize from Kuo Mo-jo's experience the way other Chinese intellectuals may have responded to the same events. If we desire a deeper understanding of the intellectual history of modern China, monographic studies of many more individuals are urgently required. The following case study of the road by which one sensitive young Chinese intellectual came to Marxism-Leninism is offered in the hope that it may make a contribution toward this end.

Chapter 1

Childhood in
Sha-wan, 1892–1905

About twenty-five miles southwest of the prefectural city of Chia-ting, in the southwestern corner of Szechwan province, there lies, on the banks of the Ta-tu River, a small market town of some 180 families called Sha-wan, or Sandy Cove.[1] It was here, on either November 10, or November 16, 1892, that Kuo Mo-jo was born. He does not remember which date is correct, but he does recall having been told that he came into the world between 11:00 A.M. and 1:00 P.M., and that he arrived feet first.[2]

Kuo Mo-jo's ancestors were originally Hakka inhabitants of Ning-hua hsien, in T'ing-chou fu, near the western border of Fukien province.[3] They had migrated to Szechwan during the second half of the seventeenth century,[4] at a time when that province was partially depopulated as a result of the bloodthirsty depredations of Chang Hsien-chung (c. 1605–1647), a famous rebel chieftain.[5] It was a legend in the family that their forefathers had come to Szechwan with nothing more in the way of worldly goods than they could carry on their backs.[6]

It was not until the time of Kuo Mo-jo's great-grandfather Kuo Hsien-lin[7] that the fortunes of the family began to improve. He accumulated considerable wealth, although Kuo Mo-jo does not know how it was acquired.[8] Judging from the poverty of his ancestors and the careers of his

7

immediate descendants, it must have been gained through some kind of mercantile pursuit. He had one son by his first wife, who died soon afterwards, and three sons and nine daughters by his second.[9]

This second wife of Kuo Hsien-lin's, whose maiden name was Ch'iu, was Kuo Mo-jo's great-grandmother. She must have been a remarkable woman, for, in addition to giving birth to twelve children, she lived to be a hundred and two years old.[10] When she reached the age of a hundred, in 1902,[11] an imposing memorial arch was erected in her honor at public expense. Kuo Mo-jo, who was about ten years old at the time, remembers this event vividly. Spanning the main road into the village from the north, this arch formed, in effect, the gateway to Sha-wan[12] and must have greatly enhanced the prestige of the Kuo family. It is recorded in the local gazetteer that this matriarch lived to see five generations of her family living under one roof.[13] In the traditional Chinese value system, life could provide no greater happiness than this, and the good fortune of the Kuo clan must have been envied throughout the entire prefecture.

It was during the lifetime of Kuo Mo-jo's grandfather, the second of Kuo Hsien-lin's four sons, that the influence of the family really became established. Together with his youngest brother, he gained control of the waterfront at Sha-wan and became a boss in the river shipping business. This made him an important person in the transportation industry of that whole area of the province.[14] He was a magnanimous person, not unlike the heroes of Chinese popular romance, and was nicknamed the Diamond Buddha.[15] From his time on, the Kuo clan constituted the single most influential kinship group in Sha-wan; but it was only after it had become thus firmly established that its members began to go to school.[16]

Kuo Mo-jo's father (1854–1939), one of whose names may have been Kuo Ming-hsing,[17] was a third son, and because of his father's improvident magnanimity he could not afford to continue his schooling beyond the age of thirteen. At that point in his career he was put to work as an apprentice in a salt well, but was recalled by his father after only six months and placed in charge of the business affairs of the family. He turned out to be a remarkably successful businessman. By dealing in oils, opium, distilled spirits, and grain, and by engaging in money changing, he was soon able to increase substantially the family's holdings in farm lands, real estate, buildings, and salt wells.[18] Although formally uneducated, he had a quick natural intelligence, which is demonstrated not only by his success in business but by the fact that he taught himself traditional Chinese medicine well enough to achieve a local reputation as an amateur doctor.[19]

Kuo Mo-jo's mother came from a very different sort of background. Her father, Tu Cho-chang, became a *chin-shih,* or metropolitan graduate, the highest degree conferred through the civil service examination system, in the special examinations held through imperial favor in 1852. This was a major distinction. During the entire Ch'ing dynasty (1644–1912) this coveted goal was achieved by only ten men from the prefecture of Chia-ting, of whom Tu Cho-chang was the last.[20] During the years immediately following, he held several official posts in Kweichow province.[21]

In 1858, the year Kuo Mo-jo's mother (1858–1932) was born,[22] there was a rebellion of the Miao tribes in Kweichow. Tu Cho-chang was the acting magistrate of Huang-p'ing chou, in the eastern part of the province, when, on the night of December 5, 1858,[23] the city was attacked by surprise. Most of the local militia were away on a mission

9

and the city was virtually defenseless.[24] Leading the remnants of the militia, Tu Cho-chang engaged the attackers in combat and was wounded. Making his way back to the yamen, he slit the throats of his three-year-old and six-year-old daughters[25] and persuaded his concubine, née Shih, Kuo Mo-jo's maternal grandmother, to commit suicide.[26] Then, with sword in hand, he went to the door and fought off the attackers until he was overwhelmed and killed.[27]

A memorial reporting Tu Cho-chang's heroic conduct was received at court on January 3, 1859. The same day, the emperor issued an edict commanding that Tu Cho-chang be posthumously awarded the distinctions due a department magistrate who had died in combat and that his concubine, née Shih, and their two daughters should be granted posthumous insignia of merit.[28] His eldest son, Tu K'ai-ch'eng, was granted the hereditary rank of *yün ch'i wei.*[29]

Kuo Mo-jo's mother, who was less than a year old when these events occurred, was rescued by a woman named Liu who was her wet nurse. This faithful servant, carrying her infant charge on her back, tried to sneak through the rebel lines, but was captured and stripped naked before being allowed to continue. Eventually she made her way to Kweiyang, the provincial capital, and later to Kunming, the capital of the adjacent province of Yunnan. In both places she supported herself and her young charge by working as a kitchen maid. It was not until several years later, when Tu K'ai-ch'eng passed through Kunming on his way to Huang-p'ing chou to bring his father's coffin home for burial, that Kuo Mo-jo's mother and her wet nurse were able to return to Szechwan.[30]

His mother spent the rest of her childhood in the ancestral home of her father's family, the village of Tu-chia ch'ang, several miles south of the prefectural city of Chia-ting.[31] She married into the Kuo family in 1872, when she was only fourteen years old by Western reckoning.[32] The match could not have been considered a very good one for the daughter of an official, but her father was dead and the family into which she married had considerable wealth and good prospects.[33]

Twenty years later, in 1892, when she was thirty-four years old, Mrs. Kuo gave birth to her eighth child. This was Kuo Mo-jo. Since two of his sisters and one of his brothers had died before he was born, he found himself the fifth child in a family which later grew to include eight. By the time he left home to go to school, he had two elder brothers, two elder sisters, one younger brother, and two younger sisters.[34]

The formal name given to Kuo Mo-jo by his parents was Kuo K'ai-chen. He did not adopt the name by which he is now known until he was a student in Japan more than twenty years later.[35] His mother claimed that on the night he was conceived she dreamed that a young leopard suddenly appeared before her and bit her between the thumb and forefinger of her left hand. Because of this dream Kuo Mo-jo was given the childhood name Wen-pao, or Cultivated Leopard.[36] It would not have been an inappropriate name for him as an adult.

It is clear from the divergent family backgrounds of his parents that Kuo Mo-jo must have become aware, from a very early period, of the two different methods of seeking power and prestige that they represented. His father's family had achieved its status by the gradual accumulation of economic power, with its corollary of local political influence, through association with the secret societies. The position of his maternal grandfather, on the other hand, had been achieved by the more arduous and uncertain, but more respectable and potentially more lucrative, pursuit

11

of status through the traditional examination system. Kuo Mo-jo was acutely conscious of the differences between the value systems represented by the family histories of his father and his mother and has often revealed an ambivalent attitude toward both of them.[37]

In China, as elsewhere, after a family has achieved wealth and local influence, the next step is usually an effort to secure greater social prestige. In the Chinese interior, even in the last decades of the nineteenth century, the only recognized route to high social standing was success in the imperial civil service examinations. Thus in 1886, half a dozen years before Kuo Mo-jo was born,[38] his family had engaged a private tutor, named Shen Huan-chang, to teach the sons of the household in a family school.[39] If this extra expense resulted in the production of even one *hsiu-ts'ai,* or "cultivated talent," the popular designation of a holder of the lowest degree in the examination system, it would prove to be money well spent, for the social prestige and financial prospects of the family would rise accordingly.

At the age of four and a half Kuo Mo-jo began formal study in the family school. This was earlier than usual, but it was at his own request. Even before he started school his mother had taught him to memorize many simple T'ang dynasty (618–907) poems. He also liked to listen to his elder brother reciting his lessons at night and found that he could remember them better than his brother could after hearing them repeated a few times. Thinking that school would be both pleasant and easy, he had little difficulty in persuading his parents, who were already impressed by his feats of memory, to let him attend. He soon found that he had made a serious miscalculation; but, since he had taken the initiative himself, his parents refused to let him drop out. Thus, in the spring of 1897, he began the traditional education, which was designed primarily to prepare him for the civil service examinations.[40]

The first book Kuo Mo-jo read was the *San tzu ching*, or *Trimetrical Classic*, as it is usually translated — a metrical compendium of conventional morals, instructive anecdotes, historical facts, and so forth, which was traditionally used as a primer.[41] After that, he moved directly on to the standard Confucian classics, including the *I ching*, or *Book of Changes*,[42] the *Shu ching*, or *Book of Documents*,[43] the *Shih ching*, or *Book of Songs*,[44] the *Ch'un-ch'iu*, or *Spring and Autumn Annals*,[45] the *Chou li*, or *Rituals of Chou*,[46] and the *I li*, or *Book of Etiquette and Ceremonial*.[47] The dating and authenticity of these books are much debated questions, but it is probably safe to say that at least parts of all of them date from the third century B.C. or earlier. They constitute some of the most difficult texts in the classical Chinese language and were not fully understood by beginning students, who were made to memorize them by rote. Along with the classics Kuo Mo-jo read the *Ku-wen kuan-chih*,[48] a famous seventeenth-century anthology of classical Chinese prose literature.[49]

Kuo Mo-jo's only respite from this rather deadly traditional curriculum was poetry, which he was required to read not for enjoyment, but because he would someday be expected to produce correct specimens of its various forms in the examinations. Nevertheless he found the poems in the popular anthologies easier to understand than the classics and enjoyed them accordingly. He read the *Ch'ien chia shih*,[50] an anthology of T'ang and Sung poetry for beginners, the *T'ang shih san-pai shou*,[51] or *Three Hundred Poems of the T'ang Dynasty*, the *T'ang shih cheng sheng*,[52] another popular anthology of T'ang poetry, and the *Shih p'in*,[53] or *Characterizations of Poetry*, by Ssu-k'ung

13

T'u (837–908), a famous ninth-century work of literary criticism which is itself a poem.[54] He particularly enjoyed the poetry of Wang Wei (699–759), Meng Hao-jan (689–740), Li Po (701–762), and Liu Tsung-yüan (773–819), but disliked that of Tu Fu (712–770) and especially that of Han Yü (768–824).[55] It is perhaps significant that the first four of these poets are famous for their lyric descriptions of nature and the last two are noted for their strict observance of the rules of prosody and their difficulty.

School was not a very pleasant place for Chinese boys in those days. In addition to the heavy load of sheer memorization that pupils were made to bear, they were also subjected to severe corporal punishment. A Chinese proverb states that "Unbeaten, no boy will ever make a man; but, by beating, he may be made into an official." [56] Since the purpose of education was the production of officials, the rod was seldom spared, and Kuo Mo-jo was subjected to it in all its rigors. The thing that upset him the most was the formality with which he was required to take down his own trousers and lie over a bench placed directly in front of the tablet erected in honor of Confucius, so that the father of Chinese education himself might the better witness his pain and humiliation.[57]

One of the pleasanter memories which Kuo Mo-jo retains from this early period of his schooling is the ghost stories he heard from his maternal uncle Tu K'ai-ch'eng. This uncle was a strange man with serious mental problems, who was quite superstitious and believed in the existence of ghosts. In the evenings, when Kuo Mo-jo and his fellow students were through with school for the day, they loved to seek him out and persuade him to regale them with tales of the supernatural, which he culled for the most part from Yüan Mei's (1716–1798) *Tzu pu yü,*[58] or *Things the Master [i.e., Confucius] Did Not Speak Of,* and the

Yüeh-wei ts'ao-t'ang pi-chi, or *Jottings from the Hut of a Scrutinizer of Trifles,* by Chi Yün (1724–1805).[59] Tu K'ai-ch'eng retold these stories so effectively that Kuo Mo-jo's hair stood on end, and he could never hear enough of them.[60]

The first significant change in the traditional educational curriculum that Kuo Mo-jo had been following came as a direct result of the Boxer Uprising of 1900. Although the Empress Dowager had quashed the reform movement after the famous Hundred Days of 1898, the humiliation of foreign intervention in 1900 led her to see the necessity for reform. On August 29, 1901, an edict was issued ordering the abolition of the stultifying eight-legged essay, previously required for all examinations, and its replacement with themes on China's political history, the arts and politics of foreign countries, and the exegesis of the classics.[61] Since education in China was largely a matter of preparation for the examinations, this step necessitated immediate changes in the curriculum all over the country. Heretofore Kuo Mo-jo had studied nothing but the classics and a little poetry, but now it became necessary for him to learn something of world affairs and to gain an elementary knowledge of the sciences. As a result of these changes in emphasis he read two works, entitled *Ti-ch'iu yün-yen,* or *The Globe in Rhyme,* and *Shih chien chieh-yao,* or *Synopsis of History,* which were written in rhymed lines of four characters each, to make the contents easier to memorize.[62]

This revolution in education was not without its humorous aspects. Kuo Mo-jo's family tutor, Shen Huan-chang, acquired an elementary mathematics textbook which had been translated from the English under the auspices of a missionary society and conscientiously mastered its contents. He then painstakingly taught his students to write

15

the Arabic numerals in their printed form, since neither he nor they had ever had an opportunity to see them written in any other way.[63]

Even in the field of traditional Chinese studies the imperial edicts on education produced a change of emphasis in the family school. Every day Kuo Mo-jo had to read and punctuate a section of the *Yü-p'i t'ung-chien chi-lan,* a chronological outline of Chinese history from the reign of the legendary Yellow Emperor through the end of the Ming dynasty (1368–1644), which was annotated by the Ch'ien-lung Emperor (r. 1736–1795) after it was compiled by his order in 1767.[64] During the same period his teacher had him read the *Tso chuan,*[65] or *Tso's Commentary on the "Spring and Autumn Annals,"* in conjunction with Lü Tsu-ch'ien's (1137–1181) *Tung-lai Tso-shih po-i,* a critique of selected passages from the above work. This exercise in comparative scholarship gave Kuo Mo-jo his first interest in textual criticism.[66]

Another result of the changes in the examination system was the revival, in the Chia-ting area, of interest in the techniques of the School of Empirical Research, which had flourished in the eighteenth and early nineteenth centuries.[67] Shen Huan-chang was not very well versed in this field, but there was an older member of the Kuo clan, named Kuo Chao-hsiu, who was. He had studied under the famous scholar Wang K'ai-yün (1833–1916) at the Tsun-ching Academy in Chengtu, the provincial capital, and was then teaching school in the village of Liu-hua ch'i, some seven miles south of Chia-ting.[68] Kuo Mo-jo's oldest brother, Kuo K'ai-wen (1877–1936), had gone there to study under him; and, as a result of this brother's influence, some of the disciplines emphasized by the School of Empirical Research, such as historical etymology and phonology, were introduced into the curriculum of the family school at Sha-wan. Thus, Kuo Mo-jo had to learn the 541 radicals under which the characters were classified by Hsü Shen (30–124) in his *Shuo-wen chieh-tzu,* the first great Chinese dictionary; and to study the *Ch'ün-ching yün-p'u,* a famous work on the phonology of the classics by Tuan Yü-ts'ai (1735–1815).[69] Kuo Mo-jo did not find these technical studies of much interest at the time;[70] but, in view of his future career as a paleographer, it is significant that he was exposed to the basic principles of historical phonology and etymology so early in his education.

On the lighter side, it was at about this time that Kuo Mo-jo first got hold of a copy of the *San-kuo yen-i,* or *Romance of the Three Kingdoms,*[71] the greatest of all Chinese historical novels. Not surprisingly, he found this popular favorite of the Chinese reading public far more exciting than his formal studies.[72]

The edict of August 29, 1901, which had abolished the eight-legged essay, was followed, on September 14, 1901, by another, which concerned the transformation of the *shu-yüan,* or private academies, into public schools. It was ordered that those in the provincial capitals were to become universities (*ta-hsüeh*), those in the prefectural cities middle schools (*chung-hsüeh*), and those in the departmental and district towns elementary schools (*hsiao-hsüeh*).[73] This order was not carried out immediately, but by the autumn of 1903 a number of new schools had been established in Chengtu, the provincial capital. Among these were the Tung-wen Hsüeh-t'ang, a secondary school designed to prepare students for study in Japan, and the Wu-pei Hsüeh-t'ang, a military academy. Kuo Mo-jo's oldest brother, Kuo K'ai-wen, who had failed in the last provincial examinations, entered the first of these, and his next oldest brother, Kuo K'ai-tso, enrolled in the second.[74]

Thanks to the efforts of Kuo K'ai-wen, it was not long

17

before a flood of new books and illustrated periodicals began to arrive in Sha-wan from Chengtu. Among them were such new periodicals as the *Ch'i-meng hua-pao,* or *Illustrated Enlightener,* a children's magazine published twice a month in Peking;[75] the *Hsin hsiao-shuo,* or *New Fiction,* a monthly magazine published in Yokohama by Liang Ch'i-ch'ao (1873–1929);[76] and the *Che-chiang ch'ao,* or *Chekiang Tide,* a patriotically nationalist political periodical published in Tokyo by the Chekiang fellow provincials' association.[77] The fact that the last two magazines were published in Japan is evidence that during the last decade of the Ch'ing dynasty, even in the Chinese hinterland, some of the most influential periodicals were those published by Chinese expatriates and students in Japan.

Kuo Mo-jo's imagination was kindled by the biographies of famous Westerners that he read in these periodicals, especially those of Napoleon and Bismarck. He was particularly moved by the sad fate of Josephine and was happy to read about Bismarck's love of dogs. There were three large dogs in the Kuo household, and as he walked about, keeping them at his heels, he fancied himself the Bismarck of the East.[78]

At least two novels among those which arrived from Chengtu with the above periodicals have stuck in Kuo Mo-jo's memory. One of these was entitled *Ching-kuo mei-t'an,* or *A Noble Tale of Statesmanship.* This was a Chinese translation of the famous Japanese political novel *Keikoku bidan,* by Yano Fumio (1850–1931), first published in 1883. It is a historical romance adapted freely from Plutarch's biography of Epaminondas of Thebes (418?–362 B.C.).[79] This work was so popular that it was translated into Chinese at least twice during the first decade of the twentieth century[80] and was also published in a dramatic version by the famous novelist and playwright Li Pao-chia (1867–1906).[81] The other novel was called *Chu-tzu chi,* or *Story of a Coolie.* It recounted the unfortunate adventures of a young Chinese ne'er-do-well who let himself be tricked into being sent to the Western Hemisphere in the coolie slave trade, where he suffered all the miseries of exploitation and maltreatment by foreigners. The vivid depiction in this novel of the hardships of the worker's life made a strong impression on Kuo. He later referred to it, in 1928, as the progenitor of Chinese proletarian literature.[82]

Kuo K'ai-wen's interest in reform was responsible for many changes in Sha-wan. He was the first to advocate the founding of an antifootbinding society, and Kuo Mo-jo's mother was the first woman in the clan to unbind her feet. It was also as a result of his urging that the female children in the family were permitted, for the first time, to study with their brothers and male cousins in the family school. He was the first person to propose the founding of a modern elementary school in Sha-wan, although after it came into existence the Kuo children continued to attend their family institution.

The teacher of the new elementary school, a man named Liu Yü-pin, who had just graduated in the first class of a newly founded normal school in Chengtu, introduced the children of the village to Western-style calisthenics for the first time. Since Shen Huan-chang was quite incapable of this sort of thing, he sent his pupils over to the new school to participate in this part of the day's activities. Kuo Mo-jo and his companions were mystified to find that the commands for the various exercises were given in what was to them an incomprehensible gibberish. It was years before he discovered that these mysterious words were the Japanese commands which Mr. Liu had been taught by his foreign instructors in Chengtu and had never bothered to translate into Chinese.[83]

During the summer vacation in 1904 Kuo K'ai-wen took two of his Japanese teachers from the Tung-wen Hsüeh-t'ang on an excursion to Mount O-mei, one of the most famous mountains in China, located just a few miles northwest of Sha-wan. During this trip they stayed with the Kuos for three days. They were the first Japanese that Kuo Mo-jo had ever seen, and despite the fact that they were living and working in China they had learned so little Chinese that he found himself unable to communicate with them.[84]

In January 1905, after the completion of his year of preparatory study at the Tung-wen Hsüeh-t'ang, Kuo K'ai-wen came back to Sha-wan for the Chinese New Year's vacation. He was to leave for Japan in February and had induced more than ten others from the same prefecture to go with him. He wanted to take Kuo Mo-jo along, and his younger brother was very anxious to go, but his parents would not permit it.

Kuo K'ai-wen, who was fourteen years older than Kuo Mo-jo, had a greater influence on him during his early years than anyone else except his parents and his teacher. He fancied himself something of a poet, an artist, and a calligrapher — in fact, as Kuo Mo-jo later remarked, a romantic. He had a collection of traditional Chinese art books, including the famous *Chieh-tzu yüan hua chuan,* or *Mustard Seed Garden Manual of Painting,* compiled by Wang Kai and others between 1679 and 1701.[85] One of these books, entitled *Hai-shang ming-jen hua kao,* or *Drawings by Famous Shanghai Artists,* contained pictures of languishing beauties, along with vaguely suggestive poetry, which contributed to the stimulation of Kuo Mo-jo's first consciously erotic feelings. It was also owing to his elder brother's influence that Kuo Mo-jo adopted the comparatively free-flowing calligraphic style of the great eleventh-century poet and statesman Su Tung-p'o (1036–1101).

In February 1905 Kuo K'ai-wen left for Japan, where he studied law and administration at Tokyo Imperial University on a scholarship from the provincial government.[86] Eight years later it was he who made it possible for his younger brother to follow in his footsteps.[87]

At the age of eleven or twelve Kuo Mo-jo had accidentally discovered the pleasures of masturbation while shinnying up a bamboo pole as part of the new regimen of foreign-style physical education. After his older brother left for Japan, he found among the latter's books copies of the *Hsi-hsiang chi*,[88] or *Romance of the Western Chamber*, a famous thirteenth-century love drama; the *Hsi-hu chia-hua*,[89] or *Tales of West Lake*, a well-known seventeenth-century collection of stories having to do with West Lake at Hangchow; and the *Hua-yüeh hen*, or *Scars of Romance*, a popular mid-nineteenth-century novel by Wei Hsiu-jen (d. 1874).[90] None of these works constitutes particularly heady fare, and only the first is of real literary merit, but Kuo Mo-jo found them sexually stimulating and avidly devoured them in secret.[91] It is not impossible that the guilt complex which figures so prominently in much of his early writing may have received some impetus from what he thought of as his inability to control these perfectly normal manifestations of puberty.

21

Chapter 2

The New School System in Chia-ting, 1906–1909

On September 2, 1905, an imperial decree announced the final abolition of the traditional civil service examinations.[1] Immediately plans were made to establish an upper-level primary school (*kao-teng hsiao-hsüeh*) in Chia-ting, which was to be located in a Buddhist temple called the Ts'ao-t'ang Ssu, just inside the north wall of the city.[2] That autumn competitive entrance examinations were held. It was decided that Kuo Mo-jo should enter the competition, and his father accompanied him to Chia-ting for the occasion.[3] The examinations were held in the old examination stalls[4] and, since a primary school graduate was now considered to be the legal and social equivalent of a *hsiu-ts'ai* under the old system,[5] there were many candidates who were thirty or forty years old. Over a thousand people competed in the first examination and, when the results were announced, Kuo Mo-jo's name was twenty-seventh out of the two hundred or so who remained in the competition. In the crucial final examination Kuo Mo-jo was rated eleventh out of the ninety candidates who were admitted. Though he was the youngest of the ten or more competitors from his home town, he had surpassed them all, which made his father very proud.[6]

School started early in 1906, with all the pupils boarding on the premises. It would have seemed to us a very strange primary school, for half or more of the students were in their thirties. Kuo Mo-jo, at the age of thirteen, was one of the youngest, and he found himself placed third from last when they lined up in assigned order for calisthenics.[7]

The principal of the school was a man named Ch'en Jun-hai, who had studied, like Kuo Chao-hsiu, at the Tsun-ching Academy in Chengtu.[8] Before the end of the semester, however, he left to become principal of a school in Liu-hua ch'i. The most terrifying person on the staff was a teacher named I Shu-hui, whose nickname was "the tiger." He taught local history and, despite his severity, Kuo Mo-jo found this a very interesting subject. He was also a staunch believer in the doctrines of the great idealist philosopher Wang Yang-ming (1472–1529).[9] This may have been Kuo Mo-jo's first contact with a set of ideas which later had considerable influence on him. A man from the Chengtu area, named Liu Shu-lin, taught history, geography, and composition. He was the most popular member of the faculty, but his choice of material for the teaching of history was rather bizarre. He used as a text the *Shih-liu kuo ch'un-ch'iu,* or *Annals of the Sixteen States,* a history of the short-lived barbarian regimes which proliferated in north China in the fourth and fifth centuries, originally written by Ts'ui Hung (d. c. 525), but later lost and reconstituted in the sixteenth century by T'u Ch'iao and Sun Hsiang-lin. The last of Kuo's teachers was Shuai P'ing-chün, a graduate of the Kōbun Normal School in Tokyo, who taught mathematics, music, calisthenics, and the classics. He taught the first three of these subjects indifferently at best, but in the last he had an approach which was new and interesting to Kuo Mo-jo. He had been a student of Liao P'ing's (1852–1932) and during the spring semester he taught his master's interpretation of the *Wang chih* (Royal regulations) section of the *Li chi.*

Liao P'ing, like Kuo Chao-hsiu and Ch'en Jun-hai, had studied under Wang K'ai-yün at the Tsun-ching Academy in Chengtu.[10] He was the last significant exponent of the late Ch'ing New Text school. This movement, which was really a form of response to the West, represented an attempt to justify progressive reform within the framework of the traditional classical learning.[11] Liao P'ing's theories were extremely unorthodox and, although ostensibly based on considerations of textual criticism, represented, in fact, a tortuous twisting of traditional Confucianism in order to make it justify change and new ideas, including a vision of progress. His claim that Confucius was actually a reformer rather than a conservative influenced the great reformer K'ang Yu-wei (1858–1927), who popularized the idea by writing an influential book entitled *K'ung-tzu kai-chih k'ao*, or *A Study of Confucius as a Reformer*.[12] It is worth noting that this school not only affirmed the existence of historical progress but predicted a future classless society.[13] In view of Kuo Mo-jo's subsequent career it is significant that it was this heterodox interpretation of the Chinese tradition to which he was exposed during his formative years.

Kuo Mo-jo did not find his studies very taxing and had plenty of free time for excursions in and around the city of Chia-ting and for amusement of other kinds. One of these was iconoclasm, in the literal sense of the word, and is reminiscent of a similar incident in the early life of Sun Yat-sen (1866–1925).[14] The school was housed in what had been a Buddhist temple, and behind the main building there was a detached structure dedicated to the worship of the deities who govern conception and fertility. Although there was a fence around it, Kuo Mo-jo managed to remove a slat and force his way in. Among the images he found inside was one of a naked boy with a skullcap on his

24

0496904

head. On removing this cap he discovered a hole in the top of the head which apparently led to a cavity in the belly and thence to the end of the penis. Concluding that this was a monkish device for abusing the credulity of superstitious women, Kuo Mo-jo knocked down all of the images and availed himself of the most universal of all gestures of contempt by urinating on them.[15]

Although he failed to take his school work very seriously, at the end of the semester Kuo Mo-jo placed first in the final examinations. This caused a great uproar, especially among the older students, who felt humiliated at being outranked by a youngster scarcely half as old as they. They made such a fuss that the understaffed and inexperienced administration capitulated and marked him down to eighth place. In the course of this wrangle he was accused by some of his fellow students of having obtained first place by fostering a homosexual relationship with Liu Shu-lin, his teacher of history, geography, and composition. Kuo Mo-jo was thirteen at the time and had been away from home for only a few months. It can well be imagined what sort of an experience this must have been for him. He said later that as a result of this incident his youthful innocence was sullied by a feeling of dislike and distrust for other people and a thirst for retaliation.[16]

Kuo Mo-jo brooded over this humiliation during the summer vacation and returned to school in the fall of 1906 resolved to try a different strategy. Attempting to stay on the right side of his teachers had produced unfortunate results, so he decided to attack them instead. Every time one of them made a mistake he was quick to pounce upon it, to the joy of the rest of the class. In this way he gradually won the respect of his fellow students, who thereafter always elected him as a delegate when they wanted to negotiate with the faculty.[17]

During the fall semester of 1906 plans were being made to establish a middle school in Chia-ting, and the primary school students were given examinations soon after the term began as a basis for selecting those who were adequately prepared to enter the new school when it opened. Kuo Mo-jo placed third in these examinations and was consequently put into the top class of his school, despite the fact that he was younger than the other students.[18]

During this semester I Shu-hui was the principal of the school. Ch'en Jun-hai, who had started out as principal at the beginning of the previous term, returned to the school to teach composition. He used as a text Pao Shih-ch'en's (1775–1855) *I-chou shuang-chi,* or *Twin Oars for the Boat of Art,* a well-known collection of essays on calligraphy and literary composition. Shuai P'ing-chün continued to teach the classics, for which course he used as a text Sun Hsing-yen's (1753–1818) *Shang-shu chin ku wen chu-shu,* or *Commentary and Sub-commentary on the New Text and Old Text Versions of the "Book of Documents."* The text of the *Book of Documents* which Kuo Mo-jo had read in Sha-wan was the Old Text version of Mei Tse (fourth century). This was his first introduction to the great controversy between the New Text and Old Text schools of interpretation of the classics.[19] Two new teachers had joined the staff for the fall semester. One of them, named Tu Shao-shang, a graduate, like Shuai P'ing-chün, of the Kōbun Normal School in Tokyo, taught mathematics and physics. The other, named Wang Ping-chi,[20] who had been a student at the Tsun-ching Academy in Chengtu, taught history and geography.[21]

At the end of the semester Kuo Mo-jo was the second in his class. When he returned to Sha-wan for the New Year's vacation in February 1907, he took advantage of his free time to pursue further some of the interests he had developed during the preceding term. He browsed through his family's copy of the *Huang-Ch'ing ching-chieh,* or *Exegetical Works on the Classics from the Ch'ing Period,* a great collectanea compiled by Juan Yüan (1764–1849). He was fascinated by Yen Jo-chü's (1636–1704) *Ku-wen Shang-shu shu-cheng,* or *Commentary on the Evidence Concerning the Authenticity of the Old Text Version of the "Book of Documents,"* which he discovered there. This was an epoch-making work which demonstrated conclusively that the Old Text version of this classic, which had circulated for close to a millennium and had been used as an official text in the traditional examination system, was a forgery. Kuo later remarked that young people love to see any kind of deception exposed, and that he found this painstaking exposition of the way in which a successful forgery had been perpetrated very exciting intellectually.

During the same vacation Kuo Mo-jo read through sizable portions of the *Shih-chi,* or *Records of the Grand Historian,* the first great history of China, compiled by Ssu-ma Ch'ien (145–c. 90 B.C.).[22] The biographies in this work have played a role in Chinese culture similar to that of Plutarch's *Lives* in the West. Kuo greatly admired Ssu-ma Ch'ien's style, and it may be significant that the biographies that he liked best were those of men who defied society in some way or risked their lives in desperate ventures. In the summer of 1909 he went on to read the book in its entirety.[23]

During the spring term of 1907 Kuo Mo-jo's activities as a student leader got him into serious trouble. The school authorities had cancelled the Saturday half-holiday, and the student body elected delegates to ask the faculty to reinstate it. Kuo Mo-jo was the representative of his class and proposed that the student body should threaten to strike if their demands were not satisfactorily met. The school administration agreed to reinstate the half-holiday, but were incensed at the threatened student strike. When they discovered that this had been Kuo Mo-jo's idea, they expelled him. It took two weeks of negotiations and the application of outside pressure from his influential relatives and friends before the authorities were persuaded to readmit him to the school.[24]

In May 1907, at the age of fourteen, Kuo Mo-jo graduated from primary school. In the fall he entered the new Chia-ting middle school, which was situated in the center of the city on the grounds where the old examination stalls had stood. At about the same time his second oldest brother, Kuo K'ai-tso, having been graduated by the Wupei Hsüeh-t'ang in Chengtu, left Szechwan for Japan.[25]

All the worst features of a transitional period were manifested in the new middle school. The principal was an incompetent political appointee and the teachers he managed to gather around him were little better. As a result the students did not pay very much attention to their studies and, taking advantage of their high social prestige, took to lording it about in public places of entertainment and engaging in troublemaking of every variety.

Kuo Mo-jo himself was responsible for precipitating a riot during the performance of a Chinese opera by his discourtesy to some members of the audience who had refused to give up their seats to him. He was in the thick of every student escapade, and engaged in every available form of dissipation. Having started to drink and learned to smoke while still in primary school, he now plunged into these manly vices with a vengeance, and went out drinking and gambling almost every night with a group of playboys from the wealthier families in Chia-ting.

He had already had several contacts with homosexuality while he was in primary school, but during his first se-

28

98108

mester in middle school he entered into a number of homosexually tinged relationships and even associated with male prostitutes.[26] It is possible that there was a relatively strong homosexual component in Kuo Mo-jo's make-up. Eventually he succeeded in overcoming it, or at least in sublimating it, but it may also have contributed to the development of the guilt feelings which play such a prominent role in his early writings.[27]

The entire staff of the Chia-ting middle school was changed before the spring semester of 1908. A new principal, Ch'in P'i-chi, took over, but the staff he recruited did not represent a marked improvement. It was during this semester that Kuo Mo-jo began the study of English and of Japanese, although the teachers in both subjects were utterly incompetent. For English they used the textbooks of the Seisoku English School in Japan, and the teacher was so inefficient that it took him a whole semester merely to teach the alphabet and the basic principles of English spelling. Kuo Mo-jo's class was divided into three sections, of which the first two were to concentrate on English as their major foreign language, and the last on Japanese. Kuo Mo-jo had such a low opinion of the English teacher that he elected to join the third section and concentrate on Japanese.

As before, the only course which stimulated him intellectually was classical studies. The teacher of this subject, a man named Huang Jung,[28] was also one of Liao P'ing's disciples. He taught the *Ch'un-ch'iu,* or *Spring and Autumn Annals,* and followed Liao P'ing in claiming that the *Kung-yang chuan,* or *Kung-yang's Commentary,* the *Kuliang chuan,* or *Ku-liang's Commentary,* and the *Tso chuan,* or *Tso's Commentary,* were all by the same hand, that the legendary emperors and dynasties of the remote past were deliberate fabrications, and that Confucius was

29

the author of the six classics.[29] Ridiculous as these theories
may be, they were all intended to enhance the role of
Confucius as a reformer. When Kuo Mo-jo reiterated this
interpretation of Confucius in his later life he was restating
in more sophisticated form an argument that had caught
his interest during his early school days.

It was at about this time that Kuo Mo-jo began to develop a strong interest in literature. The teaching in the
middle school was so bad, for the most part, that it failed
to elicit any interest, but literature was something that he
could learn to appreciate by himself. During this period
Lin Shu's (1852–1924) translations of Western fiction were
very popular in China, and it was through them that Kuo
Mo-jo gained his first introduction to Western literature.
Lin Shu may well have been the world's most prolific
translator, having produced Chinese versions of some 180
Western works, most of them novels. He knew no Western
language but worked through assistants, putting their oral
translations into flawless classical Chinese prose.[30]

The first work of Western literature Kuo Mo-jo read
was Lin Shu's translation of H. Rider Haggard's *Joan
Haste*.[31] This work, which is no longer remembered in the
West, was extremely popular in China, and Kuo Mo-jo was
deeply moved by it. He read it again and again, shed tears
over it, and fell in love with the heroine. After this first
taste of Western literature he went on to Lin Shu's translation of Scott's *Ivanhoe*,[32] which made a profound impression on him. In 1928 he wrote, "I have been deeply
influenced by Scott, although this is practically a secret of
mine since none of my friends has ever paid any attention
to this point." [33] He was also very fond of Lin Shu's translation of Charles and Mary Lamb's *Tales from Shakespeare*.[34]
He later read many of Shakespeare's plays in the original
English, but they were never as vivid to him as the fairy-

tale-like translations of the Lambs that he had read as a boy.[35]

During the same semester he had an opportunity to read the *Kuo-ts'ui hsüeh-pao*,[36] or *National Essence Review*, a famous journal which, like its editor Chang Ping-lin (1868–1936), was culturally conservative yet politically revolutionary. Chang Ping-lin participated actively in revolutionary propaganda work before 1911. He was anti-Manchu and hence antimonarchical, but was at the same time a staunch defender of the Chinese tradition, and wrote even his revolutionary appeals in a deliberately archaic literary style. Kuo Mo-jo found his writings hard to understand because of the difficulty of the language in which they were written, but looked up to him as a revolutionary.

Along with the *Kuo-ts'ui hsüeh-pao* he read the *Ch'ing-i pao*,[37] or *Journal of Pure Criticism*, the first of several periodicals edited and published in Japan by Liang Ch'i-ch'ao[38] after he was forced to flee from China as a result of the failure of the reform movement of 1898. Liang Ch'i-ch'ao, unlike Chang Ping-lin, wrote in a brilliant and lucid style which Kuo Mo-jo found intoxicating. He was particularly moved by the biographies of a series of European heroes who had fought for the independence of their countries. After reading Liang Ch'i-ch'ao he added Cavour, Garibaldi, and Mazzini to Napoleon and Bismarck in the list of foreigners whom he admired.[39]

In mid-September 1908, soon after the fall term at the Chia-ting middle school had begun, Kuo Mo-jo became seriously ill. At first he tried to ignore the symptoms, but they finally became so serious that he was forced to leave for home. Almost as soon as he arrived there he lost consciousness and remained in that state for some weeks. His family was frantic. Although his father was a respected amateur doctor he soon ran out of ideas and a number of old-style professional practitioners were called in. Even a shaman was summoned in desperation when none of their remedies proved effective. Finally, the prescription of one of the doctors led to some improvement, although it is impossible to tell whether it was really the prescription or the natural course of the disease that led to this result. Although the illness persisted for several more weeks, the crisis was past and he gradually recovered.

At the time no one knew what the disease was. In 1928, five years after he was graduated from medical school, Kuo Mo-jo diagnosed it as *typhus abdominalis*. This near-fatal illness had a significant effect on his life because of the secondary complications that accompanied it. He was left with a weakened spine and with seriously impaired hearing.[40] This must have been a serious blow for a person as self-conscious as Kuo Mo-jo. His deafness has made it difficult for him to participate comfortably in either professional meetings or social gatherings and has possibly contributed to the growth of feelings of alienation.[41] In later years he also used it as an excuse for not practicing medicine.

While recuperating from this illness, Kuo Mo-jo had a chance to do a lot of reading. It was at this time that he first became attracted to *Chuang-tzu*[42] and *Lieh-tzu*,[43] two early Taoist works, which are not only important in the history of Chinese thought, but have also played a significant role in Chinese literature because of their soaring freedom of imagination and the brilliance of their literary style.[44] He was particularly fond of *Chuang-tzu*, the style of which he later declared to be unequaled in all of Chinese literature.[45]

In January 1909 Kuo Mo-jo's second oldest brother, Kuo K'ai-tso, returned from Japan and, in March, married the second daughter of Wang Wei-yen, the district inspector of education. They had been engaged by proxy in the fall of 1907 shortly after he had left for Japan. Kuo K'ai-tso had previously been engaged to another girl, but she had died in the fall of 1907, and when the Wang family sent a go-between to seek a match for their second daughter he was engaged to her. This girl was the same age as Kuo Mo-jo, for whom she might have been a more suitable match, but he had also been engaged to another girl since his childhood. Two weeks after Kuo K'ai-tso's engagement was announced Kuo Mo-jo's own fiancée died. Had this event occurred a few weeks earlier it would probably have been Kuo Mo-jo rather than his brother who married Miss Wang. His new sister-in-law died of tuberculosis in the spring of 1910, three months after giving birth to a son.[46]

Kuo Mo-jo returned to the Chia-ting middle school after recovering from his illness and toward the end of the spring term in 1909 he got into trouble again. The geography teacher, Ting P'ing-tzu, created an uproar when he discovered a derogatory remark about himself scribbled on the wall of the students' smoking room. He threatened to resign from the staff unless the culprit was expelled, and a victim was duly discovered and sacrificed in order to save his face. Kuo Mo-jo was so incensed by this incident that when he came back to his room in a drunken stupor the night after the final examinations were over he began to heap abuse on Ting P'ing-tzu in a loud voice, and kept it up for nearly two hours. By the time he had worn himself out there was a large crowd of students outside his window cheering him on. Understandably, he was threatened with expulsion, which meant that he would not be permitted to return for the fall semester, but during the summer Ting P'ing-tzu conveniently died of diphtheria and the matter was dropped.[47]

It was not long, however, before Kuo Mo-jo was expelled

once and for all. In October 1909 a fight broke out during a theatrical performance between a group of middle school students and some soldiers from the local garrison. Several people were hurt, including one student. His classmates indignantly demanded that steps be taken to elicit a public apology from the soldiers' commanding officer. Although Kuo Mo-jo had not been present when the incident occurred, he acted as the student delegate in laying their case before the faculty. After investigating the matter the administration decided that the students were at least as much to blame as the soldiers and not only refused to demand an apology from the commanding officer but read the students a severe lecture on their conduct. The next day the entire student body went on strike. The principal happened to be out of town at the time and the faculty was unable to handle the situation; but when he returned three days later he not only quelled the strike but expelled the eight students whom he took to be ringleaders. Needless to say, Kuo Mo-jo was among them, and this time he was expelled for good.[48]

Chapter 3

Middle School, Revolution, and Marriage: Chengtu, 1910–1913

Ever since entering the primary school in Chia-ting, Kuo Mo-jo had felt the atmosphere in that provincial town to be restricting. He wanted desperately to get away from such an out-of-the-way corner and see the world. Europe or America were the places to which he most wanted to go, followed in order of preference by Japan, Peking or Shanghai, and Chengtu, the provincial capital. Since there were no other middle schools in Chia-ting, his expulsion in October 1909 turned out to be a blessing in disguise, for it provided him with an opportunity to get as far away from home as the provincial capital. In February 1910 he made the four-day journey to Chengtu in the hope of being able to continue his education there.

Kuo Mo-jo set out for Chengtu armed with letters of introduction from Wang Wei-yen, his brother Kuo K'ai-tso's father-in-law, who had just returned to Chia-ting after teaching Chinese composition for two years in a Chengtu middle school. Upon his arrival he paid a visit to Tu Shao-shang, who had been his teacher of mathematics and physics in the Chia-ting primary school, but was now a section chief in the office of the provincial commissioner of education. Tu Shao-shang provided him with further letters of recommendation and suggested that he apply for admission to the Annexed Middle School (*fen-she chung-*

hsüeh), a preparatory institution attached to the Chengtu Higher School (*kao-teng hsüeh-t'ang*). This happened to be the school in which Wang Wei-yen had taught, and when Kuo Mo-jo presented his letters of recommendation the principal, Tu Ching-chieh, gave him a two-hour written examination in his own office and admitted him to the sophomore class that very day.[1]

Among his schoolmates at the Annexed Middle School in Chengtu were quite a number of people who later achieved national prominence in the Chinese cultural and political world. Tseng Ch'i (1892–1951), the future founder of the Chinese Youth Party (Chung-kuo ch'ing-nien tang), was a class ahead of him. Wang Kuang-ch'i (1892–1936), a famous journalist and authority on Chinese music, Wei Ssu-luan, a well-known mathematician, and Li Chieh-jen (1891–1962), novelist and translator of French literature, were all his classmates; Chou Wu, the biologist, and Ch'i Shu-fen (d. 1927), the economist, were one class behind him.[2]

Kuo Mo-jo was disappointed to discover that the teaching in Chengtu was little better than that in Chia-ting and that the instruction in classical studies, in which he was particularly interested, was even worse. In this course the instructor did little more than read out loud from the *Tso chuan shih-wei,* a topical rearrangement of the material in the *Tso chuan* compiled by Ma Su (1621–1673). In the course on Chinese literature the only thing the students did in class was to go laboriously through the *T'ang Sung pa ta-chia wen tu-pen,* an anthology of the prose writings of the eight great masters of *ku-wen* in the T'ang and Sung dynasties compiled by Shen Te-ch'ien (1673–1769). A popular slogan among young people at that time was "national salvation through industrialization" (*shih-yeh chiu-kuo*), but Kuo Mo-jo found himself insufficiently motivated to master the mathematics and sciences necessary if he was to contribute to this end. On the other hand, he felt uncertain of the value of his interest in literature. Consequently, just as in Chia-ting, he neglected his studies and gave himself up to heavy drinking and other forms of dissipation.[3]

During this period the relatively conservative constitutional monarchists led by Liang Ch'i-ch'ao and K'ang Yu-wei were competing with the anti-Manchu revolutionaries led by Sun Yat-sen and Huang Hsing (1874–1916)[4] for the support of the articulate fraction of the Chinese population. In Szechwan public opinion on the whole was inclined to favor the constitutional monarchists. The students, on the other hand, were attracted to the simple solution offered by the T'ung-meng Hui, a political organization founded by Sun Yat-sen and Huang Hsing in Tokyo in 1905 which became the progenitor of the Kuomintang. The propaganda of this organization argued that all of China's problems could be solved simply by overthrowing the Manchu government. This oversimplified view of China's problems had the virtue of focusing resentment on a single target and had a great appeal for the students of the time. Sympathetic as they were with the revolutionary cause, they eagerly devoured the tales of heroism and martyrdom engendered by the unsuccessful *Putsches* of the T'ung-meng Hui.

Kuo Mo-jo and his classmates were constantly on the lookout for revolutionaries and very disappointed to discover how hard it was to find one. He had read some fictional accounts of the deeds of Russian terrorists from which he concluded that revolutionaries, since they are in constant danger of their lives, frequently have to disguise themselves as servants or workers in order to escape notice. With this in mind he began to scrutinize as closely as possible the activities of the servants in the school, but was disappointed to find not so much as a trace of revolutionary activity.[5]

Despite his interest in the revolutionary cause, the only political activity in which Kuo Mo-jo took part was more closely allied to the aims of the constitutional monarchists. During 1910 there was a nationwide movement demanding the early convocation of a national parliament. In November an imperial decree proclaimed that parliament was to be convened in 1913. This failed to satisfy all the participants in the movement, however, and further petitions were presented. In December the government adopted repressive measures which were successful in bringing the movement to a halt.[6] The province of Szechwan, owing to its relative geographic isolation, has often displayed a sort of delayed-reflex action in responding to events in other parts of the country. That is what happened in this case. Although the movement had already been suppressed in the rest of China, in early January of 1911 the students in the Chengtu Higher School distributed a mimeographed circular calling upon the students in all schools to elect delegates to a meeting to be held in the auditorium of the provincial Ministry of Education. Kuo Mo-jo was elected to represent his class.

After a rather chaotic opening the student delegates were brought to order by a teacher from the Railroad Academy (*T'ieh-tao hsüeh-t'ang*) named Liu Tzu-t'ung, who proposed that they elect a standing committee to handle correspondence, and so forth, and that they should demand the convocation of a national parliament the next year and ask the governor-general of Szechwan, Chao Erh-sun (1846–1927), to memorialize to that effect on their behalf. Liu Tzu-t'ung also suggested that they should lend added force to these requests by calling a student strike until their demands were met. These proposals were enthusiastically adopted by the student delegates. Chao Erh-sun, however, refused to comply with these demands and the student strike, effective for some time, was broken when a majority of the students were cajoled into taking their final examinations.[7] Kuo Mo-jo refused to take part in what he regarded as a betrayal of the movement and was consequently threatened with expulsion.

Having removed his belongings from the school he was in the process of moving into a hotel when he unexpectedly encountered his oldest brother, Kuo K'ai-wen, who had just arrived from Peking. After returning to China from Japan, Kuo K'ai-wen had worked for a time at Shanghai in the office of Sheng Hsüan-huai (1844–1916), who served there between 1908 and 1910 as commissioner for commercial treaty negotiations. In 1910 he had gone to Peking and competed in a palace examination where he won the degree of Bachelor of Laws (*fa-k'o chü-jen*)[8] and was appointed an attaché (*hsing-tsou*) in the Ministry of Justice, which made him an official of the seventh rank. He had just returned to Chengtu in order to take a teaching post in the provincial College of Law and Administration.

One of Kuo K'ai-wen's many visitors was Tu Ching-chieh, the principal of the Annexed Middle School, who came to ask him if he could teach two hours a week of law and economics to his senior class. Kuo K'ai-wen agreed to do so on condition that Tu Ching-chieh would reconsider the expulsion of his younger brother. Thus Kuo Mo-jo was readmitted to the school and permitted to take make-up examinations as a result of his brother's influence.[9]

On May 13, 1911, in response to a memorial by Sheng Hsüan-huai, who was now president of the Ministry of Posts and Communications, an imperial decree announced the nationalization of the major trunk line railroads in

China. The contracts for the construction of the Canton-Hankow and Szechwan-Hankow lines had been in the hands of Chinese merchants, who had encountered considerable difficulty in raising the necessary funds. When these contracts were cancelled and the government proceeded to float huge loans abroad for the purpose of financing the construction, the investors began to fear that they would not be reimbursed. Capital for these enterprises had been raised by forced sales of stock to all those who paid more than a certain fixed amount in taxes, so the number of people affected was considerable. Popular protest over the new government policy spread like wildfire and was particularly vehement in Szechwan.[10]

On June 17, 1911, a public meeting on this question was held at the Chengtu headquarters of the railroad company under the sponsorship of the Szechwan stockholders in the Szechwan-Hankow line. Although various protest organizations had already come into existence, it was at this meeting that the Railway Protection Club (Pao-lu t'ung-chih hui) of Szechwan was formally established. The antigovernment activities of this organization were destined to act as the fuse that set off the revolution of 1911.

Thanks to a happy concatenation of events Kuo Mo-jo was present at this meeting. One of his first cousins, named Kuo K'ai-ch'eng,[11] the eldest son of his father's eldest brother,[12] was an employee of the railroad company, and it was Kuo Mo-jo's habit to visit him at least once a week. June 17 was a Saturday, and when he appeared for a visit, his cousin took him along to the meeting. Kuo Mo-jo has given a vivid description of what happened that day, although its accuracy may be open to some question since it was not written until 1929. At any rate, the editors of the Chinese Historical Society considered it important enough to include in their recently published collection of

40

historical materials bearing on the revolution of 1911.[13]

After a series of orators had skillfully raised the emotions of the spectators to boiling point, it was decided that the stockholders and other responsible or influential persons present should march as a group to the office of Wang Jen-wen, the acting governor-general, and request him to memorialize the throne on their behalf. This march of several hundred dignified old gentlemen through the streets of Chengtu created a sensation. When they arrived at the governor-general's yamen they filled the entire court-yard. Wang Jen-wen came out in his robes of office, climbed onto a chair, and addressed the assemblage. He told them that he not only sympathized with their objectives but would do everything in his power to further them. This was to pour oil on the flames. As soon as the Railway Protection Club had received such indication of official sympathy it went into action, and before long all Szechwan was ablaze. Looking back in 1929, Kuo Mo-jo considered his accidental witnessing of this historic event to be the most significant experience of his years in Chengtu.[14]

During the summer of 1911 the political situation in Szechwan rapidly deteriorated, but Kuo Mo-jo had gone home to spend the summer vacation at Sha-wan[15] and was thus unable to observe in person the increasingly ominous events which took place in Chengtu. On August 3 the new governor-general, Chao Erh-feng (d. 1911), who had just returned to Chengtu from his post as border commissioner of the provinces of Szechwan and Yunnan, officially took over the duties of his office.[16] Although, like Wang Jen-wen, he undertook to memorialize the throne on behalf of the people of Szechwan, he was unable to pacify them. On August 24, upon learning that Tuan Fang (1861–1911), the government-appointed superintendent of the Canton-Hankow-Chengtu Railway, had reinstated the manager of the I-ch'ang office after he had been fired by the company, the students, merchants, and artisans of Chengtu went on strike. On August 27 in every street altars began to appear, on which incense was burned before spirit tablets dedicated to the late Kuang-hsü Emperor, who had authorized private management of the Canton-Hankow-Chengtu Railway. This was a master stroke since the officials could not very well suppress the expression of public reverence to the memory of a former emperor.

Chao Erh-feng and his subordinates saw that the situation was likely to get out of hand and repeatedly memorialized as a body, requesting a change in railway policy. Rather than make any concession the Ch'ing court ordered Chao Erh-feng to rigorously suppress all signs of discontent. On September 7, in an attempt to break the strike, Chao Erh-feng arrested some ten of the prominent leaders of the local gentry who had led the fight against railroad nationalization, including the president and vice-president of the Provincial Assembly and officers of the railroad company and the Railway Protection Club. When a great crowd of unarmed people forced its way into the courtyard of the governor-general's yamen to petition for the release of the arrested men, Chao Erh-feng became jittery and ordered his troops to open fire on the crowd, killing and wounding a considerable number.[17]

After this event a state of virtual anarchy prevailed in Szechwan. Armed clashes took place between government troops and local militia all over the province. Thus a state of war between Ch'ing and anti-Ch'ing forces had existed in Szechwan for a month before the Wuchang uprising occurred on October 10. In his autobiography, Kuo Mo-jo assigns to the people of Szechwan the credit for starting the revolution of 1911.[18]

On November 27, after Chao Erh-feng had voluntarily

surrendered his seal of office, Chengtu declared itself independent.[19] The first reaction to this event on the part of Kuo Mo-jo and his classmates was to cut off their queues. Having taken this revolutionary step for themselves, they saw to it that their teachers followed suit. Those who resisted were subjected to coercion, from which not even the principal, Tu Ching-chieh, was immune. Brandishing four or five pairs of scissors, his students surrounded him, and in the twinkling of an eye the visible sign of his subservience to the Manchu rulers was severed from his head.[20]

On December 8, 1911, some ten days after Chengtu had declared its independence, the local garrison mutinied. This event was followed by a night of unrestrained looting, and the next day a new administration took over, headed by Yin Ch'ang-heng (1886–1953).[21] The breakdown of public order, marked by the night of wanton looting, was a source of concern to the responsible members of the community, of which the students were not an insignificant part. Plans were therefore set on foot for establishing a Students' Volunteer Army, which would patrol the streets and help maintain order. Kuo Mo-jo was one of those who volunteered for this organization, but when he moved to the military barracks where they were to undergo training he was so appalled by the narrowness of the army bunks that he returned to his dormitory without even unpacking his bags.[22]

In February 1912 Kuo Mo-jo went home to Sha-wan for the New Year's vacation. There, as elsewhere in the province, law and order had completely broken down since the events of September. The local garrison in Chia-ting had mutinied, as had the one in Chengtu, and as a result large numbers of rifles had fallen into the hands of the civilian population. This only compounded the problem created by the lack of any local law enforcement agencies. In order to deal with this problem the people of Sha-wan, under the leadership of one of Kuo Mo-jo's uncles, set up a Self-Defense Corps and recruited several hundred local youths as its members. This vigilante group engaged in daily drill and issued innumerable public proclamations, most of which were composed, in the best parallel prose style, by Kuo Mo-jo.

Not to be outdone, the Yang clan, which was the most influential family among the native Szechwanese population of the village, established a rival corps. Inevitably trouble broke out between these two vigilante groups. When a member of the Yang clan joined the Self-Defense Corps which had been organized by the Kuos, the Yang group broke into his home and stole all the furniture. The Kuos decided to retaliate and, since their corps was much the larger of the two, had no difficulty in gaining control of the situation. After surrounding the home of the head of the Yang clan they blasted open the front gate with an antique cannon and, after a brief skirmish, captured Yang Lang-sheng, the son of the head of the Yang clan and leader of the rival corps. After parading him through the main street of the village, they tied him to a tree by the river and shot him.[23] That the Kuo family was able to get away with this type of high-handed activity gives some indication of the extent of its power in the local community.

The major event during Kuo Mo-jo's vacation was not this struggle over local hegemony, however, but his marriage. As previously noted, he had been betrothed as a child, but the girl had died in 1909. Since that time his mother had broached the subject of marriage with him on several occasions but he had always put her off. What was his surprise, then, on visiting his cousin one Sunday in October 1911 to be shown a family letter announcing

44

that his mother had already completed the arrangements for his marriage? The letter reported, on the authority of the go-between, who was one of his aunts, that the girl was attractive, studious, and had unbound feet. Kuo Mo-jo was taken quite by surprise, but he must have had considerable faith in his aunt's judgment, for he did nothing to stop the affair.

The wedding took place during the first week of March. It was a traditional wedding in every respect. After the ceremony the couple was escorted to the nuptial chamber and only then was Kuo Mo-jo permitted to raise the veil and take his first look at the bride. Not only did he find her unattractive, but her feet were bound and she was uneducated. Kuo Mo-jo was stunned. The celebrations lasted another two or three days, but he was scarcely conscious of what was going on around him. He does not even tell us whether or not the marriage was consummated. Within the week he set off once more for Chengtu, leaving his new wife behind him.

In 1930, when he wrote an account of his wedding, he cursed himself for opportunistically taking his chances on a happy outcome instead of either putting a stop to the whole procedure or insisting on more detailed advance information.[24] Although he recognized his mistake he did nothing to remedy it. He has married twice again, but has never divorced his first wife and does not even tell us what became of her. As late as 1924 she was still living with his parents.[25] After that we hear no more about her. This marriage and everything connected with it weighed heavily on his conscience. He said in 1930 that if there was anything in his life that he regretted it was his consent to this marriage.[26]

One of his duties on his return trip to Chengtu was to escort his sister-in-law, Kuo K'ai-wen's wife, to the provincial capital to join her husband. The previous December, after the change of government had taken place in Chengtu, Kuo K'ai-wen had received the post of minister of communications in the new military government of the province.[27] When Kuo Mo-jo and his sister-in-law arrived in Chengtu in mid-March 1912, they discovered that Kuo K'ai-wen had taken an attractive young concubine into his household. Kuo Mo-jo was also surprised to find that his brother had adopted the opium habit.[28] Thus it was a member of his own family who brought home to him in concrete terms the fact that the change in government had not effected a significant change in the habits or attitudes of the officials who staffed it.

When Kuo Mo-jo returned to Chengtu the Annexed Middle School had been abolished and he entered the Chengtu Prefectural Middle School. The teaching was terrible because all the teachers with any reputation had entered official life after the revolution created room for new talent. He did not yet know what he wanted to do in life, and the only roads open to him in Chengtu were to enter the Ts'un-ku Hsüeh-t'ang, a higher school of traditional studies, or West China Union University, a missionary institution south of the city that was popular because it presented the opportunity to learn English. Neither appealed to him. His one wish was to leave Szechwan and go to Peking, Shanghai, Japan, Europe, or America, in order of ascending preference. But where was he to get the money to do these things? When he left Sha-wan after his marriage his mother had made him promise not to go abroad,[29] so there was not to be any money forthcoming from his family. Frustration, ennui, and his guilt complex, which had been greatly aggravated by his unfortunate marriage, drove him once again to senseless dissipation. At the same time, he tells us, he affected some of the worst

46

aspects of the behavior of the old-style literati.[30] Probably no one who knew him at the time would have thought of him as anything but a rather clever playboy, typical of the wealthy young wastrels who congregated daily in the entertainment quarters of Chengtu.

The only clue we have to Kuo Mo-jo's intellectual interests during these years is a list of the books he was particularly fond of reading at the time. He tells us that in the spring of 1912 his favorite books were the *Chuang-tzu*, the *Ch'u-tz'u*,[31] the *Wen-hsüan*,[32] the *Shih-chi,* and Yen Fu's (1854–1921) translations of Thomas Henry Huxley's *Evolution and Ethics*[33] and Herbert Spencer's *Study of Sociology*.[34] The *Ch'u-tz'u* and the *Wen-hsüan* are famous anthologies of early Chinese literature, compiled in the second and sixth centuries respectively. Kuo Mo-jo later translated much of the *Ch'u-tz'u* into modern colloquial Chinese and wrote a popular historical play on the life of Ch'ü Yüan (fourth–third centuries B.C.), the major poet represented in the collection. The *Chuang-tzu* (fourth century B.C.) is one of the classics of Taoist philosophy and the *Shih-chi* is the first great history of China, but both of them have been admired almost as much for their literary style as their content. Kuo Mo-jo specifically states that the *Chuang-tzu* was his favorite book and that he considered it stylistically superior to any other work in the entire corpus of Chinese literature.[35]

How much of the content of the books by Huxley and Spencer Kuo Mo-jo assimilated it is difficult to say. The theory of evolution encountered in China few of the religious obstacles that it had to overcome in the West. The only significant ideological hurdle that it faced was the traditional Chinese penchant for explaining phenomena in cyclical terms, but this had already been weakened by the New Text school's progressive theories of history.

Hence it was not long in winning wide acceptance. It is clear from his later writings that Kuo Mo-jo accepted the Darwinian theory of evolution without qualms, but it is difficult to tell what philosophical implications, if any, he drew from it. It is possible that Spencer's pseudoscientific attempts to prove that evolution inevitably made for social progress may have laid seeds which later bore fruit in Kuo Mo-jo's acceptance of the Marxist theory of history. At one time he toyed, as other Marxists such as J. B. S. Haldane have done, with a presumed affinity between the Marxist dialectic and the laws of biology. He never got very far with these ideas, but it is possible that his early reading of Spencer's synthesis to some degree prepared his mind for such concepts. It should be added that the intellectual content of these books may have had little or no effect on him. Yen Fu's translations were famous for their elegant classical Chinese and, since Kuo Mo-jo admits that he was primarily interested in literary style at the time, it is quite possible that he read these two books largely with that consideration in mind.

In the spring of 1913 Kuo Mo-jo graduated from middle school and was admitted to the science department of the Chengtu Higher School.[36] This had formerly been the famous Tsun-ching Academy, where Wang K'ai-yün had taught, and it had an excellent library of classical works.[37] But Kuo Mo-jo was not happy there and was constantly preoccupied with the thought of somehow getting out of Szechwan and seeing the world. In June nationwide entrance examinations were held for the Army Medical School in Tientsin. This was a government-operated school at which all the students were on scholarship. Although he was not interested in studying medicine, Kuo Mo-jo took the examinations in the hope that they would enable him to leave Szechwan at government expense. When the results were announced in mid-July he found that he was one of the six candidates admitted from the province of Szechwan. He went home to bid farewell to his parents, and presumably his wife, and at the end of July set out for Tientsin.[38] He was never to see his wife again.

For the first leg of his journey Kuo Mo-jo had the company of his brother Kuo K'ai-tso, who was going to Lu-chou on business. On July 31 they set out from Chia-ting by boat and followed the course of the Min River downstream. On the morning of August 2, outside I-pin, Kuo Mo-jo got one of the greatest scares of his life. The load on their boat was unevenly distributed, which caused a distinct list. When going through the rapids where the Min River flows into the River of Golden Sand to form the mighty Yangtze their boat almost capsized. In describing this event twenty-three years later Kuo Mo-jo remarked that the terrifying scene and his reactions to it remained as vividly etched in his memory as though they had happened the day before.

The following day Kuo Mo-jo arrived in Chungking and reported to the hotel where the candidates from Szechwan had been directed to stay. There he was met by a major general who had been appointed to escort them to Tientsin. The general produced a telegram from Chengtu which reported that Tientsin had cabled instructions that the students from the provinces should delay their journeys until receipt of further notice because of the outbreak of the so-called second revolution of 1913. After giving them this news he advised them to do whatever they thought best, but strongly urged them to leave Chungking immediately, as he felt that the situation there was very precarious.

Early on the morning of August 4 Kuo Mo-jo and one of the other successful candidates for the medical school left Chungking and set out for Chengtu. In those days the trip required ten days. It was only on reaching Jung-ch'ang, about a third of the way to Chengtu, that they discovered by reading a newspaper that on the evening of the very day they had left Chungking, Hsiung K'o-wu (1881–   ), who had been in command of the Chungking garrison, declared the city independent and arrested the representatives of the provincial government who were there, including the major general who had advised them to leave.

When Kuo Mo-jo arrived back in Chengtu in mid-August he moved into the dormitory of the Chengtu Higher School, where he was permitted to stay even though the school was closed for the summer. Having nothing to do, he took advantage of the fine classical library at the school, where he devoted considerable time to reading the poetry and the parallel prose of the Six Dynasties (265–589) period, to which he was much addicted at the time. He was particularly fond of Yü Hsin's (513–581) famous "Ai chiang-nan fu," or "Rhyme-Prose Lamenting the Fall of the South," [39] and constantly intoned to himself two lines which mean, literally, "The ministers of state dealt with warfare as though it were child's play; the high officials took fine conversation to be the making of state policy." [40] It was the relevance of these lines to the current situation in China which arrested his attention.

Although Kuo Mo-jo bewailed the evils of the times, he did little to set them right. Instead he spent what time he could spare from his literary pursuits in gambling at mah-jongg with his friends. In the course of one heroic bout, which lasted for three consecutive days and nights, he managed to lose every last cent of the travel funds which had been advanced to him by the government. Since he was left flat broke by this debacle he had to leave the dormitory and move in with his sister-in-law, whose husband, Kuo K'ai-wen, was away at the time serving as the

Peking representative of Yin Ch'ang-heng. On June 13, 1913, Yin Ch'ang-heng had been transferred by Yüan Shih-k'ai (1859–1916), the president of the nascent Republic, from the post of military governor of Szechwan to that of commissioner of Szechwan border affairs, with his headquarters at Ta-chien-lu.[41] When Kuo Mo-jo finally left for Tientsin it must have been his sister-in-law who financed the trip.

Having received a telegram from Tientsin, Kuo Mo-jo set out from Chengtu again in early October.[42] Wang Ping-chi, who had taught him history and geography during his first semester in the Chia-ting middle school, but now held the post of inspector of education for eastern Szechwan, happened to be in Chengtu at the time. His younger brother, Wang Ling-chi, had recently been appointed defense commissioner of Chungking for his role in putting down the second revolution, and Wang Ping-chi wanted to go to Chungking to see him. Kuo K'ai-tso, who also happened to be in Chengtu, had been a schoolmate of Wang Ling-chi's at the Wu-pei Hsüeh-t'ang in Chengtu and later in Japan[43] and was also anxious to see his old friend. Thus the three of them set out for Chungking together. Because of reports of bandits on the main road they took a somewhat less traveled route than Kuo Mo-jo had taken two months before, cutting overland as far as Ho-ch'uan, and then taking a boat down the Fu River to Chungking. The trip took them ten days.

Kuo Mo-jo stayed for five or six days in the defense commissioner's yamen at Chungking. As soon as all the Szechwanese students who were going to the medical school in Tientsin were duly assembled they took passage down river on the steamer Shu-t'ung. Specially designed to negotiate the difficult reaches of the upper Yangtze between I-ch'ang and Chungking this was a curious craft, consisting of a powerful steam tug with a larger passenger vessel lashed to its left side.[44] Yin Ch'ang-heng, who was not satisfied with his position at Ta-chien-lu, had decided to go to Peking to seek an explanation from Yüan Shih-k'ai. Before going in person, however, he sent two groups of agents ahead, and they were on the same boat with Kuo Mo-jo and his party. Since they took up most of the cabins Kuo and the other members of his group had to sleep on the deck. This was not without its advantages, however, for they were thus in the best possible position to observe the scenery of the beautiful Yangtze gorges.

Two days after their departure from Chungking they arrived at I-ch'ang. There they changed to a Japanese-owned steamer of the Nippon Yusen Kaisha line and continued down the river as far as Hankow, which they reached three days later. The following day they took a train to Pao-ting and thence to Tientsin, where they arrived on November 3.

When Kuo Mo-jo and his party reported to the Army Medical School the next day they were disheartened to learn that they would have to take another examination on November 9. The topic for the essay question on this examination was *"t'o-tou yü yao-ni."* This combination of characters makes no sense in Chinese and Kuo Mo-jo, unable to solve the riddle, wrote down a few lines of whatever came into his head and handed in his paper. Only after the examination was over did he learn from a fellow Szechwanese student that *t'o-tou* was a Chinese phonetic rendition of the English word "total," and *yao-ni* of "unit." Thus the topic for the essay was "total and unit." This rendering of the words had been used by Yen Fu in his translation of Spencer's *Study of Sociology,* and the examiner was interested in how Spencer dealt with the concepts of society and the individual as represented in sociological terms by total, or aggregate, and unit.[45]

Kuo Mo-jo must not have read Spencer's book very carefully, for he missed the question completely. He was sure that he had flunked the examination and was afraid that he might be sent back to Szechwan. Since he was not really interested in the study of medicine in the first place, he decided to leave Tientsin before the results of the examination were announced and join his brother Kuo K'ai-wen in Peking, where he was acting as Yin Ch'ang-heng's representative in the capital.

On the morning of November 10 Kuo Mo-jo took the train from Tientsin to Peking. On his arrival he discovered that his brother had gone on a vacation trip to Japan and Korea that summer, from which he had not yet returned. He had been living in the home of a friend named Yin Ch'ao-chen (1881–   ), a member of the court in the Peking Court of Assizes, who was a *chü-jen* from Chia-ting prefecture and had studied law and administration in Japan.[46] Kuo Mo-jo settled down in the Yin household to await his brother's return.[47]

In mid-December, Kuo K'ai-wen returned to Peking and was astonished to find his younger brother awaiting him. He had left early in the summer and thus did not even know of his brother's admission to the medical school in Tientsin. He disapproved of Kuo Mo-jo's decision to leave the school, but did not reproach him for it vehemently. There was nothing much he could do to help him, for he was in financial straits himself. Earlier that month Yin Ch'ang-heng had arrived in Peking only to be placed under house arrest by Yüan Shih-k'ai. This left Kuo K'ai-wen without a job, and he was scarcely pleased to have the troubles of his younger brother added to his own. Kuo

Mo-jo had been expelled in absentia from the Army Medical School and there was nowhere else he could go to continue his education, at least until the opening of the spring semester. Kuo K'ai-wen did not know what to do with him.

On the evening of December 27, 1913, a chance visit produced a solution to the problem. Yüan Shih-k'ai had, to all intents and purposes, dissolved parliament in November, and each of the members had been paid three months' salary in advance. One of these, a former schoolmate and colleague of Kuo K'ai-wen's named Chang Tz'u-yü, had decided to use his money to make a trip to Japan, and that evening he dropped in to say good-bye to his friend. In the course of the conversation the problem of Kuo Mo-jo's future came up. Chang Tz'u-yü suggested that he continue his education in Japan and offered to take him along on his forthcoming trip.

There was an agreement at that time between the Chinese and Japanese governments whereby the Chinese government undertook to pay the expenses of any Chinese student who passed the entrance examinations to certain specified Japanese schools. The problem, therefore, was how long it would take Kuo Mo-jo to learn enough Japanese to pass these examinations. It usually took at least a year and a half. Kuo K'ai-wen told him that he would only be able to support him for six months and asked if he thought he could pass the examinations in June 1914, for they were given only once a year. When Kuo Mo-jo remained silent his brother made up his mind for him, and it was decided that he should leave for Japan with Chang Tz'u-yü the very next day.

On the evening of December 28 Kuo Mo-jo met Chang Tz'u-yü at the railway station in Peking, where they boarded a train for Mukden. The following evening they spent the night in a Japanese hotel in that city. The next day they left Mukden and, after crossing the Korean border at An-tung and passing through Seoul, they arrived in Pusan, at the tip of the Korean peninsula, on the evening of December 31, 1913. Here they stayed with the Chinese consul, K'o Jung-chieh, who was a Szechwanese and had been a schoolmate of Kuo K'ai-wen's and Chang Tz'u-yü's at the Tung-wen Hsüeh-t'ang in Chengtu.[48] They remained in Pusan for about a week before embarking for Japan, where they arrived in early January 1914.[49]

Kuo Mo-jo was twenty-one years old when he arrived in Japan. This was an important turning point in his career. Up until the spring of 1914 he had led the life of a fairly typical well-to-do young Chinese. The only external event that had had a really significant effect on his life was the abolition of the traditional civil service examination system. Because of the resultant changes in the educational curriculum, he had received a far better preparation for contact with Western civilization than had the generation before him. But he was still very much traditionally oriented. Growing up far in the interior he had not even been exposed to the hybrid civilization of the treaty ports. Japan had a fifty-year head start on China in the process of coming to terms with the West, and from the day he set foot in Japan, Kuo Mo-jo was exposed to the multifarious aspects of Western civilization. Once there he was no longer able to fall back on his family and its connections, but had to take responsibility for his own life. The short voyage across Tsushima Strait marked the end of his adolescence and the beginning of his manhood.

Chapter 4

Higher School in Tokyo and Okayama, 1914–1918

Kuo Mo-jo arrived in Tokyo on January 13, 1914,[1] and embarked immediately on what were probably the most arduous six months of his life. He had to acquire enough basic scientific knowledge and enough Japanese to pass the examinations in June. When he left Peking in December 1913 all his elder brother had been able to give him was a gold bar weighing some six ounces. If this were used up before he passed the examination and thus became entitled to a government stipend, it was not at all certain that any more money would be available.

He found himself a place to live in Ōtsuka, a section of Koishikawa located in what is now Bunkyō-ku, and enrolled in a Japanese language school in Kanda.[2] In June he successfully passed the entrance examinations to the First Higher School in Tokyo. This was a remarkable feat, by any standard, and Kuo Mo-jo reports that no other foreign student had ever passed the examinations after so short a period of residence in Japan.[3] It should be remembered, however, that he had been studying Japanese for several years before he left China, having begun the language during the spring semester of 1908, while he was still in the Chia-ting middle school.[4] Thus it seems safe to assume that he had a fairly good foundation in the language before he arrived in Japan.

The First Higher School of Tokyo was divided into three departments: liberal arts, science and engineering, and premedical. Having passed the necessary examinations, Kuo Mo-jo enrolled in the premedical department. Since by his own account he was interested in literature and found science distasteful, and in view of his attitude in the matter of the Army Medical School in Tientsin, this seems to have been a strange choice. He tells us that he made this decision because he felt that through a medical career he could be of service to his countrymen, whereas he was uncertain of the practical value of the humanities and feared that his knowledge of mathematics was insufficient to qualify him for a career in engineering or the natural sciences.[5] His detractors attribute this decision to opportunism, alleging that he took the premedical examinations because there would be fewer competitors.[6] Even if we accept this interpretation, his action does not seem to have been unreasonable. His objective was to gain admission to a Japanese school so that he would be entitled to support from the Chinese government. His financial situation made it imperative that he attain this objective after only six months of preparation. It would seem only good sense, under the circumstances, that he should elect to take the set of examinations in which he was most likely to succeed.

As soon as Kuo Mo-jo received the first installment of his government stipend, he went to Hōjō, a famous seaside resort in Chiba-ken, to spend the summer vacation. Here he enjoyed two happy months, during which he learned to swim in the waters of Kagami-ga-ura, or Mirror Bay, across which on a clear day one could contemplate the majestic calm of Mount Fuji.[7]

In September 1914 Kuo Mo-jo entered the preparatory class of Chinese students at the First Higher School in

Tokyo. This was a special preparatory year required of all foreigners, in order to equip them to compete on an equal basis with their Japanese fellow students.[8] During this year Kuo Mo-jo lived with a relative who was a third-year student in the regular course at the same school.[9] He received a meager stipend from the Chinese government of 32 yen per month, an amount equal to $15.42 in American currency at the exchange rate of the time.[10] Among his classmates during this first year of study in Japan were Yü Ta-fu (1895–1945) and Chang Tzu-p'ing (1893–1947), both of whom were later to join him in founding the Creation Society in 1921.[11]

It was also during this preparatory year that Kuo Mo-jo first met Tu Kuo-hsiang (1889–1961), who later became a prominent Communist interpreter of the history of Chinese thought. At that time he was a third-year student of economics at the First Higher School, but was also much interested in philosophy. He and Kuo Mo-jo met while attending a series of lectures given in the Hongō district of Tokyo by a Buddhist scholar named Kuei Hsing-ku on the *Ta-ch'eng ch'i-hsin lun,* or *Discourse on the Awakening of Faith in the Mahāyāna,* one of the fundamental texts of Mahāyāna Buddhism.[12] It would appear evident that Kuo Mo-jo had become interested in Buddhism at the time.[13]

The only clue we have to his state of mind during this year is an incident which occurred in the spring of 1915. Taking advantage of the fact that the European powers were too preoccupied with the war in Europe to interfere in Far Eastern affairs, Japan on January 18, 1915, presented the Chinese government with the famous Twenty-one Demands,[14] which, if accepted in their entirety, would have reduced China to the status of a Japanese protectorate. Public opinion in China was rapidly aroused and this feeling was reflected, naturally enough, among the Chinese students in Japan. By early May it looked more and more as if the Chinese government would give in, and resentment among Chinese students in Japan reached fever pitch. Many of them left their schools and returned to China in protest. On May 7, 1915, the Japanese government sent an ultimatum that the Chinese government accept its demands within forty-eight hours. That very afternoon Kuo Mo-jo and some of his classmates left Japan for Shanghai in a frenzy of patriotism. To celebrate the occasion Kuo Mo-jo wrote a traditional poem in which he expressed an eagerness to die in his country's defense. They arrived in Shanghai only to find that on May 9 the government of Yüan Shih-k'ai had accepted most of the Japanese demands.[15] The only outcome of this patriotic demonstration was that Kuo Mo-jo and his companions spent three idle days in a Shanghai hotel before returning docilely to Japan.[16]

After the completion of his preparatory year in Tokyo, Kuo Mo-jo was transferred in the summer of 1915 to the Sixth Higher School in Okayama,[17] a seaport on the Inland Sea in southeastern Honshu, where he remained for three years. It was here that he first met Ch'eng Fang-wu, also destined to be a co-founder of the Creation Society, who was one year ahead of him in the Sixth Higher School.[18]

By the time Kuo Mo-jo transferred to the Sixth Higher School in Okayama a combination of factors, including frustration and guilt over his unhappy marriage and the fact that he had been working too hard during his first year and a half in Japan, had brought him to a severe state of neurasthenia. His chest ached unbearably. He was troubled by insomnia, and the few hours of sleep he managed to get were disturbed by nightmares. He feared that he was losing his memory because he found that he was unable to remember what he read from one page to the next. He was constantly plagued by headaches and giddiness. As a result of these unpleasant symptoms he became extremely despondent and considered becoming a Buddhist monk or even committing suicide.[19]

In search of some spiritual or psychological antidote to this state of mind, in mid-September 1915 Kuo Mo-jo bought a copy of the complete works of Wang Yang-ming. He soon became interested in the technique of "contemplative sitting" (*ching-tso*) advocated by Wang Yang-ming and even bought a Japanese book by Okada Torajirō (d. 1920) on how to practice it. From then on he engaged in contemplative sitting every day for half an hour upon rising and half an hour before going to bed. He also set himself the daily task of reading ten pages of Wang Yang-ming's complete works. He found this combination of exercises very helpful both physically and mentally. Within two weeks he was sleeping more restfully and taking a more active interest in the world around him.[20]

Wang Yang-ming was the great Ming dynasty idealist who taught, in opposition to the dominant rationalist trend of neo-Confucianism, that ". . . there can be no Principle, whether in actual fact or logically speaking, unless there be mind." [21] He said, "If Heaven, Earth, spirits, and things are separated from my spirituality or consciousness, they cease to be. And if my spirituality or consciousness is separated from them, it ceases to be also. Thus they are all permeated with a single force, so how can we be separated from them?" [22] As this quotation indicates, he was not only an idealist but a pantheist. He believed in the existence of an intuitive knowledge with which all men are endowed. "Any ideas which arise are without fail automatically comprehended by this 'intuitive knowledge' of our mind. If they be good, the intuitive knowledge in our mind automatically comprehends this. But if they be evil, this too the intuitive knowledge automatically comprehends." [23] He was especially insistent on the importance of self-cultivation, by means of which one was to strive for the utmost development of one's nature.[24] Another significant element in his philosophy was the idea that only by extending or translating intuitive knowledge into action can that knowledge be made complete. He said that knowledge was the beginning of action and action the completion of knowledge. This is his famous theory of the unity of knowledge and action.[25]

The study of Wang Yang-ming had a profound influence on Kuo Mo-jo. During the following decade he constantly proclaimed his belief in pantheism, in the fullest possible development of the potentialities of the individual, and in man's intuitive knowledge of good and evil. He frequently cited Western authorities in support of these ideas, but all of them are to be found in the philosophy of Wang Yang-ming and he states specifically that it was his interest in Wang Yang-ming's thought that led him to investigate the Western thinkers who held similar views. And not only Western thinkers; for the same stimulus led him to see the *Chuang-tzu* in a new light, to read the *Tao-te ching*,[26] to study Confucian philosophy, and to develop an interest in Indian thought.[27]

He was not, however, merely influenced by Wang Yang-ming. He tells us that from 1915 to 1917 he worshiped him.[28] The word "worship" carries with it a certain religious flavor, and indeed Kuo Mo-jo admits that during this period he went through a religious phase. Despite the solace he found in Wang Yang-ming he remained depressed and uncertain of his future. He was also desperately lonely, living as he was with few friends in a foreign country. Without an adequate ideology or faith of his own, he sought everywhere for a source of comfort and became much interested in mysticism.[29]

He began to see things he had never seen before in the *Chuang-tzu*. He had always admired this work for its literary style, but now he began to think about its philosophical content. According to the *Chuang-tzu*, *Tao* is the all-embracing first principle of the universe which manifests itself in all things. All things are in a constant state of flux and thus change is the natural order of nature. Emotions are bonds, for if one comprehends the reality of inevitable change one will be unmoved, come what may, and hence free. True experience, without which there is no true freedom, comes only when the individual is one with the universe.[30] Although this sounds like the submerging of the individual in the whole, it can also be interpreted as a form of extreme individualism, for the ultimate goal is complete freedom, something which cannot be attained if the individual hampers himself with any political or social ties. The fundamental pantheism of the *Chuang-tzu* finds its characteristic expression in magnificent rhetorical and lyrical statements of man's oneness with nature. This became one of the major themes in Kuo Mojo's poetry.

While he was going through his spiritual valley of darkness he was engaged as a student in learning Latin and German and in improving the English which he had begun to study during his first semester in the Chia-ting middle school in the autumn of 1907.[31] Latin was an obvious requirement for a premedical student, and German was of prime importance because Japanese medical education was based on the German system. Kuo Mo-jo says that he had to devote twenty-four or twenty-five class hours a week to the study of German. In addition to these languages there were the regular scientific requirements for premedical students.[32] When we remember that he was studying all these subjects through the medium of a language that was not his own, it is little wonder that he was physically and mentally exhausted.

During the spring vacation of 1916 Kuo Mo-jo and Ch'eng Fang-wu went on an excursion to Miyajima, an island just off the coast near Hiroshima and one of the three most famous beauty spots in Japan. On their way back they took a cruise around the Inland Sea and were especially impressed by the beautiful Ritsurin Park in Takamatsu on the island of Shikoku.[33]

In the summer of 1916 Kuo Mo-jo went to Tokyo to visit a friend named Ch'en Lung-chi who was in the hospital with tuberculosis. He found him in Saint Luke's Hospital, an American mission institution in Kyōbashi. The treatment he was receiving there seemed to be ineffectual, and so, on Kuo Mo-jo's suggestion, he moved to a sanatorium. He died there on August 1 and Kuo Mo-jo took charge of all the necessary arrangements for the funeral.

A few days after Ch'en Lung-chi's death, Kuo Mo-jo returned to Saint Luke's Hospital to try to recover an X-ray photograph of his friend which had been left there. The nurse with whom he negotiated was named Satō Tomiko (1897–   ). She was the daughter of a Japanese Protestant minister from Sendai and raised in the Protestant faith from her early childhood. After graduating from an American mission school in her native place she had made up her mind to devote her life to charitable work. In pursuit of this objective she had left her family, moved to Tokyo, and enrolled in Saint Luke's Hospital as a student nurse. She wept when she heard that Kuo Mo-jo's friend had died and she promised that she would locate the X-ray and mail it to him. Kuo Mo-jo was strongly impressed by the purity which the girl seemed to radiate. A week or so later he received the X-ray in the mail and with it a long letter from Tomiko, written in English, in which she urged him to seek the consolations of religion. This was the beginning of a regular correspondence between them, and after Kuo Mo-jo returned to Okayama they continued to write each other as often as three or four times a week. Tomiko's idealism and deeply felt religious convictions exerted such a strong influence on Kuo Mo-jo, even through her letters, that in November 1916 he announced himself a convert to Christianity. There is no way of knowing how long he considered himself to be a Christian, but his subsequent work reveals a thorough familiarity with both the Old and New Testaments.

During the autumn of 1916 Kuo Mo-jo suggested to Tomiko that she could devote herself to the service of society more effectively if she were to enter medical school and become a doctor than if she remained a nurse. The Ichigaya Women's Medical School in Okayama held entrance examinations in March. Kuo Mo-jo felt that he could spare enough of his government stipend to pay her way through medical school if they could share their living expenses. Since her work at the hospital did not allow her any time to prepare for the entrance examinations, Kuo Mo-jo went to Tokyo in late December, during the mid-year vacation, and persuaded her to leave the hospital and come live with him in Okayama, where she could devote herself full time to preparing for the examinations. Throughout their correspondence they had referred to each other as brother and sister, and this new relationship was meant to be platonic. Kuo Mo-jo counted on his conscience and on the fact that he was already a married man to keep it that way. It was not long, however, before nature took its course, and Tomiko became a probably not unwilling victim of seduction. Kuo Mo-jo suffered agonies of guilt over what he chose to regard as a violation of the sacred character of their love.

In the spring of 1917 Tomiko was admitted to the medical school and studied there for several months. Before long, however, she became pregnant and had to leave the school and give up her plans for a medical education.[34]

Kuo Mo-jo and Satō Tomiko lived together as man and wife for twenty years and she bore him five children, but they were never formally married because he refused to divorce his legitimate wife in Szechwan. When his parents discovered what he had done they broke with him temporarily and only forgave him when his first child was born. In their letters to him, however, they referred to Tomiko as his concubine and to her children as illegitimate. This language infuriated Kuo Mo-jo. The only explanation he has given for his failure to divorce his first wife is that since she knew nothing but the traditional Chinese moral code such a step on his part might lead her to commit suicide.[35]

It is now necessary to turn our attention to one of the most important influences on Kuo Mo-jo's early development as a writer — the famous Bengali poet and author Rabindranath Tagore. Kuo Mo-jo's first encounter with Tagore occurred in the spring of 1915, during the second semester of his preparatory year at the First Higher School in Tokyo. One day the relative with whom he was living brought home with him a mimeographed selection of Tagore's poetry from *The Crescent Moon,* which was being used for supplementary reading in his English course. Included among them were the poems "On the Seashore," "Baby's Way," "Sleep Stealer," and "Clouds and Waves." Kuo Mo-jo picked them up out of curiosity and found them unlike anything he had ever encountered. They were easy to understand and were not written in any regular form. Yet they seemed to him sheer poetry with an atmosphere of freshness and tranquillity about them. It had never occurred to him that poetry could be written in such a way, and he tells us that it made him feel twenty years younger. From that time on the name of Tagore was indelibly engraved in his memory.

Tagore had become internationally prominent when he won the Nobel Prize in literature in 1913, and he immediately became popular in Japan. This popularity was still at its height when Kuo Mo-jo moved to Okayama. In the spring of 1916 he scraped together enough money to buy a copy of *The Crescent Moon* for himself. He says that he was as happy with it as a child with a picture book. In the autumn of 1916 he stumbled upon a collection of Tagore's books in the Okayama public library. Thereafter, for a period of time, every afternoon as soon as school was over he would rush to the library reading room and, with grateful tears in his eyes, would recite Tagore's poems to himself, memorizing the ones he liked best. It was, he says, as though he were experiencing nirvana. He would remain thus entranced until the street lights were turned on and it was time for him to return to his lodgings.

During these and the following years Kuo Mo-jo read everything by Tagore that he could lay his hands on, including *Gitanjali, The Gardener, The King of the Dark Chamber, One Hundred Poems of Kabir, Stray Birds,* and *Lover's Gift and Crossing.* In the fall of 1917 Tomiko was expecting a child and Kuo Mo-jo, in the hope of making some money, translated selected poems from *The Crescent Moon, The Gardener,* and *Gitanjali* into Chinese under the title *A Selection of Tagore's Poetry.* He then wrote to the Commercial Press (Shang-wu yin-shu kuan) and the China Book Company (Chung-hua shu-chü), the two largest publishing houses in China, to see if they were interested in his manuscript. Tagore was not then popular or as yet even widely known in China, which was not nearly as sensitive to world currents as Japan. Neither publishing house was interested. This exchange of correspondence, probably Kuo Mo-jo's first attempt to publish, took place sometime in August or September of 1917.

It was also Tagore who first inspired Kuo Mo-jo to try his hand at writing poetry free of the restraints of traditional prosody. Kuo had written many poems in traditional Chinese meters and has continued to do so, but they are not particularly noteworthy.[36] Kuo Mo-jo says that his first inkling of what poetry is all about came in the spring of 1913, in the Chengtu Higher School, when he chanced upon Longfellow's "The Arrow and the Song" in the fourth or fifth volume of Chamberlain's *Twentieth Century Readers,* which they were using as an English text. In some mysterious way this poem gave him a new understanding of the nature of poetry and enabled him to enjoy the lyrics in the *Shih ching* which he had earlier memorized without any sense of appreciation. It was his encounter with Tagore, however, which first inspired him to try writing poetry in a new style himself.

Kuo Mo-jo's earliest experiment in this direction was a prose poem written in English entitled "Shadow and Dream," which he presented to Tomiko in December 1916.[37] Many of his early poems, especially those written in 1918 and the first half of 1919, were inspired by Tomiko and composed under the direct influence of Tagore.[38]

It was not only Tagore's poetry but also his thought which appealed to Kuo Mo-jo. From May to September 1916 Tagore had been in Japan on a lecture tour.[39] Although Kuo Mo-jo did not hear him in person, he read the reports of his speeches in the Japanese press and was thus exposed to an explicit statement of his views as well as the more general impressions that he was able to garner from his literary works. In 1923 he subsumed his understanding of Tagore's philosophy under three headings: a pantheism in which all discrete phenomena are but manifestations of Brahma; respect for the self; and the gospel of love. It was also through Tagore that Kuo Mo-jo had been introduced to the Indian poet Kabir (1440–1518) and to the thought of the Vedas and the Upanishads, and he understood Tagore's philosophy to be essentially a restatement of the doctrines expressed in these monuments of ancient Indian culture.[40]

It is not hard to see how attractive such views might be to a mind which was already steeped in the philosophies of the *Chuang-tzu* and Wang Yang-ming. The examination of these foreign ways of thought sharpened his mind so that he now saw things in the Chinese philosophers that he had not seen before. During his third year at Okayama he even planned to write a critique of the *Chuang-tzu* and sent an elaborate outline of the projected work to Kuo K'ai-wen in Peking, but his practical-minded brother did not encourage him to continue with the project.[41]

During 1917–1918, his last year at the Sixth Higher School in Okayama, Kuo Mo-jo fell strongly under the influence of German literature. German was administered to the premedical students in such heavy doses that those who survived the treatment must have had an adequate knowledge of the language after two or three years. It is therefore safe to assume that by his last year in Okayama, Kuo Mo-jo was able to read German with some degree of fluency. Most of the language teachers in the Japanese higher schools of the time were men who had taken their degrees in the literatures of the languages in question. Thus they were accustomed to using works of literature as texts even when teaching premedical students or engineers. Kuo Mo-jo, who was trying desperately to devote his attention wholeheartedly to science — or so he tells us — was thus enticed back to literature by the subversive texts he was required to read in his third-year German class. Among the works that he was required to read were Goethe's autobiography *Dichtung und Wahrheit* and Eduard Mörike's novella *Mozart auf der Reise nach Prag*. He was also introduced to the poetry of Goethe and Heine and on his own time read works by Dostoyevsky, Turgenev, Nietzsche, Ibsen, and Björnson.[42] The love lyrics of Heine made a particularly strong impression on him. Goethe, with his not entirely successful but unremitting efforts to mingle science and poetry, had an immediate appeal for the frustrated young medical student who was trying to combine these perennial incompatibles himself. The German poet's pantheism also struck a responsive chord. It was through Goethe that Kuo Mo-jo was introduced to Spinoza, and he read through a goodly part of his *Ethica, Tractatus Theologico-Politicus,* and *Tractatus de Intellectus Emendatione.*

It is difficult to determine whether it was his love of Goethe and Tagore which led Kuo Mo-jo to pantheism or whether it was his basic pantheism which led him to appreciate poets who exhibited such tendencies. Although his fondness for these particular figures cannot be explained solely in terms of the many affinities between their thought and that of the *Chuang-tzu* or Wang Yang-ming, these similarities may well have been a determining factor. During this period and for some years thereafter he proclaimed himself an ardent believer in pantheism, which he saw as a common thread running through the philosophies of the *Chuang-tzu,* Wang Yang-ming, Spinoza, Goethe, and Tagore. And this is the thread which led him almost inevitably to Western romanticism.[43]

On December 12, 1917, Kuo Mo-jo's first son, Ho-sheng, was born.[44] Thus his growing interest in literature and philosophy coincided with a period of increased financial strain. This pressure was further intensified by a turn for the worse in Sino-Japanese relations. On March 25, 1918, two days after he had resumed the premiership of the Peking government, Tuan Ch'i-jui (1865–1936) secretly concluded the Sino-Japanese Military Mutual Assistance Convention, which gave Japan the right to send troops to north Manchuria and Outer Mongolia. Rumors of this convention soon spread abroad and on May 5 a group of Chinese students in Tokyo demonstrated their concern by establishing an organization called Corps of Chinese Students in Japan for National Salvation (Liu-Jih hsüeh-sheng chiu-kuo t'uan). The following evening, while the leaders of this group were holding a planning session in a Chinese restaurant in Kanda, the Japanese police broke in and arrested forty-six of them.[45] This created a fever of anti-Japanese sentiment among the Chinese students throughout Japan, and one of the outgrowths of this furor was the creation of a group called the Punish the Traitors Club (Chu han-chien hui). The avowed purpose of this organization was to force all Chinese students with Japanese wives to divorce them. If this seems to us an extreme way of demonstrating one's patriotism it should be remembered that this point of view was not limited to the students but was shared by the officials in the Chinese Ministry of Education. In 1910 that body memorialized on this issue and secured an imperial decree prohibiting Chinese students abroad from marrying foreigners.[46] It has been remarked by several recent observers that even today in Communist

China officials look with a jaundiced eye on mixed marriages and even on social fraternization between Chinese and foreigners of the opposite sex.[47] It is perhaps not too surprising then that Kuo Mo-jo found himself labeled a traitor.

His situation became even more difficult when it was decided that the Chinese students in Japan should return to China in a body on May 12 in protest against the Sino-Japanese Military Mutual Assistance Convention and Japanese police brutality.[48] Not only did Kuo Mo-jo refuse to repudiate Tomiko and his baby son, but he was so short of funds that he could not return to China even if he wanted to. Thus he was considered to be doubly a traitor by the more ardent patriots among his Chinese fellow students. Kuo Mo-jo was not, at least at that time, a thick-skinned man, and the abuse to which he was subjected on this occasion hurt him so deeply, he tells us, that he often wept when he had an opportunity to be alone.[49]

At the end of the spring semester of 1918, Kuo Mo-jo graduated from the Sixth Higher School in Okayama and was accepted by the Medical School of Kyushu Imperial University.[50] He devoted part of the summer to translating his favorite lyrics by Heine and completed a manuscript entitled *A Selection of Heine's Poetry*, but he had no better luck with it than he had had a year before with his anthology of Tagore.[51] Kuo Mo-jo's entry into medical school in September 1918 can be considered to mark the end of his apprenticeship. During the following year he finally found an outlet through which he was able to publish his work, and although he continued to be enrolled in the university, he had become nationally famous long before he was graduated.

Chapter 5

The Medical Student as Romantic Artist: Fukuoka, 1918–1921

Kyushu Imperial University was located at Fukuoka, a city on the northwestern coast of Kyushu, the southernmost of Japan's four main islands. In late August 1918 Kuo Mo-jo and his family moved to Hakozaki, a suburb to the north of Fukuoka situated on Hakata Bay, the scene of the famous Mongol invasions of 1274 and 1281. The Chinese government stipends had been raised during the preceding summer, so Kuo Mo-jo was now receiving seventy-two yen per month, but he was financially pressed because he had to buy textbooks and to pay the first semester's tuition of forty yen in a lump sum. They moved into the second floor of a small pawnshop near the back gate of the medical school, where they paid a monthly rent of six yen for a single room, about ten feet square, with a low ceiling and only two windows. Despite the cramped quarters it was a desirable location, for they were within a few minutes' walk of the sea, which was lined with beaches and pine woods.[1] It was an ideal place for children and for poets.

One afternoon before school had opened Kuo Mo-jo was walking along the beach in front of the famous Hakozaki Shintō Shrine when he ran into Chang Tzu-p'ing, his former classmate during the preparatory year at the First Higher School in Tokyo, whom he had not seen for three years. When Kuo Mo-jo was transferred to Okayama,

Chang Tzu-p'ing had been sent to the Fifth Higher School in Kumamoto, a city in southwestern Kyushu, where he had majored in the natural sciences. He should have graduated from higher school at the same time Kuo Mo-jo did, but because he had returned to China in early May as a protest against the Sino-Japanese Military Mutual Assistance Convention, he had been denied the right to take make-up examinations and graduate with the rest of his class. He had not even known that Kuo Mo-jo was in Fukuoka, but had come there to spend a few days swimming before school opened.

Although they did not really know each other very well they struck up a conversation, in the course of which, after discussing the paucity and low quality of the existing Chinese periodicals, they discovered that they were both interested in the idea of a magazine devoted exclusively to literature. Since nothing of this kind was being published in China at the time, they thought they might be able to start such a magazine themselves. The only people they could think of with the requisite literary ability who might be interested in joining them in such an enterprise were Yü Ta-fu, their former classmate in Tokyo, and Ch'eng Fang-wu, who had been in the Sixth Higher School at Okayama during two of Kuo Mo-jo's years there. All of this was extremely tentative, little more than youthful daydreaming, but they decided to sound out the other two on the idea and to correspond about it with each other. It was these very four who founded the Creation Society in 1921, and Kuo Mo-jo traces its genesis to this casual conversation. Two days after their talk Chang Tzu-p'ing returned to Kumamoto and Kuo Mo-jo began to attend classes at medical school.[2]

One day in late September when Kuo Mo-jo came home from school he found Ch'eng Fang-wu waiting for him.

His friend had just arrived from China, to which he had returned in May, like Chang Tzu-p'ing, as part of the student protest movement. He was acting as interpreter for a blind old man named Ch'en from his home town in Hunan, who had come to Fukuoka to consult a famous eye specialist at the university hospital. When he saw what straitened circumstances Kuo Mo-jo was in, he suggested that they should find a house big enough for all of them and move in with old Mr. Ch'en, who would pay the rent if Tomiko would do the cooking and housework. This plan was soon agreed upon, and the next day they moved into a large house near the Hakozaki Shrine, with four rooms on the second floor and two on the first. Mr. Ch'en paid three months rent in advance and he and his son, their servant, and Ch'eng Fang-wu moved into the top floor, leaving the one below for Kuo Mo-jo and his family. Two weeks later, after everything was settled at the hospital, Ch'eng Fang-wu returned to Tokyo Imperial University, where he was majoring in ordnance manufacturing. An operation was performed on Mr. Ch'en's eyes, but it was unsuccessful, and in mid-November he returned to China. Kuo Mo-jo and his family remained in the house until the rent ran out at the end of December. On the last day of the year they moved to a little two-story house by the sea with two upstairs rooms but only half a floor downstairs. The rent was six yen per month, the same amount they had been paying for a single room before. They lived in this house until April 1921.[3]

In the fall of 1918 Kuo Mo-jo wrote his first story. It was entitled "K'u-lou" (The skeleton) and was a grotesque tale on the theme of necrophilia. The outline which he gives us is reminiscent of the worst excesses of European romanticism or the Gothic horror tales of "Monk Lewis" and Charles Robert Maturin. Kuo Mo-jo thought that it was good enough to publish and submitted it to the *Tung-fang tsa-chih* (The eastern miscellany), one of the largest magazines in China. When the manuscript was rejected he indulged in the romantic act of burning it.[4]

His next story, entitled "Mu-yang ai-hua" (The sad tale of a shepherdess), was written in February and March 1919 and is the earliest example of his prose which is still preserved in published form. It is a rather crude piece of work. The story is set in northeastern Korea, a region to which Kuo Mo-jo had never been, the plot is contrived, and the characters are unreal. It is written in colloquial Chinese but the style is rather stilted. It's only notable feature is that it is purely a work of the imagination, whereas almost all of Kuo Mo-jo's later stories are autobiographical to a greater or lesser extent.[5]

On May 4, 1919, the students of Peking staged a mass demonstration against the government's weak foreign policy at the Paris Peace Conference, where it had been unable to prevent the other powers from permitting Japan to retain the special position in Shantung that she had wrested from Germany during the World War. The Peking government adopted repressive measures, which only served to set off a series of sympathetic strikes and demonstrations by students and merchants all over the country. The wave of nationalist, anti-imperialist, and antimilitarist sentiment that swept over the nation brought in its wake the further spread of the new literary ideas and iconoclastic cultural attitudes that had been brewing for several years in the small circle of enlightened intellectuals in Peking and Shanghai. This whole complex of events and trends, which is known as the May Fourth Movement, is a significant turning point in modern Chinese history.[6]

The effects of this movement made themselves felt wherever there were Chinese. In June 1919 Kuo Mo-jo and a group of his Chinese fellow students, including Ch'en Chün-che, who had been a year ahead of him at the Sixth Higher School at Okayama,[7] formed an organization called the Hsia-she, or China Society. The purpose of this organization was to collect samples of anti-Chinese writings from Japanese publications, translate and mimeograph them, and send copies to schools and newspaper offices in China. By pooling their resources they bought a mimeographing machine, and they had no difficulty in finding material, but it turned out that few of the members other than Kuo Mo-jo and Ch'en Chün-che had either the patience or the ability to turn out readable translations. Before long Ch'en Chün-che returned to his home in Chekiang, leaving the entire project in the hands of Kuo Mo-jo, who spent the summer doing the work of translating, mimeographing, and mailing all by himself.

One by-product of this enterprise had far-reaching effects for Kuo Mo-jo. The members of the Hsia-she felt that it would be desirable to subscribe to a Chinese newspaper and they chose the *Shih-shih hsin-pao* of Shanghai, which began to arrive in early September. This paper had adopted many new features as a result of the May Fourth Movement, one of which was a popular literary supplement called *Hsüeh-teng* (Lamp of learning). In the literary supplement to the first issue that arrived, that of August 29, 1919, Kuo Mo-jo encountered for the first time a new-style Chinese poem in the contemporary colloquial language by someone other than himself. It was a piece of occasional verse by K'ang Po-ch'ing, one of the early experimenters in this new poetic genre, written to bid farewell to Tseng Ch'i, Kuo Mo-jo's old schoolmate from Chengtu days, on his departure for Paris.[8] Poetry in the colloquial language that did not observe any of the traditional rules of Chinese prosody had made its bow to the reading public in the January 1918 issue of *Hsin ch'ing-nien* (New youth),[9] the leading avant-garde journal of the pre–May Fourth period. That Kuo Mo-jo remained unaware of the nature of this development until a year and a half later gives some indication of the extent to which he must have been cut off from the Chinese literary scene in the period before the May Fourth Movement.

Although Kuo Mo-jo's initial experiments with new verse forms had been in English, as early as the summer of 1918 he had written a poem in modern colloquial Chinese with rhyming lines of irregular length. It is called "The Temptation of Death" (Ssu ti yu-huo) and reads as follows:

> I have a little blade
> Who leans by the window and smiles at me.
> She smiles at me, saying:
> "Mo-jo, why must you upset yourself so?
> Come quickly and kiss me
> That I may bring you surcease of sorrow."
>
> Outside my window, blue sea water
> Calls to me unceasingly.
> She calls to me, saying:
> "Mo-jo, why must you upset yourself so?
> Come quickly, embrace me
> That I may bring you surcease of sorrow." [10]

This is not very good poetry, but it is significant that it owes nothing to the Chinese poetic tradition in concept, structure, or vocabulary. It is certainly new poetry, for it represents a complete break with the past.

Kuo Mo-jo tells us that "The Temptation of Death" was written under the influence of Tagore, and in the period since the summer of 1918 he had composed a number of other poems under the influence of Tagore and Heine.[11] When he saw the verse by K'ang Po-ch'ing his immediate reaction was that, if this was all the new poetry amounted to, there was no reason why he should not be able to publish some of his own poems. He therefore made neat copies of two of his earlier poems, "Egret" (Lu-ssu) and "Bathing in Hakata Bay with My Son in My Arms" (Pao erh yü Po-to wan),[12] and submitted them to *Hsüeh-teng*. At that time the editor of *Hsüeh-teng* was Kuo Shao-yü, who later achieved fame as a historian of Chinese literary criticism. He accepted the two poems for publication and they appeared in *Hsüeh-teng* on September 11, 1919. Kuo Mo-jo's feeling of pride at seeing his work in print for the first time produced in the subsequent months a veritable explosion of poetic activity.[13]

At this point it is necessary to say something about Kuo Mo-jo's adoption of the name under which he published these poems and by which he became known. One day while he was a student in Japan, sometime between 1914 and 1919, his parents sent him some money through a bank in Shanghai and it arrived addressed to Miss Kuo K'ai-chen (Kuo K'ai-chen *nü-shih*). This is an easy mistake to make, for the character "chen" means "chaste" and is frequently used in women's names. Kuo Mo-jo was not particularly fond of his given name to start with, so after this incident he adopted the name Mo-jo,[14] or to be more accurate, the name Mei-jo. During the Han dynasty the Ta-tu River, on which Kuo Mo-jo's home town of Sha-wan is situated, was called the Mei River (Mei-shui), and the present-day Ya River (Ya-ho), a tributary of the Ta-tu River, into which it flows shortly before it reaches Chia-ting, was called the Jo River (Jo-shui).[15] The two names were first linked together by Ssu-ma Hsiang-ju (179–117 B.C.), the famous Han poet, in his "Rebuttal to the Elders of Shu" (Nan Shu fu-lao), where the words "kuan Mei Jo" (extended the boundaries to the Mei and Jo rivers) occur.[16] Since Kuo Mo-jo's home town was on one of these rivers he felt that Mei-jo would be an appropriate name.[17] The character *mei,* however, is very rarely used, whereas there is a character pronounced *mo* which is in common usage and is written in almost the same way. Since most of his readers mispronounced his name as Kuo Mo-jo, he eventually capitulated and began to write it that way himself.[18] Thus was born one of the most famous names in modern Chinese literary history.

At about the same time that Kuo Mo-jo's poetry began to appear in *Hsüeh-teng,* he bought a Japanese book by Arishima Takeo (1878–1923) entitled *Hangyakusha* (Rebels), which was about Rodin, Millet, and Whitman. This was his first introduction to Whitman and he became completely intoxicated. He read *Leaves of Grass* and by mid-autumn of 1919 was completely under its spell. All of his most famous poems, including "Shouting on the Rim of the World" (Li tsai ti-ch'iu pien shang fang-hao), "Earth, My Mother" (Ti-ch'iu, wo ti mu-ch'in), "Good Morning" (Ch'en-an), "The Nirvana of the Phoenixes" (Feng-huang nieh-p'an), "Coal in the Grate" (Lu chung mei), "Hymn to the Bandits" (Fei-t'u sung), "The Hound of Heaven" (T'ien-kou), "The Lamp of the Mind" (Hsin-teng), and "The Lesson of the Cannons" (Chü-p'ao chih chiao-hsün),[19] were composed during the year after he first encountered Whitman, and under his direct influence.[20]

When Kuo Mo-jo began to sound Whitman's "barbaric yawp" in Chinese, the literary world took notice. Achilles Fang has described the situation as follows:

His poetry definitely strikes a new note in the history of Chinese poetry. It is neither Wordsworthian "emotion recollected in tranquility" nor Coleridge's "the best word in the best order," both of which definitions apply to most of the orthodox poems of China. With him, as with Whitman, poetry was an outlet for relieving himself of irrepressible egotism and eleutheromania, two things most solicitously suppressed by all traditionalists. . . . the emergence of Kuo Mo-jo on the Chinese poetic scene was almost miraculous; it marked the end of tradition. . . . Without the impetus given it by Whitmanism, Chinese poetry of the last thirty years could scarcely have enjoyed what little vitality it had.[21]

Whitman not only influenced Kuo Mo-jo profoundly in the matter of poetic technique, but also through the content of his message. Kuo Mo-jo had not really been much of a rebel before he encountered Whitman, who seems to have galvanized his discontent. Whitman said of his own poetry:

Not songs of loyalty alone are these,
But songs of insurrection also,
For I am the sworn poet of every dauntless rebel the world over,
And he going with me leaves peace and routine behind him,
And stakes his life to be lost at any moment.[22]

In late 1919 Kuo Mo-jo wrote a poem entitled "Hymn to the Bandits," for which these lines of Whitman might have served as an epigraph. He tells us that he was inspired to write it by his annoyance at the way in which the Japanese press persisted in referring to the Chinese students who played such a prominent role during and after the May Fourth incident as "student bandits" (hsüeh-fei). Kuo Mo-jo responded by composing a hymn in praise of the creative role of men who have been labeled bandits. It is in six stanzas, each of which deals with three men who are presumed to have something in common. In the order in which they occur, the men whose praises he sang were: Cromwell, Washington, and José Rizal; Marx, Engels, and Lenin; Sakyamuni, Mo Ti, and Martin Luther; Copernicus, Darwin, and Nietzsche; Rodin, Whitman, and Tolstoy; Rousseau, Pestalozzi, and Tagore. The fact that Kuo Mo-jo expressed his admiration for such a heterogeneous group of people indicates that he was not particularly ideologically inclined. It is interesting, however, that as early as 1919 he should have chosen to praise Marx, Engels, and Lenin. It is also significant that at this early date he already made a distinction between political and social problems, for he classified Cromwell, Washington, and Rizal as political revolutionaries and Marx, Engels, and Lenin as social revolutionaries.[23]

There is little evidence that Kuo Mo-jo was much perturbed over the terrible chaos in China before he encountered Whitman. He had paid little or no attention to internal developments in China before 1919. Yüan Shih-k'ai's monarchical ambitions and their final frustration, his death, and the resulting fragmentation of power at the hands of competing warlords are not so much as mentioned in Kuo Mo-jo's autobiography. Whitman's great concern over the internal divisions in the United States that led to the Civil War and his eloquent defense of the bloodshed that must have offended his Quaker conscience but proved necessary to assert the sovereignty of the Union over all its members may have been as influential as the May Fourth Movement in opening Kuo Mo-jo's eyes to the terrible realities of the Chinese situation.

Whitman foresaw the trend toward a great world conflict which he hoped would result in the eradication of national barriers. He wrote:

Are all nations communing? is there going to be but one heart
    to the globe?
Is humanity forming en-masse? for lo, tyrants tremble, crowns
    grow dim.
The earth, restive, confronts a new era, perhaps a general
    divine war.[24]

Kuo Mo-jo preached the necessity of bloodshed even before
he became an adherent of Marxism-Leninism; it did not
prove difficult for him to move from Whitman's prophetic
eloquence to the Communist vision of world revolution.

In his introduction to *Leaves of Grass*, Emory Holloway
says: "Whitman did not share Thoreau's distrust of science, industry, and social organization as enemies of individualism, but he did declare that political freedom,
mastery of natural resources, and industrial progress are
but necessary first steps toward a leisure in which man may
learn to think and to cultivate the aesthetic and social
arts." [25] Kuo Mo-jo came to similar conclusions. He subsequently argued that there was no inconsistency between
his belief in individualism and his conversion to Marxism-
Leninism, since the latter only indicated the recognition
on his part of the necessary priority of the "first steps" before individualism could be meaningful for any but a small
minority.

The concepts of the unity of man's intuitive knowledge
and of respect for the self, which Kuo Mo-jo had already
encountered in Wang Yang-ming and Tagore, he found
also in Whitman, who proclaimed:

I celebrate myself, and sing myself,
And what I assume you shall assume,
For every atom belonging to me as good belongs to you. . . .
These are really the thoughts of all men in all ages and lands,
    they are not original with me,

If they are not yours as much as mine they are nothing, or next
    to nothing. . . .
By God! I will accept nothing which all cannot have their
    counterpart of on the same terms.[26]

But it was Whitman's consuming sense of mission and the
feeling he conveys of being driven to create by some com-
pelling force that probably had the greatest influence on
Kuo Mo-jo. Whitman describes his own inspiration as
follows:

The urge, the ardor, the unconquerable will,
The potent, felt, interior command, stronger than words,
A message from the Heavens whispering to me even in sleep,
These sped me on.[27]

During the year after he first encountered Whitman, Kuo
Mo-jo felt himself to be driven by just such forces. This is
how he describes it:

"Earth, My Mother" was written in December 1919 just
after the New Year's vacation began. One morning, when I
had gone to the Fukuoka library to read, I suddenly felt an
attack of poetic inspiration. Running outside, I took off my
wooden clogs and walked back and forth in my bare feet on
a secluded gravel path behind the library, where from time to
time I actually lay down on the path in the hope of finding
greater intimacy with "mother earth," by feeling her skin and
accepting her embrace. . . . Under these conditions, urged
on and stimulated by the poem itself, I finally saw it to completion and dashed home to get it down on paper, feeling as
though I had been reborn. . . .
My long poem "The Nirvana of the Phoenixes" was composed during two periods of a single day. In the morning I was
in class listening to a lecture when the idea for a poem suddenly struck me and, writing in my notebook in bits and

snatches, I dashed off the first half of the poem. In the evening, just as I was about to go to bed, the inspiration for the second half of the poem struck me. Leaning on the pillow I wrote it down with a pencil as fast as I could. My whole body seemed to be suffering from the chills, so that even my teeth were chattering. . . .

From 1918 to 1919 I was frequently attacked by such compulsions. Whenever they came I would begin to write poetry like one possessed, and sometimes I could not write fast enough to keep up with my inspiration.[28]

Although Kuo Mo-jo had been in Okayama as a premedical student, more than half of his time had been taken up by language study, which further stimulated his interest in literature. At medical school in Fukuoka, however, the picture was different. There was no longer any language study as such, and he had to spend much of his time memorizing medical nomenclature in foreign languages. After less than a year of this he decided that medical school was not for him and began to consider transferring to the liberal arts. Tomiko, however, who had already borne him one child and was again pregnant, was strongly opposed to his leaving medical school. More acutely conscious of their tenuous economic situation than her husband, she argued that a knowledge of Western medicine would assure them some degree of security, and that since he had already gone this far in medicine it would be foolish to give it up now, however unpleasant he found it. Kuo Mo-jo suffered himself to be dissuaded, but not without subjecting his domestic relations to an additional strain.[29]

It was in this mood of frustration and resentment that he began, in the summer of 1919, to translate some selections from Goethe's *Faust*. He was attracted to it by the sentiments expressed in the opening soliloquy wherein Faust despairs of the value of science and of methodical thought in general and fears that excessive intellectualization has weakened his vital energies.[30] Kuo Mo-jo says that Faust's words seemed to spring from his own heart. His translation of this soliloquy was published in a special national holiday edition of *Hsüeh-teng* on October 10, 1919.[31]

Some three months after Kuo Mo-jo had begun to subscribe to the *Shih-shih hsin-pao*, Kuo Shao-yü, the editor of *Hsüeh-teng*, resigned his position and went to Europe. He was replaced by a young man named Tsung Po-hua (1897–), whose primary interest was philosophy. Kuo Mo-jo claims that Tsung Po-hua was not initially well disposed toward the new poetry, and that consequently there was a period of time during which no such poems appeared in *Hsüeh-teng*. One day, however, Kuo Mo-jo wrote him a letter discussing the philosophy of Mo-tzu (fifth century B.C.),[32] which seems to have changed his attitude, for he subsequently began to publish the backlog of poems which he had already received from Kuo Mo-jo. As a result, during the winter of 1919–1920, a poem by Kuo Mo-jo appeared in almost every issue of *Hsüeh-teng* — sometimes taking up more than half the available space.[33]

Kuo Mo-jo's letter to Tsung Po-hua was the start of a regular correspondence between them. They found each other especially congenial because of a mutual affinity for pantheism. It was through Tsung Po-hua that Kuo Mo-jo became acquainted with T'ien Han (1898–), who later became one of the leading playwrights of modern China. At that time T'ien Han was a student at the Tokyo Higher Normal School (Tōkyō kōtō shihan gakkō).[34] In February 1920, at Tsung Po-hua's suggestion, T'ien Han and Kuo Mo-jo initiated a lively correspondence, largely on questions of literature and aesthetics.[35] As early as February 29, 1920, in his third letter to Kuo Mo-jo, T'ien Han suggested that they should publish the letters exchanged in the three-way correspondence between the two of them and Tsung Po-hua.[36]

On March 15, 1920, Kuo Mo-jo's second child, a son named Po-sheng, was born.[37] Four days later, on March 19, T'ien Han took advantage of his spring vacation to come to Fukuoka and spend a week with Kuo Mo-jo. This was the first time the two had met, and Kuo Mo-jo was somewhat embarrassed by the rather hectic postnatal circumstances in which T'ien Han found the household. Nevertheless, it turned out to be a significant visit. An interesting light is thrown on Kuo Mo-jo's ambivalent attitude toward Tomiko by a conversational exchange that took place on March 20. T'ien Han asked, "After marriage, can love be preserved?" and Kuo Mo-jo responded, "Marriage is love's funeral." [38] On March 22 T'ien Han completed the preparation of the manuscript of their correspondence and, before sending it to Tsung Po-hua in Shanghai, he asked his friend to suggest a title. Kuo Mo-jo proposed *Kleeblatt,* which is German for cloverleaf, and this the title became, in the Chinese form of *San yeh chi*. The same day Kuo Mo-jo mentioned for the first time a desire to translate Goethe's *The Sorrows of Young Werther*.[39] On March 23 the two went on an excursion to the famous scenic resort of Dazaifu and in their intoxication expressed the desire to become the Goethe and Schiller of China. The following day T'ien Han returned to Tokyo.[40]

San yeh chi was published in Shanghai by the Ya-tung T'u-shu Kuan (The Oriental Book Company) in May 1920. Two-thirds of its contents were contributed by Kuo Mo-jo, whose letters took up 109 of its 166 pages. It was well received in the Chinese literary world and by 1927 had run through five editions.[41] This marked Kuo Mo-jo's first appearance before the Chinese reading public in book form. In several of the letters included in this collection he gives

1912 年在成都

Kuo Mo-jo in Chengtu, 1912.
Kuo Mo-jo, *Mo-jo wen-chi*,
vol. VI (Peking, 1958).

王獨清　　郭沫若　　郁達夫　　成仿吾

Left to right, Wang Tu-ch'ing, Kuo Mo-jo, Yü Ta-fu, and Ch'eng Fang-wu
in Canton, May 1926. *Ch'uang-tsao yueh-k'an* (Creation monthly) 1.4
(June 1926).

us a vivid picture of his thinking, especially on aesthetic issues, in the spring of 1920.

Kuo Mo-jo's correspondence with Tsung Po-hua and T'ien Han apparently helped him to recover from the mood of depression into which he had fallen in medical school. In a letter to Tsung Po-hua written on February 16, 1920, Kuo Mo-jo described his feelings as follows:

I often regret that I lack the genius of an Augustine, a Rousseau, or a Tolstoy, that I might write a naked "confession," and thus reveal myself to the world. Unless I rid myself completely of my past, my future will be enveloped in dark shadows, without any hope of development. If I do not rid myself completely of my burden of guilt, my pitiful soul will remain embroiled in a sea of tears, with no prospect of escape. In the past, the only solution I could see to my problems was death; but now I have adopted a different approach, and want to move in the direction of life. In the past I lived as a devil in darkest hell; from now on I want to live as a man in the world of light.[42]

It is clear from this quotation that Kuo Mo-jo tended to dramatize his own feelings in typical nineteenth-century European romantic fashion. He had in fact adopted not only the role of the European romantic, but also the literary theory that went with it. In a letter written to Tsung Po-hua on January 18, 1920, he said:[43]

It seems to me that only a poem which is a pure manifestation of the poetic feelings and images in the mind, a strain flowing from the well of life, a melody played on the lute strings of the heart, a tremor of life, a cry of the soul, can be a true poem, a good poem, a wellspring of human happiness, an intoxicating wine, a heaven of consolation. Whenever I encounter such a poem, no matter whether it be in modern or traditional style, whether it be by a recent or an ancient poet, whether it be Chinese or foreign, I only wish I could swallow it, book, paper, and all; I only wish I could digest it, muscles, bones, and all. . . .

It seems to me that a thing like a poem cannot be "composed." . . . Shelley put it very well when he said, "A man cannot say, 'I will compose poetry'." Goethe also said that whenever he felt the onslaught of poetic inspiration he rushed to the nearest table and, without even bothering to straighten out the sheet of paper before him, would write down, while still standing up, whatever came to him. It seems to me that this experience of Goethe's confirms the truth of Shelley's words. Poems are not "composed," but "transcribed."

To me the poet's state of mind is like a stretch of clear sea water. When there is no wind, it is as smooth as the face of a mirror, and the images of all things are reflected in it; but no sooner is there a wind than waves arise and the reflected images awake to life and movement. This wind is what we call intuition or inspiration, the waves are our rising emotions, and the moving images are the revolving stuff of imagination. To me these things are the essence of poetry and, if they can only be transcribed, the result will be poetry in both form and substance. When great waves are produced the result is strong and vigorous poetry — the "Li-sao" of Ch'ü Yüan, the "Hu-chia shih-pa p'ai" of Ts'ai Yen, the songs and ballads of Li Po and Tu Fu, Dante's *Divine Comedy,* Milton's *Paradise Lost* and *Paradise Regained,* or Goethe's *Faust.* When only ripples are produced the result is tranquil and placid poetry — the "Kuo-feng" section of the *Shih ching,* the *chüeh-chü*[44] of Wang Wei, the *tanka* of Saigyō, the *haiku* of Bashō, or Tagore's *The Crescent Moon.* The waves that create these kinds of poetry have their natural periods or rhythm, which do not permit the poet the slightest contrivance or a moment's hesitation; in fact, just as Goethe said, the poet cannot spare even the time required to straighten out the sheet of paper before him. Thus it seems to me that a poem can be represented by the formula: poem = content (intuition + emotion + imagination) + form (appropriate language). . . .

In the same letter Kuo Mo-jo went on to say:

> I think that what poets and philosophers have in common is that they both take the whole universe as their subject and the apprehension of the essence of all things as their vocation — the sole difference being that the poet's only tool is pure intuition, whereas the philosopher has the additional tool of precise reasoning. Poets are the favorites of emotion, philosophers are the caretakers of reason. Poets are metamorphoses of "beauty," philosophers are concrete manifestations of "truth." . . . But it seems to me that philosophic pantheism is the child of a marriage between reason and emotion. Philosophers who are not satisfied by the sort of dead *Weltanschauung* patched together by upholsterers naturally incline toward pantheism that they may be able to see the whole universe anew as a living, moving organism. . . . Thus, naturally, as you have pointed out, "Pantheism is the most appropriate *Weltanschauung* for a poet." [45]

We are already familiar with Kuo Mo-jo's predilection for pantheism, but here he has gone a step further by incorporating it into his literary theory as a prerequisite for the writing of poetry. This was, of course, a connection also made in nineteenth-century European romanticism, from which Kuo Mo-jo probably derived it. In his letter to Tsung Po-hua of February 16, 1920, he said:

> I am a person who has a great distaste for form and have not hitherto paid much attention to it. The things which I have written were all the results of succumbing to a momentary impulse and letting it lead wherever it might. . . . My feeling about poetry is that the best of it is natural revelation. That which is meticulously contrived is like landscape gardening or artificially stunted miniature trees, fit only for the delectation of the wealthy upper classes. But among the phenomena of the natural world — the vastness of the virgin for-

est, the delicacy of the wild flower by the roadside, the movement of great waves at sea, the stillness of a mountain spring or dew, the anger of thunder and lightning, the ecstasy of the pure moon and bright stars — there is not one which does not reveal itself naturally to everyone so that all may enjoy it. Aristotle says, "Poetry is the imitation of nature." It seems to me that these words of his refer not only to what the realists mean by being true to life in describing things, but also the idea that the most important thing in the creation of poetry is natural revelation. The birth of a poem, like the existence of natural objects, ought not to require even the slightest artificial contrivance. . . .

The fundamental task of poetry is lyrical. Writing which is lyrical, even though it does not adopt the forms of poetry, is poetry nonetheless. For example, the free verse and prose poetry of today is an expression of the fact that the poets of recent times, in their unwillingness to accept any restraints, have broken away from all previously established forms and concentrated on trying to catch the essence of poetry and thus facilitate its natural revelation. But within this natural revelation there are natural harmonies and natural pictures, because the emotions themselves have the functions of music and art. Poems are composed out of the melodies and colors of emotions. The language of poetry is not a human effort to express emotion, but emotion's expression of itself. It seems to me that real poetry, good poetry, can only come into existence when one has reached this state in which substance and form are completely undifferentiated.

Of all the literary forms poetry was the earliest to develop. One can find clues to this fact by investigating the question from the point of view of either the race or the individual. The languages of primitive men and of young children are expressions of poetry. Primitive men and young children derive fresh sensations from everything in their environments, these sensations give rise to irrepressible emotions, and these emotions, in turn, are expressed in melodic language. The process which produces this language is the same as that which produces poetry; this is why the best examples of lyric poetry are folk songs. . . .

The primitive cells of which poetry is composed are simple intuition and generalized emotion. As the human race gradually became civilized and the individual brain gradually became more complex, it sought to differentiate and develop its various intuitions and emotions. It was at this point that imagination began to play a part in the production of poetry. To draw a dubious analogy, intuition is the nucleus of the poetic cell, emotion is the protoplasm, imagination the centrosome, and poetic form merely the cell membrane, that is to say, a thing secreted by the substance of the cell itself.

I have recently tended to favor a monistic theory of poetry. It seems to me that the purpose of creating poetry is to create a "man," or, to put it in other words, to refine his emotions. The value of artistic discipline can only be established on the basis of refinement of the emotions. Forms which have already been developed by others should not be imitated. Forms which have already been developed by others can only imprison one. As far as form is concerned, I favor absolute freedom and absolute subjectivity.[46]

As a final illustration of Kuo Mo-jo's attitudes in the spring of 1920, I will quote a passage from a letter he wrote to Tsung Po-hua on March 30. It describes his feelings when riding on the train between Fukuoka and Dazaifu with T'ien Han and is somewhat less theoretical than the preceding quotations.

Fly! Fly! All is verdant life and sparkling light dancing before our eyes. Fly! Fly! Fly! My ego has melted into this mighty all-enveloping rhythm! I have become one with the entire train, one with all nature! . . . I have discovered the secret of poetry, the embryology of poetry! Nature and the poet are one.[47]

91

The number of famous persons whom Kuo Mo-jo either discusses or mentions in these letters is extraordinary. The following is a list of the men he refers to, in chronological order: Confucius, Aristotle, Lao-tzu, Mencius, Ch'ü Yüan, Ts'ai Yen, Mu Hua, Kuo P'u, St. Augustine, T'ao Ch'ien, Wang Wei, Li Po, Tu Fu, Han Yü, Tu Mu, Saigyō, Nichiren, the emperor Kameyama, Meister Eckhart, Dante, Kabir, Michelangelo, Milton, Spinoza, Newton, Bashō, Rousseau, Gray, Goldsmith, Wieland, Lavater, Knebel, Goethe, Schiller, Malthus, Napoleon, Beethoven, Coleridge, Southey, Shelley, Carlyle, Heine, Emerson, Millet, Marx, Whitman, Baudelaire, Dostoyevsky, Tolstoy, Rodin, Hoffding, Liliencron, Verhaeren, Wilde, Maeda Eun, Bergson, Tagore, Hauptmann, Maeterlinck, Symons, Gorky, Fukuda Tokuzō, Arishima Takeo, Kuriyagawa Hakuson, and Max Weber (the cubist painter and poet).

There are several interesting things about this list, the most striking of which is the preponderance of non-Chinese figures. Only one-fifth of those mentioned are Chinese, and no Chinese is referred to who lived after the T'ang dynasty. We find eleven Germans, the same number of Englishmen, eight Japanese, six Frenchmen, and a scattering of people from other countries. Goethe, Heine, Shelley, and Whitman, in that order, are the people referred to most often. Even without the obviously derivative nature of the passages on literary theory which were quoted above, it would be quite clear from this list of names alone that during this period of his life Kuo Mo-jo's understanding of literature, his attitude toward it, and the models he chose to emulate were predominantly Western.

In May 1920 Tsung Po-hua gave up his position as editor of *Hsüeh-teng* and went to Germany to continue his studies. He was replaced by Li Shih-ts'en (1892–1934), who later became a prominent philosopher. Kuo Mo-jo continued to submit poetry to *Hsüeh-teng* and Li Shih-ts'en continued to print it, but Kuo Mo-jo gradually became dissatisfied with the treatment he received, since for some reason Li Shih-ts'en always seemed to put his poems at the bottom of the page, underneath the work of other writers. Finally he discovered that one of his poems had been printed at the bottom of the page, underneath a poem by someone else which was plagiarized from one that he had previously published in the same periodical. This so irritated him that he stopped submitting his poetry to *Hsüeh-teng*.[48]

Tsung Po-hua's departure for Germany increased Kuo Mo-jo's sense of frustration and futility, and he began to play with the idea of giving up his medical education and returning to China. On July 10, 1920, he suddenly made up his mind to go to Shanghai, and, leaving Tomiko and the children behind, took a train to Moji, the nearest port of embarkation. In Moji he went to visit a former schoolmate from Szechwan named Ho Kung-tu (d. 1921),[49] who was in a private hospital convalescing from an illness. Ho suggested that Kuo Mo-jo postpone his trip long enough so that they could travel to Shanghai together at the end of the month. Kuo Mo-jo readily agreed to his friend's suggestion and returned to Fukuoka on July 19.[50]

That very day he received a letter from Chang Tung-sun (1886–   ), the editor of the *Shih-shih hsin-pao*, saying that the Kung-hsüeh She, or Cooperative Study Society, wished to publish Chinese translations of some of the most famous works of foreign literature, of which Goethe's *Faust* was one, and asking him if he would undertake to do a complete translation of this work. Kuo Mo-jo was surprised but overjoyed by this unsolicited offer and, giving up his plans of returning to China, promptly wrote to Chang Tung-sun accepting the proposal. The task so excited him that he got up every day at four or five o'clock in the morning and worked until late at night, sometimes even skipping his meals. Within four weeks he translated all of Part I, revised it, and made a fair copy. He started on Part II, but decided that it was complex and overlong, and that Part I could stand well enough by itself. He wrote to the Kung-hsüeh She explaining his decision, but for some reason never received a reply. When his classes resumed he no longer had any time to work on the manuscript, so he put it away in a drawer. A month or two later when he decided to take another look at it one day, he found that more than a third of the manuscript had been completely destroyed by a family of rats who had made a nest in the drawer. His state of mind was not improved by Tomiko's comment that this catastrophe was clearly an omen intended to show him that he ought not to devote himself to literature.[51]

In surveying his development during this period from the vantage point of 1932, Kuo Mo-jo said:

The translation of *Faust* exerted a very bad influence on me. In my brief experience of writing poetry there were three or four metamorphoses. During the first period I imitated Tagore. This was before the May Fourth Movement, and I strove for brevity and tranquility in my poetry, with rather little success. During the second period I imitated Whitman. This was during the high tide of the May Fourth Movement, and I strove to make my poems vigorous and robust. This must be counted my most memorable period. During the third period I imitated Goethe. Somehow, imperceptibly, the passion of the second period was lost and I ended by making a game of versification. It was under Goethe's influence that I began to write poetic dramas. . . . It goes without saying that this influence was complemented by the "neo-romanticism" that was popular at the time and the school of "expressionism" that had recently arisen in Germany. In particular it was the disjunctive, diffusive expressionism of the school of that name that found a most suitable culture medium in my disjunctive, diffusive brain. Ernst Toller's *Die Wandlung* and Georg Kaiser's *Die Bürger von Calais* were the works I admired the most. Some of the members of this school worshiped Goethe, taking his words *"von Innen nach Aussen"* as their motto; and I, who had finished translating *Faust,* Part I, felt an even greater kinship. But this influence was actually a limiting one, which it later cost me no small effort to cast off.[52]

In this quotation it is Goethe's philosophy of composition that Kuo Mo-jo has singled out as a significant influence and condemned. There was, however, more to his feeling of affinity with Goethe. The basis of Goethe's *Weltanschauung* was pantheism. Karl Viëtor sums up Goethe's views as follows: "Nature and spirit, phenomenon and essence, are one; the infinite is distributed in purely finite, independent, individual phenomena which together constitute a great all-embracing unity. Unity in multiplicity is the essence of the world." [53] Goethe's view of the universe is similar to that which had already attracted Kuo Mo-jo to the *Chuang-tzu,* Wang Yang-ming, Tagore, and Whitman.

The way in which Goethe reacted to life may have had as much of an appeal for Kuo Mo-jo as his thought. Karl Viëtor says of Goethe:

. . . an incessantly active urge to poetic production, operating intrinsically and extrinsically, constituted the central point and basis of his existence. This poetic productivity was maintained because of the effect which immediate experiences exercised upon it, so that he found it constantly necessary to maintain activity by assimilating or rejecting, whether he dealt with books, people, or social groups. He always had either to work in active opposition or to attempt to produce something similar. Only this untiring maintenance of production was possible for him.[54]

Kuo Mo-jo had already been stimulated by Whitman's example into the belief that he was driven to create by a "potent, felt, interior command, stronger than words." Goethe provided him with another model that he was not slow to emulate. Like Goethe he has demonstrated a tendency to either imitate or oppose the persons and models with which he has come in contact, and his "untiring maintenance of production" has been formidably impressive.

Kuo Mo-jo's first experiments with drama were written about this time under the influence of Goethe, and, to a lesser extent, of Wagner.[55] He lists four works that resulted directly from this influence: "Wild Cherry Blossoms" (T'ang-ti chih hua), "The Rebirth of the Goddesses" (Nü-shen chih tsai-sheng), "The Tragedy at the river Hsiang" (Hsiang lei), and "The Two Princes of Ku-chu" (Ku-chu chün chih erh tzu).[56] The first three were written in 1920 and the last in November 1922. None of them can be considered a complete work of art. Kuo Mo-jo originally planned ten acts for "Wild Cherry Blossoms," but wrote only five. He published the second scene of Act I in 1920 and Act II in 1922 and destroyed the rest.[57] The other three examples referred to are merely tableaux or scenes.

All of these pieces are concerned with figures from early Chinese history or mythology, but Kuo Mo-jo admits that he only used them as mouthpieces for his own ideas.[58] "The Tragedy at the river Hsiang" is about Ch'ü Yüan, the first great Chinese poet, who is believed to have been banished by his prince on the basis of slander and misunderstanding, to have wandered about China expressing his resentment in magnificent allegorical poetry, and to have finally drowned himself in despair in a tributary of the river Hsiang in what is now Hunan province. This figure of misunderstood genius has always held a special fascination for Kuo Mo-jo, and he readily admits that he identifies himself with him. In "The Rebirth of the Goddesses" he used the struggle between Chuan Hsü and Kung Kung, two figures from ancient Chinese mythology, to symbolize the struggle for control over China that was then going on between the northern and southern warlord factions and the rebirth of the goddesses to symbolize the rise of a new and beautiful China after the antagonists have destroyed each other. For this work he used the last eight lines of the second part of *Faust* as an epigraph.[59]

Although Kuo Mo-jo states that Goethe's influence over him was dominant during this period, he links it with that of the German expressionists. Expressionist drama has been described as being marked by the exchange of ideas instead of dramatic action, types instead of characters, little background, and no psychological development.[60] Kuo Mo-jo's early experiments with drama fit this description perfectly. The expressionist movement as a whole was characterized by antimilitarism and a passionate internationalism, and these themes were also employed by Kuo Mo-jo. But there was another side to the picture. Ernst Toller, whom Kuo Mo-jo specifically mentions, was also a Marxist and a Communist. It may have been from this element in the expressionist school that Kuo Mo-jo got some of the ideas whose later development led to his repudiation of Goethe and his espousal of Marxism-Leninism.

In the second scene of the first act of "Wild Cherry Blossoms," Nieh Ying says that the root of eternal conflict is the private ownership of land, which came as a result of the abolition of the collective well-field system; this in turn came as a result of the empire's being in the possession of a single family, thanks to the fact that the emperor Yü, unlike his predecessors, chose to pass on his inheritance to his own son instead of to the best qualified man he could find, thus founding China's first dynasty.[61] This was written in September 1920. In Act II, which was not published until May 1922, but was probably written about the same time, Nieh Cheng says: "We believe that all the unhappiness in the world is the result of inequality of wealth. We believe that the most senseless system practiced by mankind is the private property system." [62] Although as early as 1919 Kuo Mo-jo had sung the praises of Marx, Engels, and Lenin in "Hymn to the Bandits," it was not until some years later that he acquired any real knowledge of Marxism-Leninism. It is therefore significant that as early as September 1920 he had become convinced of the immorality of the private property system.

It was not only ideological considerations, however, that helped to prepare the way for Kuo Mo-jo's gradual move toward Marxism. Emotional factors were perhaps equally important. The success of the Russian Revolution and the heroic figure of Lenin early cast their spell over him. In his poem "Good Morning," written in January 1920, he hailed the new Russia in the following words:

Ah! Ah! Oh Russia, of which I stand in awe!
Good morning! Oh Pioneer, of whom I stand in awe![63]

In April 1920, in his poem "The Lesson of the Cannons," Kuo Mo-jo described a dream sequence in which the figures of Tolstoy and Lenin appear before him. When he asks what they have to teach him, Tolstoy replies that he loves the ancient Chinese philosophers Mo-tzu and Lao-tzu for their universal love and pacifism. He says that Heaven (*t'ien*) and the Way (*tao*) are one. Then, after describing an ideal society without law courts, prisons, soldiers, or foreign relations, he ends by saying that all would be well if everyone could only be like the peasant. Suddenly Lenin interrupts him, crying:

Comrades! Comrades! Comrades! . . .
Fight to destroy the classes!
Fight to liberate the peoples!
Fight to remake society!
The bearers of the highest ideal are the peasants and workers!
The final victory is ours!
Comrades! Comrades! Comrades! . . .

At this point Kuo Mo-jo is awakened by the vehemence of Lenin's cries.[64]

Kuo Mo-jo's admiration for Lenin was based more on respect for his role as a dynamic individual than on any real ideological commitment. During this period his romantic ego was running away with him and he tended to identify himself with all the great historical and literary figures he encountered in his reading. In January 1921 he began to write an autobiographical novel. He never finished it, but the opening fragment was published in 1922. In this work he compares his own fate to that of Su Wu (140–60 B.C.), the famous general of the Former Han dynasty who spent nineteen years as a prisoner of the Hsiung-nu. It is true that Kuo Mo-jo, like Su Wu, was in a foreign country, but since Kuo Mo-jo was there of his own volition the comparison seems dubious. He goes on to describe himself as the protagonist in a tragic drama.[65] This kind of romantic self-dramatization has remained a characteristic of Kuo Mo-jo's work even after his announced conversion to Marxism-Leninism in 1924.

In December 1919 Kuo Mo-jo was inspired by reading Carlyle's *On Heroes, Hero-worship, and the Heroic in*

History to compose a poem, entitled "Snowy Morning" (Hsüeh chao), the last words of which were: "Oh, Hero poet! Oh Proletarian poet!" [66] It is clear that he thought of himself in these terms, and his tendency to see himself in a variety of heroic roles was probably reinforced by reading Carlyle. The angry Scotchman's explosive attacks on sham and hypocrisy and his distrust of democracy may have had some influence on Kuo Mo-jo's thinking, but his preachments on the cult of the hero seem to have had a profound and lasting effect.

At this point it is necessary to revert to the question of the founding of a periodical devoted solely to literature which Kuo Mo-jo and Chang Tzu-p'ing had discussed in September 1918. Sometime during the intervening period Kuo Mo-jo, Yü Ta-fu, Hsü Tsu-cheng, Liu K'ai-yüan, T'ao Ching-sun, and Ho Wei started a small literary magazine of their own. The title of this periodical was the English word *Green,* and the contents seem to have been written largely, if not entirely, in Japanese. The editor was Ho Wei, and Kuo Mo-jo was an important contributor. It appears to have been an annual, but it ceased publication after only two issues because of difficulties in finding a typist.[67] Since these young men were widely separated in Tokyo, Kyoto, and Fukuoka, it is surprising that they were able to publish anything at all. They must have been a highly motivated group. All of them, with the exception of Liu K'ai-yüan, later contributed to the publications of the Creation Society.

The question of undertaking something more ambitious than *Green* was raised in the fall of 1920. Later in that year Chang Tzu-p'ing, who was then studying geology at Tokyo Imperial University, Ch'eng Fang-wu, and T'ien Han held two or three meetings in the rooms of Yü Ta-fu to discuss this question. During the second of these meetings T'ien Han undertook to find a publishing house in China. Ch'eng Fang-wu kept Kuo Mo-jo informed of these proceedings by mail. A number of Chinese students in Kyoto, including Cheng Po-ch'i (1895–   ), Mu Mu-t'ien (1900–   ), Chang Feng-chü, and Hsü Tsu-cheng, were also involved in these plans.[68] All of these people later contributed to the publications of the Creation Society. The fall of 1920 and the spring of 1921, during which this group of young Chinese students in Japan engaged in the meetings and correspondence mentioned above, can be considered to be the gestation period of the Creation Society.

In the spring of 1921 Kuo Mo-jo was also motivated to write by the desire to become a member of an organization called the Ping-ch'en Hsüeh-she, or 1916 Society. This organization was founded in Tokyo on December 5, 1916, by forty-seven Chinese students who were studying in the Tokyo area,[69] and was destined to become one of the most important scholarly organizations in China under the name of the Chung-hua Hsüeh-i She (Chinese arts and sciences association), which it adopted in June 1923.[70] On January 21, 1921, Chang Tzu-p'ing, who was a member of this organization, wrote Kuo Mo-jo a letter in which he offered to propose his name for membership. On January 24 Kuo Mo-jo wrote in reply that shortly after the society was founded he had been proposed for membership by Wu Yung-ch'üan and Ch'en Ch'i-hsiu, but had asked to postpone the proceedings until he had produced a sufficiently significant piece of work to justify his membership. Later on Tseng Ch'i, his schoolmate from the Annexed Middle School in Chengtu, had offered to propose his name again, but he had refused on the same grounds as before. Now with Chang Tzu-p'ing bringing up the issue for the third time, Kuo Mo-jo was already fairly well known, but he still asked to postpone the question until he could complete an

101

article to be entitled "The Pompeii of Chinese Intellectual History," so that he might enter the society together with a significant example of his work.[71] This wish was fulfilled when "The Pompeii of Chinese Intellectual History" was published in the May issue of the society's journal *Hsüeh-i*, or *Wissen und Wissenschaft*, as it was somewhat pretentiously entitled in German.

This article represents Kuo Mo-jo's first attempt to write intellectual history. In it he compares the effect on Chinese intellectual history of Ch'in Shih Huang-ti's burning of the books in 213 B.C. to the eruption of Vesuvius which buried the city of Pompeii. He says, "The well-field system, which was initiated by the Yellow Emperor (traditional dates 2697–2597 B.C.), is the earliest instance of the practice of communism in our country." [72] He then goes on to assert that Chinese society before the Hsia dynasty (traditional dates 2205–1766 B.C.) was a democracy and that the change, during the reign of Yü (2205–2197 B.C.), the founder of the dynasty, from public to private ownership of property was the origin of all subsequent strife. He asserts that Chinese thought was free, rational, and creative before the Hsia dynasty and became so once again during the Warring States period (403–221 B.C.), but that throughout the Hsia, Shang (1766–1122 B.C.), and early Chou (1122–770 B.C.) dynasties, and from the Ch'in period (221–209 B.C.) on, this free, rational, and creative thought was stifled under the weight of religion, superstition, and restriction. He calls the Hsia, Shang, and Western Chou periods the first of China's dark ages and the post-Ch'in period the second.[73]

This essay is jejune, to say the least, and it is no accident that it is not included in the current edition of Kuo Mo-jo's collected works. Nevertheless, it is significant that as early as the spring of 1921 he attributed communism, democracy, freedom of thought, rationality, and creativity to the golden age of China's prehistoric past and assigned the two thousand years of the post-Ch'in empire to the dark ages. One is inevitably reminded of the "primitive communism" and "feudalism" which characterize the same periods in the Marxist scheme of periodization which he later came to accept.

Many of the members of the 1916 Society which Kuo Mo-jo joined in the spring of 1921 were also members of a more exclusive organization called the Young China Association (Shao-nien Chung-kuo hsüeh-hui).[74] This group was founded in Peking on June 30, 1918,[75] and included among its members Tseng Ch'i, Wei Ssu-luan, Chou Wu, Wang Kuang-ch'i, and Li Chieh-jen, all of whom had been schoolmates of Kuo Mo-jo's in the Annexed Middle School in Chengtu. Kuo Mo-jo's correspondents and friends Tsung Po-hua, T'ien Han, Cheng Po-ch'i, and Tso Shunsheng (1893–1969) were also members. Kuo Mo-jo was anxious to belong to this group, but he was never permitted to do so. The qualifications for membership were moral as well as intellectual and they were taken so seriously that no more than 108 members were ever allowed to join.[76] Kuo Mo-jo was excluded on the grounds that he was living with a Japanese woman without having divorced his legal wife.[77] I suspect that his failure to return to China in May 1918 in protest against the signing of the Sino-Japanese Military Mutual Assistance Convention may also have had something to do with it, since the founders of the Young China Association were all ardent patriots. Whatever the case may be this rebuff must have wounded him deeply.

With all these cultural projects in his head Kuo Mo-jo was becoming less and less interested in medicine. In February 1921 he made up his mind to transfer from the medical school at Fukuoka to the Liberal Arts Department (*bun-ka*) of Kyoto Imperial University. It was Ch'eng Fang-wu who dissuaded him from taking this step by arguing that one did not have to go to school to study literature and that it gave him an added advantage over other writers to have a sound foundation in the sciences.[78] Tomiko, who had already borne him two children and was soon to be pregnant with another, also argued strongly against such a move on the grounds that a practical skill such as medicine was more reliable as a means of making a living than literature. Kuo Mo-jo heeded the advice of his friend and his wife but remained very badly frustrated. He did not feel that he could be a good doctor because of his deafness, which made it difficult for him to use a stethoscope. One day Tomiko accidentally came upon him sitting in his room all by himself and trying to listen to his heartbeat with a stethoscope. He had a look of pained frustration on his face. When she realized how much he was troubled she regretted having objected so strongly to his desire to concentrate on literature.[79] By this time, however, it was too late to do anything about it during that academic year.

Though Kuo Mo-jo acceded to Ch'eng Fang-wu's advice, he does not seem to have taken the importance of developing a sound foundation in the sciences too seriously. During the spring of 1921 he paid little attention to his medical studies, but stayed in his room all day reading literature and philosophy. Among the books he read at this time were Hamsun's *Hunger*, Flaubert's *Madame Bovary*, Zola's *L'Oeuvre*, Maupassant's *Bel-Ami* and *Sur l'eau*, Johan Bojer's *The Great Hunger*, and plays by Ibsen, Hauptmann, and Galsworthy. The more he read this kind of literature the less interested in medicine he became and the more he found himself wanting to go back to China.[80]

At this juncture Kuo Mo-jo received the news that his

friend Ch'eng Fang-wu, who had been studying ordnance manufacturing (*zōhei-ka*) at Tokyo Imperial University, was about to abandon his final examinations and return to China. He had been living with a fellow Hunanese named Li Feng-t'ing, who had graduated from a private college of law and administration in February and returned to Shanghai. There Li learned that the T'ai-tung Book Company (T'ai-tung t'u-shu chü) was planning to reorganize its editorial offices into three departments which would deal with law, literature, and philosophy. Li Feng-t'ing had been offered the job of editor of the law department and Li Shih-ts'en, who had replaced Tsung Po-hua as editor of *Hsüeh-teng* in May 1920, had agreed to become editor of the philosophy department. Li Feng-t'ing thereupon wrote to Ch'eng Fang-wu holding out the possibility that he might be able to get a position as editor of the literature department. When Ch'eng Fang-wu learned of this he made up his mind to skip his final examinations and sail for Shanghai at the end of March. He wrote Kuo Mo-jo to this effect and told him that his ship would make a stop at Moji, a port in northern Kyushu, on April 1.[81]

No sooner did he learn of his friend's plans than Kuo Mo-jo made up his mind to meet the ship at Moji and accompany Ch'eng Fang-wu to Shanghai. Without more ado, he obtained a half-year's leave of absence from the school authorities[82] and, saying good-bye to his wife and children, took the night train from Hakozaki to Moji on March 31, 1921. Kuo Mo-jo did not choose a very convenient time to leave, for earlier that day their landlord had come to collect the rent and told them that they would have to move out within the week because he was planning to rebuild the house.[83] A week after Kuo Mo-jo's departure his family moved to a small one-story Japanese-style house in downtown Hakozaki.[84]

On April 1, 1921, Kuo Mo-jo met Ch'eng Fang-wu's ship at Moji and they continued to Shanghai together. During the short voyage across the Yellow Sea he was seasick, but Ch'eng Fang-wu had a German edition of Turgenev's novels with him and Kuo Mo-jo took advantage of his hours in the bunk to read *Fathers and Sons* and *Virgin Soil*. Echoes of Bazarov's nihilism were soon to appear in his work and in 1924 he translated *Virgin Soil* into Chinese.

They landed in Shanghai on the morning of April 3. This was Kuo Mo-jo's first sight of China since his short-lived return of May 1915. Two poems which he wrote on this occasion bring out the unreality of his expectations and the rapidity of his disillusionment. While still aboard ship in the Huang-p'u River he wrote a poem entitled "The Mouth of the Huang-p'u" (Huang-p'u chiang k'ou)[85] in which he expressed heartfelt joy at returning to this peaceful countryside, the homeland of his ancestors. The next day he wrote a poem entitled "Impressions of Shanghai" (Shang-hai yin-hsiang)[86] in which he declared that he had been rudely awakened from a dream and had become thoroughly disillusioned. The people in the streets of Shanghai were now seen to be nothing but walking corpses.[87] This incident reveals how far out of touch he had become with the realities of life in China. After seven years in Japan he had apparently forgotten the miserable circumstances under which the vast majority of his countrymen lived.

Kuo Mo-jo's arrival in Shanghai brought to an end another chapter in his life. During his first three years at Fukuoka, from 1918 to 1921, he had begun to express concern over the situation in China, but this was in large part a response to the concern expressed by the Western authors he read over similar issues in their own countries.

Walt Whitman's concern over the dangers of disunity in the United States and Ernst Toller's condemnation of the evils of the World War in Germany may have had as much to do with the development of his attitude toward the situation in China as the impact of that situation itself. He had been cut off from China, and there is little evidence, before he discovered Whitman, that he felt deeply concerned over what was happening there. After 1919 he had begun to write about China in terms of a rather crude symbolism; but it was not until his arrival in Shanghai in April 1921 that he was brought face to face with Chinese realities. His difficulty in coming to terms with them became an important factor in his subsequent drift toward Marxism-Leninism.

Chapter 6

The Heyday of the Creation Society: Shanghai and Fukuoka, 1921–1924

Shortly after their arrival in Shanghai on the morning of April 3, 1921, Kuo Mo-jo and Ch'eng Fang-wu went to the editorial offices of the T'ai-tung Book Company. There they discovered that the projected reorganization of the editorial department had never taken place. Li Feng-t'ing had joined the faculty of the Anking College of Law and Administration (An-ch'ing fa-cheng hsüeh-hsiao), and Li Shih-ts'en already had his hands full editing *Hsüeh-teng* and the magazine *Min-to*.[1] Chao Nan-kung, the manager of the company, which was owned by certain elements in the Political Science Clique (Cheng-hsüeh hsi), a right-wing Kuomintang group,[2] was unable to give Ch'eng Fang-wu either the formal contract or the salary that he had promised. On the other hand, he was quite willing to retain him on an informal basis and offered to do the same for Kuo Mo-jo. This seemed satisfactory to Kuo Mo-jo, who had not been offered a job in the first place, but entirely unsatisfactory to Ch'eng Fang-wu.[3]

Disgruntled by this turn of events, they decided to get away from it all by spending what was left of the money which Ch'eng Fang-wu had received for his traveling expenses on a weekend excursion to the famous West Lake outside Hangchow. They took the night train from Shanghai to Hangchow on April 8, and during the trip Kuo

Mo-jo wrote four poems. The third of these is an example of the self-dramatization and artless hyperbole which mars so much of his poetry.

The train runs southward,
It and my thoughts forming a cross:
With all my heart I long for my mother in Szechwan to the
    west,
With all my heart I long for my children in Japan to the east,
Am I not like another Christ crucified![4]

The following day he was inspired to write another poem by the sight of an Asiatic "Man with the Hoe" laboring beside the famous Thunder Peak Pagoda (Lei-feng t'a) on the shores of West Lake. He ends the poem with the lines:

> I wanted to fall down before him,
> Call him: "My father!"
> And lick away the mud on his shoes.[5]

Unfortunately we can only surmise how the old man might have reacted had he actually been accosted in such a manner by the young poet. Two days and six poems later, on April 11, Kuo Mo-jo and his companion returned to Shanghai by the afternoon train.[6]

After two or three weeks of futile waiting in the hope that a decent job might materialize, Ch'eng Fang-wu decided to go home to Changsha, where he thought he could get a job at an arsenal managed by a former schoolmate of his from Tokyo Imperial University. Kuo Mo-jo was not offered a definite job or promised a fixed salary, but was informally employed by the T'ai-tung Book Company and allowed to share a room on the premises with the acting literary editor, a man named Wang Ching, to whom he soon took an active dislike.[7]

The editorial offices of the T'ai-tung Book Company were located in a three-story building called Te-fu Li on Ma-huo Lu, practically next-door to the racetrack, in the downtown section of the International Settlement in Shanghai. The ground floor of this building served as a warehouse, and the upper floors were used not only as editorial offices but as a dormitory for the editors. Among those who lived and worked in the same building while Kuo Mo-jo was there were Chang Ching-lu (1898–) and Shen Sung-ch'üan, both of whom later became prominent in the publishing business, Teng Chün-wu, a young Szechwanese poet who later contributed to the publications of the Creation Society, and I Chün-tso (1899–) and Lo Tun-wei, co-editors of a popular magazine called *Chia-t'ing yen-chiu* (Family studies), who later became prominent editors under Kuomintang auspices.[8]

The atmosphere in this curious ménage was casual in the extreme, and several of the participants have written vivid descriptions of it. I Chün-tso recalls:

Life in the editorial offices on Ma-huo Lu was quite intriguing. All day long we consumed the noodles of which our northern proprietor was so fond. Whenever lunch or supper time rolled around, the loud-voiced northern cook would shout, "Come get your noodles!" as though he were vending his wares in a roadside snack shop, whereupon we "editors" would tumble downstairs, tearful with hunger, and gobble up a bellyful, wiping off our mouths with the backs of our hands. . . .

We didn't have any fixed salaries. If you needed a hat, Chao Nan-kung would take you to a hat store and buy you one. If it was a shirt you needed, he would take you out and purchase one for you. That was the way it went. Although the T'ai-tung Book Company was doing a pretty good business, its expenses were great. Chao Nan-kung was both chivalrous and magnanimous, so that he was always in debt. He didn't have any spare cash to give to his friends, but he was well enough known in commercial circles to get credit when he needed it, and it was thus that we survived. We found this intriguing as well as convenient. Whenever we needed anything, all we had to do was to seek out the proprietor, and he was sure to oblige. . . .[9]

Under these unusual conditions Kuo Mo-jo worked for the T'ai-tung Book Company from the first week of April through the last week of May 1921. During this period he translated Thomas Gray's "Elegy Written in a Country Churchyard," [10] retranslated Theodor Storm's novella *Immensee* from a faulty version made by a former schoolmate of his named Ch'ien Chün-hsü, prepared a new edition of the *Hsi-hsiang chi* (Romance of the western chamber) in which the text was punctuated and presented in the format of Western drama, and edited the collection of his own poetry that was published in August 1921 as *The Goddesses* (Nü-shen).[11] Although his name was already known to readers of *Hsüeh-teng* and the other periodicals in which he had occasionally published, it was the appearance of *The Goddesses* that first brought him real recognition as a poet.

It was also during this period that Kuo Mo-jo first became acquainted with some of the leaders of the Literary Research Society (Wen-hsüeh yen-chiu hui). This organization, which had been founded in January 1921, included many of the figures who had risen to prominence in the period of the May Fourth Movement, and it had already begun to publish the first Chinese magazine devoted to literature in the new vernacular forms. It tended to stress "art for life's sake" as opposed to "art for art's sake," which the Creation Society was to champion during its early period.[12] Not long after Kuo Mo-jo returned from his excursion to Hangchow he received a letter from Cheng Chen-to (1897–1958), one of the founders of the Literary Research Society, suggesting that they meet on a certain Sunday at Pan-sung Yüan, a famous park on the outskirts of Shanghai. When Ch'eng Fang-wu learned of this he told him that the previous year, in Tokyo, T'ien Han had received a letter from members of the Literary Research Society, which was still in its period of gestation at the time, suggesting that he and Kuo Mo-jo should join in the forthcoming enterprise, but that he had neither answered the letter nor forwarded it to Kuo Mo-jo. Ch'eng Fang-wu had seen the letter in T'ien Han's room but had forgotten to tell Kuo Mo-jo about it. From this Kuo Mo-jo concluded, naturally enough, that T'ien Han disapproved of the idea.

When he arrived at Pan-sung Yüan on the appointed Sunday he was met by Cheng Chen-to, Shen Yen-ping (1896–   ), better known by his penname as Mao Tun, the new editor of the *Hsiao-shuo yüeh-pao* (Short story monthly), and K'o I-ts'en, who had been one of the editors of *Hsüeh-teng*. He was already acquainted with K'o I-ts'en, who had come to visit him with Li Shih-ts'en, but this was his first meeting with Cheng Chen-to and Shen Yen-ping. During the course of the day Cheng Chen-to asked him to join the Literary Research Society, but Kuo Mo-jo declined on the grounds that if T'ien Han did not want to join he preferred to follow suit for fear of offending his friend. He did, however, offer to cooperate with them without formally becoming a member of the organization.[13]

The most important thing that Kuo Mo-jo accomplished during the spring of 1921 was to persuade Chao Nan-kung to undertake the publication of the literary magazine which he and his friends had dreamed of ever since the summer of 1918. At the end of May he made a trip to Japan in order to work out the details concerning the projected magazine with his colleagues. Chao Nan-kung paid his round-trip fare and gave him a hundred *yüan* in cash and a gold bracelet for his wife, which he sold for forty-three *yüan*. This was the only remuneration he received for his two months' work in the editorial offices of the T'ai-tung Book Company.[14]

On May 31, 1921, Kuo Mo-jo arrived in Fukuoka and spent the night with his family.[15] The next day he took the night train from Fukuoka to Kyoto. Upon his arrival there he went to visit Cheng Po-ch'i at the Third Higher School, where he was a student. This was the first time they had met, although they had been corresponding for some time after having been put in touch with each other by T'ien Han. Cheng Po-ch'i was in the middle of his final examinations so it was inconvenient for him to entertain Kuo Mo-jo at the time. Instead, he took him to see Li Shan-t'ing (d. 1927), a former schoolmate of Kuo Mo-jo's at Okayama, who was then studying under Kawakami Hajime (1879–1946), the pioneer Japanese Marxist, in the economics department of Kyoto Imperial University. Kuo Mo-jo was suffering from an upset stomach and was too sick to do anything but spend the day in Li Shan-t'ing's room, where he also stayed overnight. His host was a Marxist, and Kuo Mo-jo asked him to explain the fundamentals of Marxism to him, but he was unsatisfied by what he heard. Li Shan-t'ing suggested to him that he read Kawakami Hajime's magazine *Shakai mondai kenkyū* (Studies of social problems), but he did not take up this suggestion at the time.

The next morning Kuo Mo-jo and Li Shan-t'ing were invited to tea by Chang Feng-chü, who had also invited Shen Yin-mo (1882–   ), the famous poet, calligrapher, and educator, who was then doing some research at Kyoto Imperial University. That afternoon Cheng Po-ch'i took Kuo Mo-jo to see Mu Mu-t'ien, later a prominent contributor to the publications of the Creation Society, who was then a second-year student at the Third Higher School. The following day Li Shan-t'ing took him on an excursion to Lake Biwa, and that evening he caught the night train for Toyko at the station in Ōtsu. While on the train he worried about the magazine they were planning and decided that with the number of contributors available they could not hope to bring out anything more ambitious than a quarterly. He could not make up his mind whether to call it *Ch'uang-tsao* (Creation) or *Hsin-i* (Magnolia).[16]

On the morning of June 5 Kuo Mo-jo arrived in Tokyo and went to Yü Ta-fu's apartment, only to learn that he was sick and in the hospital. He located his room at the Kyōun Hospital in Surugadai shortly after noon and found that he was not seriously ill and would probably be able to leave in a few days. They spent the afternoon and evening discussing the literary scene in Shanghai and their plans for the magazine. Yü Ta-fu approved of the name *Ch'uang-tsao* and promised to provide ten to twenty thousand words of material for each issue. That night Kuo Mo-jo slept in an adjoining room which he had to share with two nurses.[17]

The next day he went to find T'ien Han, who was living in the suburbs of Tokyo in a monastery called Getsuin Shōja, which had been rented by a group of Chinese students, and where Ch'eng Fang-wu had also lived at one time. T'ien Han was still enrolled in the Higher Normal School (Kōtō shihan gakkō), but was not paying much attention to his studies. Kuo Mo-jo stayed overnight with T'ien Han and his fiancée, I Sou-yü (d. 1923). They had lunch in Tokyo the next day with T'u Mo, who had been a schoolmate of Kuo Mo-jo's at the Sixth Higher School in Okayama, and then went to see *The Cabinet of Dr. Caligari* at a theater in Kanda.

The following morning, June 8, 1921, Kuo Mo-jo returned to Yü Ta-fu's apartment on the third floor of the Daini Kaiseikan and found that he had already come back from the hospital. They decided to hold a meeting that afternoon and were able to round up Chang Tzu-p'ing, Ho Wei, and Hsü Tsu-cheng for the purpose. It was agreed to adopt the name *Ch'uang-tsao* (Creation) and to publish the magazine as a quarterly for the time being, postponing more ambitious plans until such time as they could more accurately assess their resources. They also determined to begin publication as soon as possible and to prepare the material for the first issue during the summer vacation. Kuo Mo-jo maintains that this meeting marked the formal inauguration of the Creation Society.[18]

His mission accomplished, Kuo Mo-jo returned to Shanghai sometime during the latter half of June and continued to work for the T'ai-tung Book Company. It was during this summer that he began to work on a translation of Goethe's *The Sorrows of Young Werther*. In July he received a letter from Li Shih-ts'en once again asking him to join the Literary Research Society, but he again refused on the same grounds as before.[19] Cheng Chen-to also came to visit him several times, and through him he met Yeh Sheng-t'ao (1893–), the novelist and short story writer,[20] and Chu Ch'ien-chih (1899–), the philosopher.[21] At this time there were also quite a few former schoolmates of his employed in the editorial offices of the Commercial Press, the greatest publishing house in China. These included Cheng Chen-wen, Chou Ch'ang-shou, and Ho

Kung-kan, all of them members, like himself, of the Ping-ch'en Hsüeh-she (1916 Society). They came to visit him at the T'ai-tung Book Company in Ma-huo Lu from time to time and he occasionally repaid their calls by dropping in at the editorial offices of the Commercial Press in Chapei.[22] It is apparent that Kuo Mo-jo had an entrée to the most prominent circles in the literary and publishing worlds of Shanghai.

On August 5, 1921,[23] the Creation Society made its first formal bow before the public with the publication of Kuo Mo-jo's collection of poems entitled *The Goddesses,* which was published as the first volume in the *Creation Society Collectanea* (Ch'uang-tsao she ts'ung-shu). This not only brought Kuo Mo-jo immediate fame as the most vigorous of the new poets, but also brought the name of the Creation Society to the attention of the public.

In mid-August, Chao Nan-kung received a letter from Kuang Ming-fu, the president of the Anking College of Law and Administration, to which Li Feng-t'ing had gone, asking him to recommend a teacher of English to him. Chao Nan-kung suggested to Kuo Mo-jo that he take the job and carry on his editorial activities from Anking. Kuo Mo-jo refused the job because he did not feel that his English was good enough, but recommended Yü Ta-fu for the position. He also decided at this time to return to Japan and continue his medical studies and suggested to Chao Nan-kung that if Yü Ta-fu would take the position at Anking he could also take over from him the responsibility for editing the new magazine. After Chao Nan-kung had reluctantly agreed to this proposal, Kuo Mo-jo wrote to Yü Ta-fu in Japan. Why should he have suddenly decided on such a move? He says that he took this step because he found the atmosphere in Fukuoka more con-

116

ducive to creative writing, because he had begun to see the validity of his wife's arguments concerning the value of a medical diploma, and because he felt uncertain of his ability to handle all the responsibilities involved in the publication of the *Creation Quarterly*.[24] Although he fails to mention it, perhaps an equally powerful motive was the presence of his wife and children in Japan.

Yü Ta-fu agreed to this proposition and arrived in Shanghai sometime in early September, with the T'ai-tung Book Company footing the bill for his trip. Shortly before Kuo Mo-jo's departure for Japan, Kao Meng-tan (1870–1936),[25] the general editor of the Commercial Press, gave a dinner party at which Hu Shih (1891–1962) and Kuo Mo-jo were the guests of honor. This was the first time that the two men had met. Hu Shih was in Shanghai at the invitation of Kao Meng-tan in order to make up his mind whether or not to become his successor as general editor of the Commercial Press. The conversation at the dinner party indicated that they had been considering the possibility of offering Kuo Mo-jo a position on the new editorial staff, but since he had already told them that he was planning to return to Japan, no offer was made.[26]

Sometime in mid-September, Kuo Mo-jo left Shanghai to return to Fukuoka. The T'ai-tung Book Company bought a second-class ticket for him and also gave him an additional sixty *yüan*. Yü Ta-fu, Cheng Po-ch'i, Teng Chün-wu, and a new friend named Pi Jui-sheng went down to the dock to see him off. Just before the ship sailed he discovered that his wallet had been stolen by a pickpocket. He was bailed out of this embarrassing predicament by Yü Ta-fu and Pi Jui-sheng, who were able to give him a total of seventy-seven *yüan* between them. This money was later repaid to them by the T'ai-tung Book Company.[27]

Shortly after his departure the Wuchang Higher Normal School (Wu-ch'ang kao-teng shih-fan hsüeh-hsiao) offered him a position as professor of literature and even sent him a contract in care of the T'ai-tung Book Company; but by that time he had already returned to Fukuoka to continue his medical studies.[28]

On October 5, 1921,[29] Kuo Mo-jo received a copy of the *Shih-shih hsin-pao* in which he saw an advertisement inserted by Yü Ta-fu announcing the forthcoming publication of the *Creation Quarterly*, the first issue of which, it was promised, would appear on January 1, 1922. This was not an ordinary advertisement, for it stated that the purpose of the new magazine was to counterbalance the influence of a certain group that had monopolized the literary world.[30] This charge was clearly directed against the Literary Research Society, the members of which had been on good terms with Kuo Mo-jo during the spring and summer. The bombshell thus launched by Yü Ta-fu was an effective publicity stunt, but it laid the foundation for an antagonism between the Literary Research Society and the Creation Society which came to depend more on their rivalry than on any fundamental difference in their basic outlooks.

After his return to Fukuoka, Kuo Mo-jo had to take make-up examinations for the ones he had missed at the end of the preceding academic year. In what spare time he had at his disposal he finished three other tasks: a revision of Mu Mu-t'ien's translation of the fairy tales of Oscar Wilde, the completion of his own translation of Goethe's *The Sorrows of Young Werther,* and the preparation of material for the first issue of the *Creation Quarterly*. By November he had collected all the material necessary for the first issue with the exception of Yü Ta-fu's story "Mang-

mang yeh" (Endless night) and had sent the manuscripts to
Yü Ta-fu in Anking. Publication was delayed until May 1,
1922, however, due to Yü Ta-fu's slowness in finishing
"Mang-mang yeh," which was not completed until sometime in February or March.[31]

At the end of June 1922 Kuo Mo-jo's summer vacation
began and he returned to Shanghai with a hundred *yüan*
sent him by the T'ai-tung Book Company for traveling
expenses.[32] He arrived in Shanghai on July 2.[33] Because of
overcrowding at the main office of the T'ai-tung Book Company on Ma-huo Lu, Chao Nan-kung purchased a two-story
house at 121 Min-hou Nan Li, off Hardoon Road.[34]
About a week after his return to Shanghai, Kuo Mo-jo
moved into this house.[35]

During the summer vacation Cheng Po-ch'i also came to
Shanghai and joined Kuo Mo-jo in the editorial offices of
the T'ai-tung Book Company. He brought with him two
manuscripts which he had received from his friend Wang
Tu-ch'ing (1896–1940), who was then studying in France.
These were a long Whitmanesque autobiographical poem
entitled *Shina* (China)[36] and a translation of Tagore's *The
Crescent Moon*. Kuo Mo-jo decided that *Shina* was beyond
saving, but he put so much time and effort into revising
the translation of *The Crescent Moon* for publication that
he claims it was as much his own work as that of Wang
Tu-ch'ing.[37]

It was at this time, during the summer of 1922, that
Kuo Mo-jo first began to turn his attention to political
problems. A group of his friends who were on the editorial
staff of the Commercial Press wanted to publish a magazine
of political comment but thought it would be preferable
not to have it published by their own company. Kuo Mo-jo
was instrumental in persuading the T'ai-tung Book Com-

pany to publish it for them. This group, which was originally formed under the leadership of Ch'en Shen-hou
(1885–1922), advocated the restoration of constitutional law
and disarmament by peaceful means. Because Kuo Mo-jo
was a personal friend of some of the members and because
he had helped them to secure a publisher, he was invited to
attend their meetings. One effect of going to these meetings was to impress upon him how ignorant he was of political problems. In August 1922 Ch'en Shen-hou died unexpectedly and it was feared that the group might dissolve,
but it held together despite this loss under the leadership
of Ho Kung-kan. The magazine, which began to appear
shortly after Ch'en Shen-hou's death, was entitled *Ku-chün*
(Isolated army), and the group therefore became known
as the Ku-chün She (Isolated army society). Kuo Mo-jo
wrote a song entitled "Ku-chün hsing" (Song of the isolated army) for the first issue of the magazine.[38]

In July, Ho Kung-kan paid Kuo Mo-jo a visit and announced that Kao Meng-tan was anxious to have him sign
a contract with the Commercial Press, the terms of which
stipulated that he would be paid at the rate of five *yüan*
per thousand words of original material and four *yüan* per
thousand words of translation. This was the treatment the
Commercial Press gave its best writers and Kuo Mo-jo
must have been flattered to receive such an offer, but he
did not sign a formal contract at the time out of a desire to
preserve his independence.[39]

On July 23, 1922,[40] Yü Ta-fu arrived in Shanghai and
moved into the house on Min-hou Nan Li with Kuo Mo-jo.
During the summer Chang Wen-t'ien (1898–   ), later a
famous Communist, Wu Ming, the poet and politician,
Wang Fu-ch'üan, the literary historian, and Chu Tzu-
ch'ing (1898–1948), the famous poet and essayist, were

120

frequent visitors, although Kuo Mo-jo says they came more to see Yü Ta-fu than himself.[41]

On August 5, 1922, the anniversary of the publication of Kuo Mo-jo's influential book of poems *The Goddesses*, Yü Ta-fu organized a dinner party in his honor at I-p'in Hsiang, a famous Shanghai restaurant. It was attended by many of his former schoolmates from Japan as well as Cheng Chen-to, Mao Tun, Hsieh Liu-i (1897–1945), the translator and literary historian, and Huang Lu-yin (1898–1934), the woman short story writer.[42] All were members of the Literary Research Society. It is apparent that their feud had not yet developed to the point where they were no longer on speaking terms with one another.

During July and early August, Kuo Mo-jo translated into modern vernacular Chinese forty poems from the *Shih ching*, the oldest anthology of Chinese poetry. His preface to this collection is dated August 14, 1922. It was published during the same month[43] under the title *Chüan-erh chi* (Cockleburs), from the name of the first poem included.[44] This was the first attempt ever made to translate ancient Chinese poetry into the modern vernacular[45] and aroused so much controversy that the discussions it gave rise to were later published in a separate volume.[46]

On September 3, 1922, Kuo Mo-jo embarked from Shanghai to return to Fukuoka accompanied by a friend named Fei Che-min. He arrived at Moji on September 5, but was forced to spend twenty-four hours in a quarantine station on an island in the harbor. This experience prompted him to compose the following verse:

How brightly shine the lights of Moji across the water!
How murky is the ocean by night!
Oh, Napoleon on St. Helena,

And Prometheus under the Caucasus,
I know what your torments must have been! [47]

The next morning, despite his night of vicarious Promethean agony, Kuo Mo-jo was able to catch the 8:30 train and arrived safely home in Fukuoka two hours later in the middle of a rainstorm.[48]

Soon after his return to Fukuoka, Kuo Mo-jo and his family moved into the Hōyōkaku, a luxurious resort hotel on the shore of Hakata Bay which had been sold to a railroad company and was temporarily vacant while awaiting remodeling. The caretaker of this enormous building was a friend of theirs and offered them the opportunity to live there rent-free if Tomiko would help with the cleaning. Kuo Mo-jo's friend T'ao Ching-sun, a writer and musician, moved into the empty building with them.[49]

During September, while living amidst the empty splendors of the Hōyōkaku, Kuo Mo-jo revised an autobiographical story entitled "Wei-yang" (Unfinished) which had originally been written in 1921,[50] composed eleven poems,[51] and translated Fitzgerald's version of *The Rubáiyát of Omar Khayyám* into Chinese.[52]

Before leaving Shanghai, Kuo Mo-jo and Yü Ta-fu had agreed to ask Ch'eng Fang-wu to move there and take responsibility for the affairs of the Creation Society during their absence.[53] Thus in early October, after Kuo Mo-jo had left for Japan and Yü Ta-fu had returned to his job at the Anking College of Law and Administration, Ch'eng Fang-wu came to Shanghai from Changsha and moved into the house on Min-hou Nan Li.[54] That autumn T'ien Han came to Shanghai from Tokyo in order to take a job on the editorial staff of the China Book Company (Chung-hua shu-chü) and moved into a house on Min-hou Pei Li. One day when T'ien Han was visiting in the house on Min-hou

Nan Li he accidentally came across a letter from Ch'eng Fang-wu to Kuo Mo-jo which was severely critical of him. He became so upset that he not only broke with Ch'eng Fang-wu but severed his relations with the Creation Society.[55]

On November 23, 1922, Kuo Mo-jo completed his one-act play "Ku-chu chün chih erh tzu" (The two princes of Ku-chu).[56] At about the same time he translated a selection of poems by Shelley, compiled a chronological biography of the English poet,[57] and composed ten new poems of his own.[58] Sometime in 1923 he translated Gerhart Hauptmann's novel *Der Ketzer von Soana,* although his translation was not published until 1925.[59] On February 28, 1923, he finished a three-act historical play called *Cho Wen-chün*[60] about the young widow who eloped with Ssu-ma Hsiang-ju, the famous Han dynasty poet.[61] During the same month his third son, Fo-sun, was born.[62]

In March 1923 Kuo Mo-jo finally graduated from medical school. On learning of this event his parents sent him three hundred *yüan* and asked him to return to Szechwan. Kuo Mo-jo planned to move temporarily to the countryside somewhere near Shanghai for as long as it would take him to complete his translation of *Faust* and then perhaps return to Szechwan.[63] This was not, however, to be the way things worked out.

The same month he received a letter from Chang Feng-chü asking him to come to Peking and join Chou Tso-jen (1885–1965) and himself on the staff of Peking University, the most prestigious in China, which was about to establish a department of Far Eastern literature. Kuo Mo-jo says that he refused this flattering offer on the grounds of incompetence, since he had received no formal education in the literary field.[64]

On April 1, 1923,[65] Kuo Mo-jo and his family embarked

for Shanghai in a third-class cabin[66] on the *Kasuga-maru*.[67] The same day he wrote a poem entitled "Farewell to Japan" (Liu-pieh Jih-pen) in which he proclaimed that he never expected to return to her shores.[68] On April 2 they arrived in Shanghai and moved into the house on Min-hou Nan Li.[69]

The following day[70] Yü Ta-fu, who had just given up his job at the Anking College of Law and Administration, arrived in Shanghai and moved into the T'ai-tung Book Company offices at Ma-huo Lu. Now for the first time Kuo Mo-jo, Ch'eng Fang-wu, and Yü Ta-fu were all in Shanghai at the same time. During the month of April they laid plans for the publication of a second periodical, to be called the *Creation Weekly* (Ch'uang-tsao chou-pao),[71] the first issue of which was published on May 13, 1923.[72]

Also during the month of April, Kuo Mo-jo made the acquaintance of Liang Shih-ch'iu (1902–   ), who later become an outstanding literary critic, and began to correspond with Wen I-to (1899–1946),[73] the famous poet and scholar, who was then a student at the School of the Art Institute of Chicago. In September 1923, it was Kuo Mo-jo who arranged for the publication of Wen I-to's first book of poems by the T'ai-tung Book Company.[74] Between April and June, Kuo Mo-jo wrote seven articles, eight poems, and a short story, translated a song from Goethe's *Wilhelm Meister,* and began to translate Nietzsche's *Also Sprach Zarathustra.*[75]

Sometime in early July 1923 the local alumni of the Japanese Higher School (kōtō gakkō) system held a dinner party in Shanghai. One of the people present was Chang Chi-luan (1888–1941), the editor of the *Chung-hua hsin-pao* (China news), an organ of the right-wing Political Science Clique.[76] During the dinner party he asked Kuo Mo-jo if the Creation Society could produce a daily literary section for his newspaper, designed to take up half a page. The paper would be willing to pay a hundred *yüan* a month for such a contribution and would give the Creation Society a free hand in its editorial policy. Kuo Mo-jo agreed to consult with his colleagues about the proposal, and when he did so they decided to accept the offer. The title of this new literary effort, *Creation Daily* (Ch'uang-tsao jih), was chosen by Kuo Mo-jo, who also designed the woodblock print which decorated its masthead. The first issue was published on July 26, 1923.[77]

During the autumn of 1923 when the Creation Society was at the height of its influence, simultaneously publishing the *Creation Quarterly,* the *Creation Weekly,* and the *Creation Daily,* it began to collapse from within. In the second half of September, Yü Ta-fu received a letter from Professor Ch'en Ch'i-hsiu of Peking University, a well-known economist, asking if he could come to Peking and teach two hours of statistics a week in his place while he was on a visit to the Soviet Union. When Kuo Mo-jo learned of this offer he advised against accepting it, but was surprised to find that Yü Ta-fu wanted to go and that Ch'eng Fang-wu also supported the idea. When he asked what was to become of the three periodicals they were publishing, Yü Ta-fu replied that as far as he was concerned they might just as well suspend publication. In this way Kuo Mo-jo was rudely awakened to something he should have noticed before: thanks to the high-handed way in which he played his self-appointed role as leader of the organization he had begun to alienate his colleagues.[78] Yü Ta-fu claims that he accepted the offer from Peking because of financial difficulties.[79] In all probability he was tired of his uncertain status in Shanghai and simply wanted the security of a regular job. On October 5, 1923, Kuo Mo-jo and Ch'eng Fang-wu went down to the dock to see

Yü Ta-fu off when he embarked for Tientsin on his way to Peking.[80]

Kuo Mo-jo and Ch'eng Fang-wu now found themselves in a very depressing state of affairs. A vivid picture of their discouraging situation just after Yü Ta-fu's departure is available in the diary of Hsü Chih-mo (1896–1931), the famous poet. There we find the following entry for October 11, 1923:

Hu Shih showed us some of Kuo Mo-jo's new poems. In content, form, and style they mark a falling off. Can it be that *The Goddesses* have fled forever? Hu Shih, Chu Ching-nung (1887–1951), and I walked to 121 Min-hou Li to pay Kuo Mo-jo a visit. It took us some time to find the place. Kuo Mo-jo came to the door himself, holding an infant son, in diapers. He was barefooted, wore an old student's uniform, and appeared rather haggard; but he has a broad forehead and wide chin and seems congenial and easy to make friends with. When we came in there were guests already there, including T'ien Han, who also had an infant son in his arms; but almost before we knew it, he had left, taking his son with him. All I remember is that his face is long and narrow. Kuo Mo-jo's living quarters are extremely cramped and the furnishings haphazard. His children swarm about in the midst of all this, calling upon their father to fondle and comfort them when they fall down and to wipe away their tears and snivel when they cry. None of them can speak Chinese. From the kitchen the sound of wooden clogs could be heard, which must have been his Japanese wife. After we had been seated and had run through the usual formalities, Ch'eng Fang-wu came downstairs and joined us, but refused to say anything. Hu Shih tried his best to break the awkward silence by finding some topic of conversation, but there seemed to be a barrier of ice between the hosts and their guests, which failed to melt even after a considerable period. From time to time Kuo Mo-jo would smirk and stare at us, I don't know why. Chu Ching-nung did not say a single word, but that was simply because there seemed to be no way to get a conversation going. At 5:30 we took our leave and departed. Hu Shih was very much surprised by the awkwardness of this meeting and said that the last time he had been there, when Yü Ta-fu was present, the house had been in somewhat better order and the conversation had flowed more naturally. Actually, with only their four hands they are maintaining a daily, a monthly [*sic.*, should be weekly], and a quarterly periodical, which is bound to be a rather unfortunate state of affairs. Moreover, they are not making enough to live on very comfortably and may even be destitute. No wonder their stock in trade is rebellion and lack of restraint.[81]

On the next day, October 12, 1923, Hsü Chih-mo's diary continues as follows:

Just now Kuo Mo-jo came to see me and brought his eldest son along with him. The conversation went much more naturally today. . . . He is going to go to work for a Red Cross hospital in Szechwan at the beginning of the year. He is also fed up with Shanghai. He gave me a copy of *Cockleburs,* a collection of his translations from the *Shih ching.* The idea is a very good one.[82]

The following day Kuo Mo-jo entertained Hu Shih and Hsü Chih-mo at the Mei-li Ch'uan, a well-known Shanghai restaurant, and got sufficiently carried away in his drunkenness to kiss and embrace Hu Shih. Two days later, on October 15, 1923, Hu Shih and Hsü Chih-mo gave a return feast for Kuo Mo-jo and his friends.[83] These excerpts from Hsü Chih-mo's diary not only give us a vivid glimpse of Kuo Mo-jo's domestic situation at the time, but also indicate that he was not yet by any means on such bad terms with Hu Shih and his circle as he was later to be.

Another fact which emerges from these diary entries is that Kuo Mo-jo was planning at the time to return to

Szechwan and embark on a medical career. As early as 1922 his oldest brother, Kuo K'ai-wen, who was then working in Chungking, had arranged a job for Kuo Mo-jo on the staff of the Red Cross Hospital there. At the time of his graduation from medical school in March 1923 his parents had written to him asking him to return to Szechwan, and the Red Cross Hospital had sent traveling expenses to him in Japan, which he failed to receive because he had already left for Shanghai. Since that time his brother had repeatedly written to him urging him to take the job,[84] and his remark to Hsü Chih-mo indicates that he had finally decided to do so. This resolution does not seem to have lasted very long, however, since on December 13, 1923, we find him writing to Liang Shih-ch'iu that he no longer intends to return to Szechwan.[85] Nevertheless, it was not until mid-March of 1924 that he finally made up his mind to reject the offer.[86]

One day in mid-October 1923, Yin Chu-fu, the manager of the *Chung-hua hsin-pao,* came to see Kuo Mo-jo and tactfully suggested that they should bring the *Creation Daily* to an end whenever it was convenient for them to do so, because the newspaper was finding it difficult to make ends meet and wanted to rid itself of this additional expense. Kuo Mo-jo surmised that the real reason for this request was probably pressure from Chang Shih-chao (1881–   ), one of the conservative leaders of the Political Science Clique, of which the *Chung-hua hsin-pao* was an organ, who was opposed to the use of the vernacular written style. Whatever the reasons for this request may have been, Kuo Mo-jo and Ch'eng Fang-wu could not but comply. Thus the *Creation Daily* ceased publication with the hundredth issue on November 2, 1923.[87]

If Kuo Mo-jo had lost one job he soon acquired another. Beginning with the issue of November 1, 1923, he became one of the two editors of *Hsüeh-i* (*Wissen und Wissenschaft*), the monthly journal of the Chinese Arts and Sciences Association (Chung-hua hsüeh-i she), to which the 1916 Society had changed its name in June 1923.[88] He remained on the masthead as one of the editors of this journal until the issue of April 15, 1927.[89] He was also active in other activities of this organization. On January 20, 1924, at a meeting of the directors of the Chinese Arts and Sciences Association it was decided to elect a committee to make plans for the future establishment of an Arts and Sciences College (Hsüeh-i ta-hsüeh) in Shanghai. Kuo Mo-jo, along with Wang Chao-jung, Ho Kung-kan, Fan Shou-k'ang, and Chou Ch'ang-shou, was one of the five members elected to this committee.[90] In March 1924, despite his own comparative penury, he pledged himself to contribute two hundred *yüan* toward the expenses of founding Arts and Sciences College. On March 16, 1923, Kuo Mo-jo addressed the annual meeting of the Chinese Arts and Sciences Association, which met from March 15 to March 17 in the building of the provincial department of education at Hangchow, on the subject "The Social Nature of Literature." [91] He tells us that he derived the ideas for this speech from Ruskin's *Unto This Last,* Grosse's *Die Anfänge der Kunst,* and Jean-Marie Guyau's *L'Art au Point de Vue Sociologique,* but that it was a dismal failure because of the inherent contradiction in his desire to prove the social utility of art without giving up the importance he attached to the artist's need for self-expression.[92]

During this period of Kuo Mo-jo's life the contradictions were accumulating thick and fast. The *Creation Daily* had been discontinued in November 1923, the last issue of the *Creation Quarterly* had come out in January 1924,[93] and it was apparent that sooner or later the *Creation Weekly* would follow suit. As if this were not enough, his family

129

was a source of even greater anxiety. Neither Tomiko nor his three children could speak a word of Chinese and they were extremely unhappy in Shanghai. It was certainly true that the children had been much better off in Japan, where they had had access to free medical care and a healthful outdoor environment. In addition, Tomiko had always wanted her husband to practice medicine and had been consistently opposed to his literary activities. All these factors led to constant quarrels between them, and constant domestic pressure was put on him to abandon the Creation Society and return to Japan. Meanwhile in mid-February 1924 he received a telegram from the Red Cross Hospital in Chungking offering him the directorship of the hospital and a salary of four hundred *yüan* a month, but he did not even reply to the telegram.[94] Finally Tomiko took matters into her own hands and insisted on returning to Japan with the children whether he came with them or not. Kuo Mo-jo, in desperation, agreed to let them go and promised to follow them as soon as he could wind up the affairs of the Creation Society. Cheng Po-ch'i had come to Shanghai during his winter vacation and was about to return to Japan, so Kuo Mo-jo decided to send his wife and children back under his friend's protection. They set sail at 8:50 A.M. on the morning of February 17, 1924, aboard the *Nagasaki-maru*.[95] Within a few days of their arrival back in Fukuoka, Tomiko was able to rent a house with a garden and some orange trees for twenty yen a month.[96]

In mid-March 1924 Kuo Mo-jo received a visit from two representatives of the Red Cross Hospital in Chungking, who had come all the way from Szechwan, at the behest of the head of the local Red Cross, to persuade him to accept the offer. They presented Kuo Mo-jo with a money order for a thousand taels of silver to cover any expenses he might have to incur. Despite this handsome treatment, he finally turned down the offer once and for all. He claimed that he did this not only because he did not want to practice medicine, but because he felt that if he and his family were to move to Szechwan there would inevitably be a tragic conflict with his parents over the question of his first wife.[97]

Originally Kuo Mo-jo had not planned to leave Shanghai until the *Creation Weekly* had published its fifty-second issue in May, but he was thrown into such an unhealthy psychological state by his wife's precipitate departure that he resolved to leave the affairs of the Creation Society in the hands of Ch'eng Fang-wu and rejoin his family a month earlier. He embarked on April 1, 1924,[98] on the *Kasuga-maru*, the same ship on which he had come to Shanghai with his family only a year before.[99] Ch'eng Fang-wu joined Chou Ch'üan-p'ing and Ni I-te, two of the younger contributors to the publications of the Creation Society, in coming to the dock to see him off, and he was accompanied on the voyage by Huang Hui-ch'üan, a wealthy Szechwanese friend, who had purchased a first-class ticket for him.[100] On his departure from Shanghai, Kuo Mo-jo swore an oath that he would never again set foot on Chinese soil.[101]

The last issue of the *Creation Weekly* appeared during the first week of May 1924.[102] This event marked the end of the first period of the Creation Society, which then lay dormant for more than a year until it was revived in the summer of 1925. Yü Ta-fu arrived in Shanghai during the first week of May to join Ch'eng Fang-wu in presiding over the wake.[103] An abortive attempt was made, with Yü Ta-fu acting as the middleman, to keep the *Creation Weekly* alive by combining it with the *T'ai-p'ing Yang* (The Pacific Ocean), a liberal political magazine edited by a group of students of political science, economics, and law who had studied in Europe or in the United States.[104] It was proposed by the editors of the *T'ai-p'ing Yang* that the two periodicals should be combined into one, which would retain the title *Creation Weekly*. The first half of this joint undertaking, which was to be devoted to political matters, would be compiled in Peking and then sent to Shanghai, where the Creation Society would compile the second half, devoted to literature, and arrange for publication in that city as before. Negotiations over this proposed merger dragged on from April through July 1924,[105] but nothing came of them. Kuo Mo-jo admits that it was probably foolish not to agree to this proposal, but states that what he and Ch'eng Fang-wu objected to was that the contributors to the *T'ai-p'ing Yang* savored too much of the gentry or bureaucracy for their taste.[106] This is probably an example of the hostility, cutting across all ideological lines, which persisted throughout the 1920's and 1930's in China, between intellectuals who had studied in Japan and those who had returned from Europe or the United States.

A few weeks after Yü Ta-fu returned to Peking in mid-May 1924,[107] Ch'eng Fang-wu left Shanghai for Canton, where his elder brother, Ch'eng Shao-wu (d. 1924), held the post of quartermaster-general to the Second Army, under the command of his fellow Hunanese T'an Yen-k'ai (1876–1930),[108] one of the most influential figures in Sun Yat-sen's newly reorganized Kuomintang government. Once there he accepted a position as professor on the staff of the College of Sciences (Li-hsüeh yüan) of Kwangtung University (Kuang-tung ta-hsüeh), and a teaching position in the newly founded Whampoa Military Academy, under the directorship of Chiang Kai-shek.[109]

While Yü Ta-fu and Ch'eng Fang-wu were winding up the affairs of the Creation Society and then going their separate ways to Peking and Canton, Kuo Mo-jo was busily engaged in translating a book of essays by the pioneer Japanese Marxist Kawakami Hajime entitled *Social Organization and Social Revolution* (She-hui tsu-chih yü she-hui ko-ming).[110] This book was the instrument of Kuo Mo-jo's conversion to Marxism-Leninism, and it is therefore appropriate to halt here temporarily in the progress of our narrative and take a look at the intellectual developments which mark his progress from romanticism to Marxism-Leninism between 1918 and 1924.

Chapter 7

From Romanticism to Marxism-Leninism, 1918–1924

During the period between 1918 and 1924 two general trends are distinguishable in Kuo Mo-jo's thinking and attitudes. The first was toward romanticism, which was already apparent in *San yeh chi* and which was given additional impetus by his translation of *The Sorrows of Young Werther*. The second, gradual but fairly steady, was toward Marxism-Leninism. These two tendencies were not in any way mutually exclusive. It was the disintegration of the Creation Society and his increasing lack of confidence in his abilities as a creative writer, as much as the pressure of external events and the demands of his contemporaries, that tempered his romanticism. Yet his acceptance of Marxism-Leninism did not mark a sharp break with romanticism, and his conduct since 1924 would tend to substantiate the thesis that he has remained something of a romantic at heart. Although these two strands were interwoven in his thinking, I shall try to separate them for the purpose of analysis.

Kuo Mo-jo finished translating *The Sorrows of Young Werther* during the fall and winter of 1921, and the preface he wrote for it on January 22 and 23, 1922, reveals the extent to which the work had influenced him. In it he singles out five strains in the young Goethe's thought to which he responded sympathetically.[1]

First: his emphasis on emotion. Kuo Mo-jo cites with approval the concept that what one can discover through reason can be discovered by anyone else in the same way and that therefore the heart is the unique source of individuality. Thus, one should not seek to analyze or dissect the universe with its myriad phenomena by means of reason, but should rather synthesize and create it for one's self by means of the heart and emotions. In this way one can create his own paradise wherever he may find himself.[2]

Second: his pantheism. Kuo Mo-jo says:

Pantheism is atheism. If all natural phenomena are manifestations of God, and I also am a manifestation of God, then I am God, and all natural phenomena are manifestations of me. When a man has lost his Self and become one with God, he transcends time and space and sees life and death as one. But when a man becomes aware of his Self, he sees only the alternation and inconstancy of the external appearance of the myriad phenomena of the universe and of his own external appearance, and a feeling of sorrow about life and death, being and non-being, is born within him. . . . Energy is the source from which all things are created, it is the will of the universe, the thing in itself—*Ding an Sich*. If one can achieve union with this energy, one will be aware only of life and not death, only of constancy and not change. The body will find itself in paradise wherever it is, forever in a heaven where the soul is flooded with eternal happiness. . . . Man, in the final analysis, seeks only this eternal happiness. If one seeks this eternal happiness, one must first forget the Self. Goethe finds the prescription for forgetting the Self not in quietude but in action. With the same energy with which a lion strikes its prey, with the whole body and the whole soul, one must seek self-realization in the fulfillment of every moment. One must devote oneself to everything with one's entire energy. . . . This is not a doctrine that the lukewarm and the middle-of-the-roaders can apprehend.[3]

Third: his praise of nature. Kuo Mo-jo says:

He sees nature as a manifestation of the one God. Nature is the awesome appearance of the body of God. Therefore Goethe does not deny nature. He affirms nature, he treats nature as a benign mother, a friend, a lover, and a teacher. He says, "Henceforth I will take refuge only in nature. Only nature is inexhaustibly bountiful, only nature can produce a great artist. . . . All conventions and rules tend to destroy the real feeling and expression of nature." He loved nature, he worshiped nature, and nature gave him inexhaustible sympathy, comfort, and guidance. Therefore he was against mere dexterity, against accepted morality, against the class system, against accepted religion, and against superficial learning. He considered books to be dregs, written words to be dead bones, and almost took art itself to be superfluous. . . . How true! When one loses oneself in nature there are times when even poetry and art seem superfluous; how much the more is this true of scholarship, morality, religion, and class.[4]

Fourth: his admiration of primitive life. Kuo Mo-jo says:

The life of primitive man is the simplest, the purest, and the closest to nature. Those who worship nature and sing its praises cannot help admiring primitive life. . . . In the tiller of the soil . . . is to be found the most honest sincerity, the most devoted energy, the most fervent love. It is he who is best able to pour his entire energy into everything he does. Living for every moment, his is the very epitome of a life of self-realization.[5]

Fifth: his respect for children. Kuo Mo-jo says:

Why should children be respected? Select a child at random for observation. You will find that there is not a moment of the day when he does not devote his entire self to the tasks of creation, expression, and enjoyment. The life of a child is the life of a genius in miniature, it is the epitome of a life of self-realization.[6]

This exposition of the "elective affinities" he felt for certain elements in Goethe's early thought is an excellent summary of much of Kuo Mo-jo's own thinking between 1918 and 1923. Most of his pronouncements during this period were either echoes of these ideas or could be logically derived from them. He has said of himself that he was a romantic as early as the summer of 1918,[7] and I think he can be legitimately so characterized from that time on until at least the summer of 1923. Arthur O. Lovejoy has remarked in his famous address "On the discrimination of romanticisms": "The word 'romantic' has come to mean so many things that, by itself, it means nothing. It has ceased to perform the function of a verbal sign." [8] Yet no other word so adequately describes Kuo Mo-jo's thinking and attitudes during this period. There were logical inconsistencies between the tenets held by different varieties of European romanticism, and there were logical inconsistencies in Kuo Mo-jo's thinking — in which strands from these diverse sources were interwoven with others out of the Chinese past. But he thought of himself primarily as an artist rather than a philosopher and has never been rigorously logical in his thinking. He regarded himself as a romantic, and I think that the term can properly be applied to him.

A useful working definition of romanticism is given by Iredell Jenkins in *The Dictionary of Philosophy*. On the philosophic side:

Romanticism holds that Spirit, or the Absolute, is essentially creative; the ultimate ground of all things is primarily an urge to self-expression, and all that it has brought into being is but a means to its fuller self-realization. . . . From this basic view there springs a metaphysic that interprets the universe in terms of the concepts of evolution, process, life, and consciousness. . . . The metaphysical process is the process by which the Absolute seeks to realize itself, and all particular things are but phases within it. Hence the epistemology of romanticism is exclusively emotional and intuitive, stressing the necessity for fullness of experience and depth of feeling if reality is to be understood. Reason, being artificial and analytical, is inadequate to the task of comprehending the Absolute; knowing is living, and the philosopher must approach nature through inspiration, longing, and sympathy.

On the aesthetic side:

The essence of romanticism, either as an attitude or as a conscious program, is an intense interest in nature, and an attempt to seize natural phenomena in a direct, immediate, and naive manner. Romanticism thus regards all forms, rules, conventions, and manners as artificial constructs and as hindrances to the grasp, enjoyment, and expression of nature. . . . Romanticism stresses the values of sincerity, spontaneity, and passion, as against the restraint and cultivation demanded by artistic forms and modes. It reasserts the primacy of feeling, imagination, and sentiment, as opposed to reason. . . . It commands the artist to feel deeply and freely, and to express what he has felt with no restraints, either artistic or social. It seeks in works of art a stimulus to imagination and feeling, a point of departure for free activity, rather than an object that it can accept and contemplate.[9]

If this definition is accepted, Kuo Mo-jo was certainly a romantic in this period; for every element in it can also be found in his preface to *The Sorrows of Young Werther*.

It has already been pointed out that in Kuo Mo-jo as a poet the influence of Whitman is much more pronounced than that of Goethe. It is also significant that Kuo Mo-jo never repudiated Whitman, as he most emphatically did Goethe. In 1932 he declared Goethe not even worthy of veneration:

It is Goethe's energy that is capable of arousing respect, but his achievement was actually limited. How does he compare with his somewhat younger contemporary and fellow country-man Karl Marx? To be blunt, he comes off little better than a firefly in the light of the sun. He was a poet of the period when German feudal society was being transformed into a capitalist society. At the outset he was a trumpeter celebrating the capitalist revolution, but after he became a minister of the duchy of Weimar he retreated into the feudal camp. His aristocratic airs and his monarchism really leave an unpleasant taste in the mouth.[10]

This combination of hero worship and crude class analysis betrays the hand of Kuo Mo-jo the Marxist-Leninist. It is now our task to try to trace the path that led him through the mists of romanticism to what he perceived to be the clear daylight of the Marxist-Leninist world view. There were quite a few elements in Kuo Mo-jo's romanticism that, given a new interpretation or a slightly different emphasis, could have played a significant role in facilitating his transition to Marxism-Leninism. Some of these appear in his preface to *The Sorrows of Young Werther*.

In this work Kuo Mo-jo seems to take a rather strong stand in favor of emotion and intuition as against reason. Such an attitude, of course, would constitute a barrier to the acceptance of Marxism-Leninism. This was an overstatement of his point of view, however, for he elsewhere declares himself in favor of a much better balanced view of the roles of intuition and reason. In this case he also derives his view from Goethe:

139

"Der Drang nach Wahrheit und die Lust am Trug." This phrase of Goethe's, it seems to me, reveals completely the contradictions in our youthful psychology. Truth is to be sought after, but illusion must also be explored; reason is to be extended, but intuition cannot be rejected. This is not only the inherited feeling of the Chinese people, but is, to be sure, a natural inclination shared by all mankind. Goethe's life was the very crystallization of these conflicting tendencies, and yet, for all that, was no less perfect. As I see it, we need be neither partial nor indiscriminate: where it is appropriate to apply reason, we should apply it to the best of our ability; and where it is appropriate to employ intuition, we should do so without hesitation.[11]

Thus it is apparent that despite his romantic emphasis on intuition he did not reject the role of reason. As time went on he gave it greater and greater scope.

Kuo Mo-jo's discussion of pantheism in the preface is particularly significant. He starts out by equating pantheism with atheism, thus indicating that when he uses the term God in the succeeding lines he means by it an absolute that is not spiritual. Such a conception of the absolute, as he goes on to describe it, does not differ essentially from the *Tao* of the *Chuang-tzu*. In fact, the first two-thirds of his discussion under the heading of pantheism sound very much like a paraphrase of ideas clearly expressed in that work. There seems to be an inconsistency between the assertion that action rather than quietude is the prescription for forgetting the Self and the declaration that one must seek the fullest possible self-realization. It is possible that Kuo Mo-jo reconciled these apparent contradictions by means of Wang Yang-ming's doctrine concerning the unity of knowledge and action. At any rate, the important things to note are that Kuo Mo-jo interpreted his pantheism atheistically, in fact, although he does not say so here, materialistically; that he believed action to be the road to self-realization; and that he condemned half-measures and compromise. All of these factors served to facilitate his acceptance of Marxism-Leninism.

Kuo Mo-jo's understanding of the relationship between the artist and nature leads him to condemn all conventions and rules. He then extends this principle to include opposition to accepted morality and religion and the class system. Elsewhere in the same preface he says: "Art is a manifesto of revolution against the existing morality and the existing society. To criticize such art from the standpoint of the traditional morality is like trying to carry ice through fire." [12] It has already been pointed out that Kuo Mo-jo was opposed to the private property system. Once again it is notable that every one of the things he singled out for attack is also an object of attack in the *Chuang-tzu*.

Kuo Mo-jo's remarks on the primitive life are reminiscent of the eighteenth-century idealization of the "noble savage." There is a deeper significance to them, however. His explanation of the origin of the private property system, which has already been referred to, indicates that as early as 1920 he believed that there had been a "golden age" of primitive collectivism in prehistoric China, and that this was an ideal type of society. It is again to be noted that the *Chuang-tzu* also posited the existence of such a society and obviously hoped to see it restored. From this state of mind it was not a difficult leap to acceptance of the Marxist-Leninist belief in the primitive communism of the past and the classless society of the future.

Kuo Mo-jo's remarks on the respect due to children are closely related to his feelings about primitive man. In fact, he linked the two together and gave them joint credit as the originators of poetry: "Poetry was the first of all the forms of literature to develop. . . . The language of primitive peoples and of children is an expression of poetry. Primitive peoples and children have fresh, novel feelings about their environment, and irresistible emotions develop from these feelings, which are given expression in melodic language. The development of this sort of language is the development of poetry." [13] According to current Chinese Communist literary theory all the vital elements in literature have sprung from the people. Until the twentieth century the people in China were the peasants and thus the tillers of the soil whom Kuo Mo-jo associated with primitive man. It must be noted, however, that this particular theory was not yet current in China in 1924. This correspondence between Kuo Mo-jo's romantic beliefs and contemporary Chinese Communist literary theory is not, therefore, immediately relevant to his conversion.

All of these elements in Kuo Mo-jo's romanticism tended to facilitate his acceptance of Marxism-Leninism; but they are also to be found in the Chinese tradition, particularly in the *Chuang-tzu,* which was one of his favorite books from a very early age. There are thus certain strands of continuity between the Chinese tradition to which he was exposed in his youth, the romanticism that he espoused between 1918 and 1923, and the Marxism-Leninism of his post-1924 period.

In view of these considerations and the admiration he expressed for Marx, Engels, and Lenin as early as 1919 in his "Hymn to the Bandits," [14] it is curious that such a comparatively long time elapsed before he made any serious attempt to understand Marxism-Leninism.

On May 26, 1921, Kuo Mo-jo wrote a prefatory poem to *The Goddesses* in which he said:

I am a proletarian:
Because except for my naked self,

I have no private property of my own.
The Goddesses is something that I gave birth to myself,
And perhaps I could say that it belongs to me,
But I would like to become a communist,
So I am going to share it with the public.[15]

Writing in 1932, Kuo Mo-jo described the development of his political thought a decade earlier as follows:

Although my political thinking was comparatively advanced, it was not in any way organically related to my literary activity. In the introductory poem to The Goddesses I said, "I am a proletarian" and "I would like to become a communist"; but this was only playing with words, for in reality the very concepts of the proletariat and of communism were still unclear in my mind. In "Wild Cherry Blossoms" I expressed some bloody ideas, but they, too, were only concerned with the extermination of evildoers and were rather strongly tinged with anarchism.[16]

It will be remembered that on the night of June 1, 1921, while he was in Kyoto making final arrangements for the establishment of the Creation Society, Kuo Mo-jo stayed with Li Shan-t'ing, a former schoolmate from the Okayama days, who was then enrolled in the economics department of Kyoto Imperial University. Li Shan-t'ing, who was a disciple of Kawakami Hajime, the pioneer Japanese Marxist who taught at the university for twenty years between 1908 and 1928, was so enthusiastic about his creed that he was known to his classmates as the "Chinese Marx." This meeting took place less than a week after Kuo Mo-jo had announced his desire to become a communist, and he was sufficiently interested to ask Li Shan-t'ing for an explication of the fundamentals of Marxism, with the following results:

He spoke to me of the "formulas of the materialist interpretation of history," of the "inevitable collapse of capitalism," and of the "dictatorship of the proletariat," but failed to give me the impression that he had a real grasp of the essentials, so that I was quite unable to make head or tail of it all. He suggested that I read Kawakami Hajime's magazine *Studies of Social Problems*, but since I did not feel any particular need to do so at the time, I did not immediately take up his suggestion.[17]

As we have already seen, it was the process of translating a book by Kawakami Hajime that eventually effected Kuo Mo-jo's conversion to Marxism-Leninism in 1924.

A letter written on October 10, 1921, the tenth anniversary of the outbreak of the 1911 revolution, reveals a significant fact about Kuo Mo-jo's thinking during this period that set him apart from the majority of his contemporaries. In it he remarks, "I have long since freed myself from the bonds of narrow nationalism." [18] On the same subject he said in 1932: "At the outset the Creation Society did not stand for any isms on the positive side. On the negative side it is possible to say, at the very least, that it did not stand for nationalism." [19] Kuo Mo-jo's repudiation of nationalism, which was possibly influenced by the passionate internationalism of the German expressionists, and Ernst Toller in particular, may have made his transition to Marxism-Leninism easier, for this was the period when the Comintern was stressing internationalism and the world revolution.

In 1932 Kuo Mo-jo described his political outlook in 1921–1922 as follows:

My own way of thought was inclined toward revolution. I felt that, no matter what, the existing situation in China had to be destroyed, and that in order to destroy the existing situa-

tion it would be necessary to adopt positive and bloody measures. This way of thinking was really still an idealistic way of
thinking, however, for I thought that once China's evildoers
had been entirely rooted out a good state of affairs would
naturally ensue. This was really in no way different from the
"government by good men" that Hu Shih was advocating.[20]

Up to this time Kuo Mo-jo had never shown a trace of
anti-Western sentiment, but in the fall of 1922 he published a fragment in the second issue of the *Creation Quarterly* that revealed both a marked change in his attitude
toward Tagore and an incipient hostility toward the West.
It runs as follows:

Last night I dreamed that I met Tagore.
He said to me, "You Chinese poets are nothing but a bunch
of performing monkeys."
I said, "What do you mean by that?"
He said, "All you can do is imitate; sometimes East, sometimes West. Despite your fancy duds, you're coming out at the
elbows."
"What a joke," I replied heatedly. "You're really nothing
but an old monkey yourself. You're better than we are only
in so far as the Westerners have seen fit to reward you with
more of their money."
He struck at me with his cane, and I woke up, sorry to have
destroyed such a great idol.[21]

This petulant attitude was probably the result of having
lived for two summers in Shanghai's International Settlement, where the patronizing air of many Westerners caused
much justifiable resentment among sensitive Chinese intellectuals. He had not yet revealed any familiarity with
the Leninist theory of imperialism.

It was in November 1922 that Kuo Mo-jo wrote "The

145

Two Princes of Ku-chu," the last of the poetic dramas which he composed under the influence of Goethe. The protagonists of this dramatic fragment are two legendary recluses of ancient China, Po I and Shu Ch'i, who flee from the corruption of the world in order to preserve their purity and finally die of starvation in their mountain retreat. Kuo Mo-jo's approval of their conduct gives us a clue to his own attitudes at the time. He was thoroughly disgusted with the disorder and corruption he found in China, but his basic reaction was to try to keep himself uncontaminated at all costs. This thoroughly unrevolutionary attitude did not prevent him from once again drawing an idealized picture of the primitive society that had once existed in China, and this time labeling it specifically as communistic.[22] Thus as early as 1922 he identified his picture of the ideal society with what he called communism. Since there is no evidence that he then had any understanding of Marxist-Leninist theories of the stages of societal development, it is probable that this was merely a semantic association. It is nonetheless a significant one.

During the same period that he was writing "The Two Princes of Ku-chu," Kuo Mo-jo also wrote a poem entitled "Nine Stanzas in Ancient Style Lamenting the State of the World" (Ai-shih ku-tiao chiu shou). In the last of these stanzas he expresses the wish to see all China covered with red flags. In 1932 he described his state of mind when writing this poem as follows:

Here I openly made use of the word "red," but the odd thing is that in all these verses, although I attacked the politicians, the warlords, the bureaucrats, the party members, and the educators, I never even mentioned the people who were standing behind these puppets pulling the strings [i.e., the imperialists]. From admiration for these members of the "Lumpen-proletariat" [certain rebels and assassins from Chinese history whom

146

he mentions in the poem], I wanted, at one jump, to see China communized. Lying prone on a wicker couch dreaming of communization — there you have a true picture of me at the time.[23]

Here Kuo Mo-jo is criticizing himself for not having understood the Leninist theory of imperialism. He visualized an ideal communistic society in the past and hoped to see it restored in the future, but was not yet prepared to do anything about it. In some respects his vision is reminiscent of the theory of Liao P'ing, to which he had been exposed in his early schooldays, which interpreted the golden age depicted in certain of the Confucian classics as a mirror image of the utopia of the future.

For some reason there seems to have been a rather drastic shift in Kuo Mo-jo's attitudes during the month of May 1923. On May 2, in an address delivered at Shanghai University, he was still using his romantic jargon. Among other things he said that art has no intrinsic purpose, although after it is produced it may have social effects, just as a tree does not grow in order to serve man, although once it has grown man may use it for lumber.[24] But on May 18, barely more than two weeks later, he wrote a manifesto entitled "Our New Literary Movement" which expresses very different sentiments. This document still contains many romantic elements, but it reveals a marked shift of emphasis and is full of Marxist-Leninist jargon. In it we find such phrases as "the oppression of greedy capitalists from abroad" and "we are being trampled under foot by the demon of capitalism." Kuo Mo-jo goes on to say, "The bourgeois temperament has taken too deep root among the promoters [of the colloquial literature movement] and their collaborators. We must extirpate it, root and branch." He ends with the following peroration:

147

The present situation in China leaves only two roads open to us. We must either maintain our own purity by retiring to the mountains and woods, thus becoming friends of nature but deserters of life; or we must commit ourselves to total struggle and, as warriors in the melee of life, declare war on our pernicious society. Our spirits summon us to take the latter path and will not allow us to quail. We must roar like the tempest and erupt like a volcano. We must utterly sweep away and reduce to ashes all the corruption that exists. We must devote ourselves wholly to this end, body and soul. . . . Before there was light there was chaos, before there can be creation there must be destruction. New wine cannot be put into old wineskins. Before the phoenix can be reborn he must suffer cremation. Amid the present chaos our first task must be destruction. Our spirits are red hot with the fires of rebellion.

We attack the demon of capitalism.

We attack accepted moralities which are not based on the individual.

We attack the accepted religions which negate human life.

We attack the unreasonable barriers that restrict man's life.

We attack the literary tendencies produced by the foregoing.

We attack the servile literature which accommodates such tendencies.

It is the task of our movement to manifest through literature the spirit of the proletariat, naked humanity.

It is our objective to destroy the lair of the demon with bombs of life.[25]

In this manifesto the romantic elements still predominate, but the emotional, if not yet intellectual, acceptance of certain elements of Marxism-Leninism stands out very clearly. This manifesto is significant historically because it was one of the first calls for proletarian-oriented literature issued in the Chinese literary world.

The somewhat confused state of Kuo Mo-jo's thinking during this period is illustrated by a letter he wrote to

148

Tsung Po-hua in Germany on May 20, 1923, in which he compares Eastern and Western civilizations. He begins by rejecting the idea that the civilization of the East is characterized by stillness and that of the West by movement and points out that the great differences between the Greek and Hebrew cultures or between the Chinese and Indian cultures are only obscured by such facile dichotomies. He then declares that the spirit of ancient Chinese culture was akin to that of classical Greece and that science probably would have developed in China, just as it did in the West, had it not been for the burning of the books (in 213 B.C.) and the influx of Buddhism. According to Kuo Mo-jo, Buddhism played the same role in inhibiting scientific advance in China that Christianity played in Europe during the Middle Ages. He then defends science against the charge that it undermines spiritual values and produces a crass materialism, which resulted in Europe in the holocaust of the World War, by maintaining that, on the contrary, science, and particularly the scientific attitude, is needed everywhere if there is to be any hope of progress. He says that the World War was the inevitable result of the extreme development of capitalism, that farsighted thinkers had long since predicted the catastrophe that capitalism would bring upon the human race, and that during the war itself great men of action had arisen and succeeded in overturning the system that was responsible for their sufferings. He then remarks, "In the final analysis, Marx and Lenin are the heroes to whom we young people should look with veneration." At the end of the letter he calls for a dynamic, progressive, yet at the same time transcendental attitude on the part of youth.[26] This letter is clearly a response to the controversies over Eastern and Western civilization and science and metaphysics that were raging in Chinese intellectual circles at the time.[27] It reveals the somewhat muddled thinking of this transitional period in Kuo Mo-jo's development, but it leaves no doubt as to where his sympathies lay.

On May 27, 1923, Kuo Mo-jo wrote a remarkable series of five poems that reveal very clearly the changes taking place in his attitudes and the violence of the emotions which accompanied them. They will be presented in an arbitrary order, since the original sequence in which they were written is not indicated.

The first poem, entitled "To Encourage My Friends the Unemployed," reads as follows:

> My friends, we need not despair! Do not despair!
> It must be our task to destroy the demon's lair!
> What sort of employment is there for anyone under the
>   capitalist system?
> We are no more than dogs of the capitalists with collars
>   about our throats!
> My friends, we ought rather to congratulate ourselves that
>   we are free!
> We ought rather to congratulate ourselves that we are free,
>   my friends!
> If we are not strong enough to destroy the demon's lair,
> We can join hands and choose starvation rather than
>   compromise our principles.
> My friends, we need not despair! Do not despair!
> Let us rally our spirits and vow to destroy the demon's
>   lair! [28]

Although Kuo Mo-jo was scarcely a proletarian and was not himself slaving for any capitalist, this poem indicates that he must have begun to take an interest in Marxist-Leninist theory. His own troubles were as much neurotic as economic and capitalism was little more than embryonic in China at the time, but Marxist-Leninist theory made it into a convenient scapegoat for his personal difficulties as well as those of his country.

The second poem is entitled "My Miserably Incarcerated Friends." In the first verse the tenements of Shanghai are compared to prisons from which all of nature's sights and sounds are cut off. The second and third verses continue:

> My miserably incarcerated friends —
> In such an environment as this
> Are we anything more than convicts?
> We are imprisoned in impenetrable fog,
> We are trapped in the demon's lair.
> A demon all of gold
> Sits on top of us,
> So that we dare not make the slightest move.
> Oh, Oh,
> We dare not make the slightest move!
> But we must go to the soldiers!
> We must go to the masses!
> My friends, it is useless to deplore the situation,
> Words are no longer of any use! [29]

Here Kuo Mo-jo expresses for the first time a wish to go to the people. Although he did not immediately heed his own exhortation, these lines became Communist slogans during the Sino-Japanese War.

The third poem is entitled "Singing and Laughing in the Gardens of the Rich." Here Kuo Mo-jo, in his resentment of the rich, lashes out against even the birds that sing and the flowers that bloom in their gardens, and wishes that he had a weapon with which to slaughter and uproot them. The last verse reads:

> Oh, thick-skinned, shameless nature
> All you do is toady to the rich!

151

>   The praises that I have sung you in the past,
>   I hereby wipe out with a stroke of the pen.[30]

Here Kuo Mo-jo discovers that even the beauties of nature, with which he had so often felt himself in mystic communion, are available only to those who can afford them. It is the inequality of distribution that bothers him. He is not really repudiating nature, but only setting it aside until such time as everyone will be able to enjoy it as much as he does.

The fourth poem is entitled "The Grapes of Wrath." In the first two verses Kuo Mo-jo calls on the poet to take the ugly side of things, as well as the beautiful, as his province. He points out that there is an unpleasant side to everything and that one should not look at things with one eye closed. The last verse reads:

>   Oh nature, you of the myriad contradictions,
>   I will never again allow myself to be infatuated by your
>   cold countenance.
>   The incurable wrath of this human world
>   Will furnish the grapes out of which I henceforth make
>   my wine.[31]

This is merely an elaboration of the theme of the third poem, with the addition of a promise that he will henceforth write about real human problems instead of composing incantations to nature.

The fifth poem is entitled "A Seeker after Strength," and reads as follows:

>   Begone! Oh, feelings of uncertainty!
>   No longer entangle my white-hot heart!
>   Like a poor moth who strikes against a lamp
>   You will burn up forthwith!

Begone! Oh, specious attractions of nihilism!
No longer knock secretly at the iron door of my heart!
Poor smile-peddling whore,
Go marry yourself to a businessman!

Begone! Oh, spirit of negation!
Begone! Oh, delicate embroidery needle!
I will hold the *Koran* in my left hand,
And in my right, a sword! [32]

These poems make it clear that iconoclasm was no longer
enough for Kuo Mo-jo; he had had enough of the tortures
of uncertainty; piecemeal solutions did not suffice; having
exorcised nature and beauty he was trying to dispel his
lingering doubts in the search for a fighting faith to which
he could grant unqualified allegiance.

On September 4, 1923, Kuo Mo-jo wrote an article entitled "The Artist and the Revolutionary" in which he
said:

There are those who say that the artist and the revolutionary cannot be united in one person. Those who make this sort
of statement usually fall into one of two categories: the per-
verse dwellers in the ivory tower who avoid reality, or the
toughs who do not understand the spirit of art but pride themselves on being activists. The first category is made up of those
who advocate art for art's sake. They offer up their lives to art
and worship idols of their own creation. Although this attitude
is somewhat affected, it can still be forgiven; for there is absolutely no such thing as art completely disassociated from human life. Moreover, it is really unimportant whether an artist
advocates art for art's sake or art for life's sake so long as what
he produces is art. It does not matter whether we say a knife
is for killing chickens or for killing people, what we demand
of it is that it have the characteristics of a knife. This is easy
enough to comprehend. As for the second category of people,

some of them do not claim that art is absolutely useless but would have it that artists are capable only of speech and not action. They make speech and action into two separate entities, and they do the same with revolution and art. . . . If an artist decides to make use of his art as revolutionary propaganda, we ought not to discuss whether or not it is proper for him to produce revolutionary propaganda, but whether or not the vehicle he uses for his propaganda is art. If the vehicle he uses for his propaganda is art, then he is, of course, an artist. This kind of artist who uses his work for revolutionary propaganda is just like the activist who practices revolution with a bomb. They are alike in making a real contribution to the revolutionary cause. We need not expect the activist to produce propaganda art, and we need not expect the revolutionary artist to go out throwing bombs. . . . I want to take this occasion to make a bold statement. All real revolutionary activity is artistic activity. All sincere activists are pure artists. All sincere artists are also pure revolutionaries.[33]

In early October 1923 Kuo Mo-jo drafted a manifesto for the All-China Arts Association. Part of this document reads as follows:

> There is a close relationship between the people and the origins of art; but since the rise of the system of private production art has become the monopoly of the privileged classes.
> The fewer the people's opportunities for contact with art become the more they deteriorate.
> When art loses its popular base it, also, deteriorates.
> The interaction of these two factors has produced the decadence of the Chinese people and the decadence of Chinese art.
> This is the twentieth century, and it will not stand for the continued existence of the system of private production.
> This is the twentieth century, and it will no longer allow art to remain the monopoly of the privileged classes.

We must rescue art and give it back to the people!
It is not our goal to try to bring art down to the level of the
    people,
It is our goal to try to raise the people into the realm of
    art.[34]

There is a noticeable evolution here from what started as the romantic concept that art springs from the primitive, but the document remains more romantic than Marxist in that the decadence of the Chinese people is explained more in terms of art than economics.

Only a few days later, however, Kuo Mo-jo moved a step further. On October 11, in an essay entitled "My Views on Tagore's Visit to China," he said:

European disorder is the result of defective institutions, and the East is perishing in the toils of the private property system. Although the diseases are different, they stem from the same root. I believe that the materialist interpretation of history offers the only clue to the solution of the world situation. Until the economic systems of the world have been transformed, such things as the manifestations of Brahma, the dignity of the Self, and the gospel of love can only be the morphine or cocaine of the propertied and leisured classes, while the members of the proletariat are left to soak themselves in sweat and blood. Peace propaganda is the greatest danger the world faces today. Peace propaganda is only a protective device of the propertied classes. Out of it are forged the chains of the proletariat.

He went on to say that although he was not ill-disposed toward Tagore as an individual, he hoped that his Chinese audience would not be led astray by his thinking.[35] This essay contains Kuo Mo-jo's first mention of the materialist interpretation of history and his first explicit statement regarding the absolute priority of economic reform. He had covered quite a lot of ground in the ten years since he first encountered Tagore in 1914.

As has already been mentioned, Yü Ta-fu left Shanghai for Peking on October 5, 1923, the publication of the *Creation Daily* was suspended on November 2, the last issue of the *Creation Quarterly* appeared in January 1924, and Kuo Mo-jo's wife and children left for Japan on February 17. This series of events only served to exacerbate the sense of desperation with which Kuo Mo-jo was casting about for a solution to his own and his country's problems. During the period between the departure of his family and his own return to Japan in the first week of April, he almost had a nervous breakdown. His state of mind at that time is forcefully delineated in a series of autobiographical stories he wrote during February and March 1924 entitled "The Crossroads," [36] "The Saints," [37] "Purgatory," [38] and "The Cross." [39] All of them reveal feelings of inferiority, inadequacy, guilt, depression, resentment, and paranoia. In "The Saints" he describes himself in the third person: "He was much like the heroes in many of Turgenev's novels. He wanted very much to sacrifice himself to the world of reality, but he was constantly troubled with doubt and always ended up a victim of futility." [40] In "The Cross" he describes the state of desperation he is driven to by a letter from his wife telling of the hard time she is having in Japan. He feels terrible anguish and guilt and even contemplates the killing of their children and a mutual suicide. He promises to follow her anywhere, even to death, and berates himself for trying to make a career for himself in the creative arts, for which he has no talent. Finally he rejects his role as an artist.[41] These four stories paint a convincing picture of a man dominated by feelings of guilt and paranoia, in roughly equal proportions. His was a psyche ripe for religious conversion.

Kuo Mo-jo has described his state of mind in February and March 1924 as follows: "At that point I had certainly come to the crossroads in my life. . . . I utterly stripped away the affectations that had hitherto served me as protective armor. Only a fearful force can bring a man to take an irrevocable step, or, to put it more bluntly, to care no longer about his face." [42] It was an emotional crisis that brought Kuo Mo-jo to the point of taking an irrevocable step, but, as we have seen, a considerable reorientation in his intellectual outlook had already taken place. Here is his own description of this process:

In my own thinking I was depressed to find myself in a dilemma from which I did not see how I could either advance or retreat. I had always been somewhat stricken with a tendency to the left, and while publishing the *Creation Weekly* had sung a pretty radical tune, saying that I would "go to the masses" and "go to the soldiers"; but when all the shouting was over, I was still upstairs in my room at Min-hou Nan Li. I had shouted about it, but had not done anything about it and had to bear the interminable reproaches of my conscience. The pantheism of my earlier thinking, the so-called development of the individual, so-called freedom, and so-called expression had somehow, imperceptibly, been rooted out of my mind. Marx and Lenin, who had previously been on the borders of my consciousness, had gradually pushed Spinoza and Goethe out of it and taken over the central place in my thinking. When Lenin died early in 1924, I was as deeply grieved as if the sun had set forever.[43] But of Marxism-Leninism I certainly had no very clear understanding, and it was at that time that I developed the desire to investigate this system of thought.[44]

Since Marxism-Leninism had been a fairly prominent current in the Chinese intellectual world since about the time of Kuo Mo-jo's arrival in Shanghai in 1921, or slightly before,[45] it may well be asked why such a long time elapsed before he got around to seriously investigating it. This is a particularly pertinent question because, as I have tried to demonstrate, there were very few real obstacles to the acceptance of Marxism-Leninism in his thinking during this period and, in fact, he was drifting in its direction all the time. The only explanation I have to offer is based on a remark he made in June 1923, when he said: "Ch'eng Fang-wu and I share a certain idiosyncrasy. Whatever most people say is a good thing we are unwilling to believe in." [46] I suspect that one reason he delayed the study of Marxism-Leninism for so long may have been that he felt it beneath his dignity to do what so many of his contemporaries, and particularly his rivals, were doing. At any rate, the disintegration of the Creation Society and of his domestic, economic, and psychological situations finally pushed him into it.

The instrument of Kuo Mo-jo's conversion was a book of essays on Marxist problems by Kawakami Hajime entitled *Social Organization and Social Revolution*. These essays had originally appeared in Kawakami's journal, *Studies of Social Problems,* which Li Shan-t'ing had unsuccessfully recommended to Kuo Mo-jo in June 1921. He began the translation of this book soon after his return to Fukuoka in April 1924, and the task occupied him for about fifty days.[47] Even before the translation was finished, Kuo Mo-jo wrote a letter to Ch'eng Fang-wu on April 18, 1924, in which he said: "When I think about it, the last year in Shanghai is like a confused dream." "For the last two weeks I have been doing nothing but reading and translating Kawakami Hajime's *Social Organization and Social Revolution*. I am afraid it will take me at least another three weeks to finish it. I now have a dream which is sustaining my life." [48]

In another letter to Ch'eng Fang-wu, written on August 9, 1924,[49] Kuo Mo-jo spells out the significance of this dream as follows:

Fang-wu! We have been born in a most meaningful age; the age of a great revolution in human cultural history! I have now become a thoroughgoing believer in Marxism. For this age in which we live Marxism provides the only solution. . . .
I came here with the intention of translating the book *Social Organization and Social Revolution,* which you did not entirely approve of. Although I, too, am not one hundred per cent satisfied by its contents — for example, I do not think that the author's disapproval of plans for an early political revolution is in accordance with the basic principles of Marx — nevertheless, I have derived no small benefit from translating it. The dislike for individualistic capitalism and the faith in social revolution that I held only vaguely in the past are now reinforced by the light of reason and are no longer merely emotional reactions. The translation of this book constitutes a turning point in my life. It has awakened me from my semi-somnolent state, it has delivered me from my uncertainty before the crossroads, it has rescued me from the shadow of death. I am deeply grateful to the author and profoundly grateful to Marx and Lenin. . . . The thing which has amazed me the most in translating this book is the fact that men like Lenin and Trotsky,[50] whom we have been accustomed to regard as little more than desperadoes, have such subtle minds and are such dedicated scholars. We read too few books, by and large, and how often we are misled into evaluating people on the basis of general report.[51]

In this letter Kuo Mo-jo not only announces his conversion to Marxism-Leninism but admits that he had never given it any serious study in the past.

The translation of Kawakami's book also induced Kuo Mo-jo to revise his theories on art and literature. In the same letter to Ch'eng Fang-wu he wrote:

My understanding of literature has completely changed. It is no longer a problem of literary technique but one of the literature of yesterday, the literature of today, and the literature of tomorrow. The literature of yesterday was composed for the delectation of an aristocracy that was not even conscious of the fact that it had usurped a position of favor and precedence in human life. . . . The literature of today is the literature of those who are now on the revolutionary path, the cry of those who are oppressed. . . . It is a revolutionary literature. I recognize that it is a transitional phenomenon, but it is an inevitable phenomenon. And what is the literature of tomorrow? Ah, Fang-wu, it is the literature of which you have so often spoken, which transcends time and space. But it can only come into being after the realization of socialism. Once socialism has been realized great literary geniuses will be able to freely develop their potentialities to the utmost. Only then, when there are no longer any classes, and when life's only troubles will be due to natural and physiological causes, will man be able to return to his true nature. Only then will literature be able to take pure human nature as its subject. Only then will a pure literature become possible. To talk of a pure literature at present is only possible in the dream world of the young, amidst the comforts of the well-to-do, in the euphoria of the drug addict, in the drunkenness of the alcoholic, and in the hallucinations of the starving.[52]

Although Kuo Mo-jo had proclaimed himself a convert to Marxism-Leninism and repudiated his romanticism, this letter clearly indicates that his romanticism had not been successfully exorcised. All he had done was to project it into the future, where its realization was to be an indication of the perfection of the Communist utopia.

Kuo Mo-jo's acceptance of Marxism-Leninism in 1924 did not mark a break with the Chinese tradition as he understood it. In fact certain elements in that tradition may have tended to predispose him in favor of Marxism-

Leninism. The same can be said of the role romanticism played in his thinking. As a matter of fact he was able to justify his acceptance of Marxism-Leninism to himself and to others as the only available compound of "knowledge and action" that gave promise of making possible the achievement of his traditional and romantic ideals.

Epilogue

Kuo Mo-jo left Shanghai to rejoin his family in Fukuoka on April 1, 1924.[1] His entire financial assets consisted of a sum of one or two hundred *yüan* which he had borrowed from a friend in Shanghai.[2] He took with him to Japan a complete set of Goethe's works, in German; a collection of Kawakami Hajime's essays on Marxism, in Japanese; and a German translation of Turgenev's *Virgin Soil*. His plans, in the order of their importance, were: to write, in commemoration of his Japanese wife, a novel which he had been projecting for some time under the title *Pure Light* (Chieh-kuang), to see his wife and children again, and, after completing the novel, to enter the physiology department of Kyushu Imperial University and devote the rest of his life to pure scientific research.[3]

Kuo Mo-jo's plans did not long survive the pressure of realities. Finding himself in financial difficulties, he soon saw the danger of relying on the uncertainties of inspiration in order to feed his family and decided to devote himself to the more prosaic but more certainly remunerative task of translation. On April 18, 1924 he wrote to Ch'eng Fang-wu: "For the last two weeks I have been doing nothing but reading and translating Kawakami Hajime's *Social Organization and Social Revolution*. I fear it will take me at least another three weeks to finish it. I now have a dream which is sustaining my life, and have discarded my intention of studying physiology." [4] Thus we find that within a matter of two weeks Kuo Mo-jo had either postponed or discarded the first and third of the plans he gave as reasons for his return to Japan. Although he assigns it only second place, his desire to see his wife and children was the only one of his plans that was immediately fulfilled, and we are probably safe in assuming that it was, in fact, the primary reason for his return.

After completing the translation of Kawakami's book, Kuo Mo-jo consented, at the request of the T'ai-tung Book Company, to write a preface for their forthcoming punctuated edition of the complete works of Wang Yang-ming. In preparation for this task he spent the first two weeks of June in restudying Wang Yang-ming's works and became so interested that he planned to do an extensive study of his philosophy. He completed the preface on June 17, but gave up the plan for a longer study when he found that he would not receive any remuneration for it.[5]

Kuo Mo-jo had been much influenced by the *Chuang-tzu* and Wang Yang-ming in his early years. The fact that he undertook to do an extensive study of Wang Yang-ming's philosophy only a few weeks after he had become a Marxist-Leninist reveals that he had not lost interest in his earlier mentors. After describing the events of June 1924, in a section of his autobiography written in 1937, Kuo Mo-jo devoted a lengthy paragraph to an evaluation of the *Chuang-tzu* and Wang Yang-ming:

The thought of Chuang-tzu is generally considered to be nihilistic, but I feel it to be very close to that of Spinoza. He considers all the phenomena of the universe to be manifestations of a single ultimate reality. When man understands this essential concept he sees all phenomena as one and thus rids himself of individual, personal desires. Such a conception can bring quiescence in personal life and eliminate conflict in government. Chuang-tzu can, in fact, be considered a universalist.

Moreover, it seems to me that his literary style is unsurpassed in all of classical Chinese literature. Although the substance of Wang Yang-ming's thought is Zen Buddhism masquerading in Confucian garb, it does not really differ in any respect from that of Chuang-tzu. The ultimate reality which Chuang-tzu calls the *Tao* is referred to by Wang Yang-ming as intuitive knowledge. On the one hand he advocates contemplative sitting, that one may apprehend intuitive knowledge, while on the other hand he advocates the expression of this knowledge in conduct, so that one's life may reveal a unity of knowledge and action. Even though his premises may be questionable, it seems to me that his advocacy of "disciplining oneself through action" is an antidote to the shortcoming of all mystics. Moreover, his own career . . . is the best illustration of the validity of his theories. . . . My respect for him has continued to the present day.[6]

At the end of April, when he was still but halfway through his translation of Kawakami, Kuo Mo-jo had made a three-day trip to Tokyo in order to collect from the local representative of the Szechwan provincial government the sum of three hundred yen for traveling expenses which he had failed to collect on his way home after graduation from medical school the year before. This money enabled him to pay the family's debts and the rent for the month of May, but there was not enough left over to pay the rent for June.[7] For some reason Kuo Mo-jo never received any compensation for his preface to the works of Wang Yang-ming.[8] On top of this, the Commercial Press, which had accepted his translation of Kawakami's book, decided to issue it as part of a collectanea, and therefore, according to established precedent, offered him no cash payment but only the promise of future royalties. As a result of these events, Kuo Mo-jo and his family were forcibly evicted from the house in which they were living at the end of

June and had no alternative but to move temporarily into the one-room upper story of the same small pawn shop where they had lived for a while when they first came to Fukuoka in 1918.[9]

Finding it impossible to do creative writing under such crowded conditions, and desperately in need of something which could be sold for ready money, Kuo Mo-jo spent all of July and the first third of August in translating Turgenev's novel *Virgin Soil* into Chinese.[10] On August 9, immediately after finishing the translation, he wrote a long letter to Ch'eng Fang-wu in which he described in detail his reactions to Kawakami and Turgenev and told his friend that he was determined to return to China and devote himself to literary propaganda in the cause of the social revolution. This document is the most important source we have for Kuo Mo-jo's thinking during this period.

After starting out with a discussion of the difficulty of pursuing pure research in the China of that day, Kuo Mo-jo launches suddenly into an impassioned description of the ideal world which he believes man can achieve for himself if he will but act upon the Marxist-Leninist creed. I will let him speak for himself.

A world in which everyone will be able to develop his talents in accordance with his natural proclivities, in which everyone will be able to devote himself to truth in the hope of making some contribution thereto, in which everyone will be able to find freedom, in which everyone will be able to attain nirvana, such is the most ideal, the most perfect of worlds. Is such a world but the utopia of a dreamer? Is it but the ivory tower of an aesthete? Not so! Not so! I now believe that it can be realized with certainty on this earth! I believe that the era characterized by the principle "From each according to his capacity, to each according to his need," foretold by scientific socialism, will eventually come, and I believe that "an association in which the free development of each is the condition for the free development of all" can be established. If we should not be destined to see the coming of such an era and the establishment of such a society in our lifetimes — and it goes without saying that we cannot be so destined — then the only course which we, who cannot develop freely, living as we do in this unfree age, should pursue is to devote our efforts to bringing about their realization, that our fellow men may partake equally of nature's bounty, and that our posterity may soon be free of life's material bonds and thus permitted free and complete development of their individualities.

Fang-wu! We have been born in a most meaningful age, the age of a great revolution in human cultural history! I have now become a thoroughgoing believer in Marxism. For this age in which we live Marxism provides the only solution. Matter is the mother of spirit. A high development and equal distribution of material civilization will be the placenta of a new spiritual civilization. Fang-wu! We who live in this age of transition can only perform the function of midwives. We cannot now become pure scientists, pure artists, or pure thinkers. If one wishes to become such, it goes without saying that one must possess the necessary genius, but one must also have the material prerequisites. Naturally we must admire those geniuses who have been able to achieve such pure development of their personalities before the realization of the social revolution; but if they have not had wealthy fathers, they have had wealthy patrons. Take a look, for example, at the greater and lesser lights of the Italian Renaissance; at Newton, Goethe, and Tolstoy; or at Tagore, who has recently been received in China as a sage! If they were not satellites of the aristocracy they were members of the aristocracy themselves, and only because they were lucky enough to be so blessed were they able to develop their talents. Those who are not so blessed die of starvation or disease before they get anywhere! How many real geniuses have ever been able to develop freely and completely? Fang-wu! I have awakened. That frustration and weariness which we both feel — and which I fear is felt by the entire body of Chinese youth — stems from the fact that we lack the good fortune to be able to seek self-perfection for ourselves, and that we cannot discover a means of making free development possible for all. Our internal demands cannot be brought into harmony with the external conditions. No longer finding any signposts along our path, we have sunk into inactivity; and thus we are frustrated, weary, uncertain, and even think frequently of suicide. Fang-wu! Now that I have awakened to realization of all this, my thinking, which used to be deeply imbued with individualism, has been completely altered. It is also as a result of this awakening that I have given up my determination to study physiology. This sort of awakening has been disturbing my spirit for the last two or three years, but I have stayed hard abed in a state of half-sleep. Now I am wide awake, Fang-wu! Now I am wide awake. My thinking has not been consistent in the past, but I feel now that it has a single focus of concentration. I feel that I have found the key to the contradictory problems which I was once unable to solve. Perhaps my poetry will die as a consequence of this, but since nothing can be done about it, the sooner it dies the better.[11]

The striking element which emerges most clearly from this eloquent statement is the extent to which Kuo Mo-jo's attention remains focused on the problem of self-expression and full development of the potentialities of the individual. It is clearly the ends rather than the means of Marxism-Leninism which attract him. He has surrendered nothing of his earlier beliefs but has rather given them added dignity by positing the possibility of their fulfillment as the distinguishing characteristic of the ideal society toward which history is inevitably moving. The very act of renouncing his quest for personal freedom in order to seek it on behalf of the masses is a heroic and romantic gesture. This does not, however, detract from the sincerity of his commitment.

Later on in the same letter Kuo Mo-jo discusses his reactions to *Virgin Soil*. He had read the book twice before, once in the spring of 1921 and again in 1923,[12] so he was already thoroughly familiar with it before he began the task of translation. This is what he has to say about it.

The strongest impression which I now retain of this book *Virgin Soil* does not come from its fluent and elegant style . . . or from the personalities of its leading characters, but from the ideas concerning the social revolution with which it is animated. Turgenev recognized quite clearly the two important prerequisites for social revolution — the political and the material, or economic. He made Markelov represent the radicals in favor of political revolution and Solomin represent the moderates in favor of increasing the material forces of production. He saw to it that Markelov's approach met with failure, but enthusiastically endorsed the limited achievements of Solomin. As I see it, his thinking is clearly that of the socialist revisionists. But it is Markelov who has succeeded today, fifty years later, and Turgenev's "anonymous Russia" has become the Russia of Lenin. Turgenev's prophecy has obviously been proven wrong, but this in no way detracts from the value of the book. The realization of the social system envisaged by socialism cannot but depend, in the final analysis, on the fulfillment of the necessary material conditions. Even when a socialist political revolution succeeds in an underdeveloped country the path which must subsequently be followed is that of Solomin, for in order to attain prosperity the forces of production must be increased. Lenin has divided the social revolution into three stages: the first is the period of preparation (propaganda), the second is the period of struggle, and the third is the period of management of production. At present the Russian revolution has passed through only the first two stages and is just beginning to enter the third and longest period.

Fang-wu! Is not the Russia of the seventies, after the emancipation of the serfs, just like our China of the twenties, after the overthrow of the Manchus? We, too, are progressing toward a social revolution. . . . And is not the life of the bureaucrats as it is depicted in this book . . . a photographic likeness of the conduct of China's bureaucrats, new and old? . . . Nejdanov's doubts, Markelov's radicalism, Solomin's good sense, and Mariana's heroism are all to be found, both good and bad, in the personalities of young Chinese men and women. Even if we restrict ourselves to the circle of our personal acquaintances we can discover no few examples of Chinese Nejdanovs, Markelovs, Solomins, and Marianas. This is, no doubt, another reason why I like this book and why I decided to translate it, for in it we can see the reflections of our own faces. Nevertheless, the only lessons which this book can teach us are negative ones. It makes us see that Nejdanov's doubts are of no help to the cause, that Markelov's extremism can only result in failure, that Solomin's sensible moderation only makes the road ahead discouragingly long, and that Mariana's heroic submission is too lacking in self-determination. What we must emulate is the "anonymous Russia" which Turgenev never knew but which is already known to us — the Russia of Lenin.[13]

It is interesting to note that Kuo Mo-jo, like so many other Chinese before and since, found a peculiar affinity between the problems of the discontented intellectuals in nineteenth-century Russia and in twentieth-century China. We can be sure that however much Kuo Mo-jo would like to have been either a Markelov or a Solomin, he felt himself to have the greatest affinity with Nejdanov, the classic figure of the "superfluous man," the ineffectual and alienated intellectual. But it was just this tendency in himself that he wished to fight against. We have seen that he accepted Lenin's theory of the three stages of the social revolution, and it was obvious that China was still in the first stage. It was propaganda then that was needed, and he resolved to throw himself into the fray.

Fang-wu! We have taken the revolutionary path and our literature can only be revolutionary literature. As far as contemporary literature is concerned, I cannot see that any such thing exists except in so far as it serves to promote the social revolution. Only in so far as it serves to promote the social revolution does it deserve to be called literature; otherwise it has about it the stench of meat and wine or the fragrance of narcotics and can count for nothing. Only one road is open to us in real life and, therefore, if literature is the reflection of life, only this sort of literature can be real. Fang-wu, this is my definite belief, and having once arrived at it, I see literature in true perspective and my faith in it is restored. This is the period for propaganda and literature is a propaganda weapon. I am no longer uncertain as to the course which I must pursue.

Fang-wu, I am going to return to China. On the revolutionary road China occupies the most strategic point. I hope to spend the latter half of my life meaningfully. I intend to return to China sometime in September. I will take my wife and children with me so that we can live or die together. After completing the translation of *Virgin Soil,* I have murdered the Nejdanov in my heart.[14]

This letter represents possibly the highest pitch of radical fervor that Kuo Mo-jo ever achieved. Unfortunately the Nejdanov in his heart proved to be a tougher customer than he had bargained for. By October 4, 1924, he was already confiding to his diary some doubts about the validity of Marxism.[15] He returned to Shanghai with his family on November 16, 1924,[16] where he continued to support himself by free-lance writing and part-time teaching; but nothing he wrote between August 1924 and July 1925 would indicate that he was a Marxist-Leninist. In the period after the May Thirtieth Movement in 1925 he began, for the first time, to develop personal contacts with members of the Chinese Communist Party.[17] But it was not until March 1926 that he moved to Canton and began to participate actively in the revolutionary political movement.[18] During the Northern Expedition he held a succession of high posts in the General Political Department[19] and when the break came, in 1927, between the Kuomintang and the Chinese Communist Party, he sided with the latter.[20] Finally, six years after he had declared in his preface to *The Goddesses* that he would like to become a communist, and three years after he had announced his conversion to Marxism-Leninism, in the course of the disastrous retreat from Nanchang to Swatow, in August and September 1927, he joined the Chinese Communist Party, at a time when its fortunes were at their lowest ebb.[21]

It was perhaps the act of a romantic, but it was an act based on intellectual convictions as well — convictions which he had first formulated in the spring and summer of 1924. The chain of circumstances which enabled Kuo Mojo to finally allay the lingering doubts of the Nejdanov in his heart must lie outside the scope of this work. Suffice it to say that by the summer of 1924 the ideological foundations had been laid for the career of the most versatile Chinese intellectual of our day. If I may borrow a stock phrase from the repertory of the traditional Chinese storyteller: "If you want to know what happened next, pray wait for the explanation in the next installment."

Notes

Bibliography

Glossary

Index

ABBREVIATIONS USED IN THE NOTES

CTCK   *Ch'uang-tsao chi-k'an* (Creation quarterly)

CTCP   *Ch'uang-tsao chou-pao* (Creation weekly)

CTHP   Kuo Mo-jo *Ch'uang-tsao shih-nien hsü-pien* (Ten years of creation continued)

CTSN   Kuo Mo-jo, *Ch'uang-tsao shih-nien* (Ten years of creation)

FCCH   Kuo Mo-jo, *Fan-cheng ch'ien-hou* (Before and after the 1911 revolution)

MJWC   Kuo Mo-jo, *Mo-jo wen-chi* (Collected literary works of Kuo Mo-jo)

SYC   T'ien Shou-ch'ang, Tsung Po-hua, and Kuo Mo-jo, *San yeh chi* (Cloverleaf)

WTYN   Kuo Mo-jo, *Wo ti yu-nien* (The years of my youth)

Notes

1. CHILDHOOD IN SHA-WAN, 1892–1905.

1. *Lo-shan hsien chih,* comp. Huang Jung et al. (Chengtu, 1934), 1:28. For a map showing Sha-wan in relationship to Chia-ting, see the first map at the front of this work. For a more detailed map showing the location of Sha-wan in Kuan-O hsiang, the rural district in which it was situated, see the eleventh map in the same work. For Kuo Mo-jo's own description of Sha-wan, see *WTYN,* pp. 3–7.

2. *WTYN,* p. 13. Apparently, for the sake of convenience, Kuo Mo-jo has settled on the date November 16, 1892, for public celebrations of his birthday. See Kuo Mo-jo, "Wu-shih nien chien-p'u," originally completed on September 25, 1941, in Chang Ching-lu, comp., *Chung-kuo hsien-tai ch'u-pan shih-liao* (Peking, 1954–1959), III, 318–319.

3. *WTYN,* pp. 9–10. See also Fu Lien-chang, *Tsai Mao chu-hsi chiao-tao hsia* (Peking, 1959), p. 92, which gives an eyewitness account of a speech Kuo Mo-jo made in T'ing-chou in September 1927, in which he said, "I was also a citizen of T'ing-chou three hundred years ago." The fact that Kuo Mo-jo's ancestors were of Hakka origin is not mentioned anywhere in his autobiographical writings. It was called to my attention by Professor Lo Hsiang-lin, of the University of Hong Kong, a leading authority on Hakka history, who told me in a personal communication of November 1963 that Kuo Mo-jo had told him so himself while they were both in Chungking during the Sino-Japanese War. For the fact that there had been a Hakka clan named Kuo, which claimed descent from the famous T'ang general Kuo Tzu-i (697–781), living in the T'ing-chou fu area, see Lo Hsiang-lin, *K'o-chia shih-liao hui-p'ien* (Hong Kong, 1965), p. 209. For the reasons why Ning-hua hsien played such an important role in Hakka migrations, see ibid., pp. 377–387. For a map showing the routes of Hakka migration, see Kuo Shou-hua, *K'o-tsu yüan-liu hsin-chih* (Taipei, 1964), map facing p. 1.

4. For the great Hakka migrations to Szechwan in the late seventeenth and early eighteenth centuries, see Lo Hsiang-lin, *K'o-chia shih-liao hui-p'ien,* pp. 10–12. Also see Ho Ping-ti, *Studies on the*

Population of China, 1368–1953 (Cambridge, Mass., 1959), pp. 139–143.

5. Chang Hsien-chung occupied Szechwan from 1644 to 1646. See James B. Parsons, "The Culmination of a Chinese Peasant Rebellion: Chang Hsien-chung in Szechwan, 1644–46," *Journal of Asian Studies,* 16.3:387–400 (May 1957), especially pp. 393–398.

6. *WTYN,* pp. 9–10.

7. The name of Kuo Mo-jo's great-grandfather is given in *Lo-shan hsien chih,* 9:50b, where he is described as a *ch'u-shih,* or retired scholar. This is just a euphemistic way of indicating that he never had any official rank.

8. *WTYN,* p. 16.

9. Ibid., p. 17.

10. *Lo-shan hsien chih,* 9:50b.

11. For the date, see ibid., 5:50.

12. *WTYN,* pp. 28–29.

13. *Lo-shan hsien chih,* 9:50b.

14. *WTYN,* p. 18.

15. *SYC,* p. 109. The term is Chin-kang Fo.

16. *WTYN,* p. 18.

17. Ibid., p. 147.

18. Ibid., pp. 18–19.

19. *SYC,* pp. 109–110; *WTYN,* pp. 21 and 135.

20. *Lo-shan hsien chih,* 8:59b. See also *Tseng chiao Ch'ing-ch'ao chin-shih t'i-ming pei lu, fu yin-te,* comp. Fang Chao-ying and Tu Lien-che (Peiping, 1941), p. 183.

21. *Lo-shan hsien chih,* 9:22b.

22. *WTYN,* p. 14.

23. For the date, see *Ch'in-ting p'ing-ting Kuei-chou Miao-fei chi-lüeh,* comp. Ch'en Pang-jui et al. (Peking, 1896), 7:21b.

24. Ibid., 7:20b.

25. *Lo-shan hsien chih,* 9:23 and 10:3. For their ages, see *SYC,* p. 110.

26. *Lo-shan hsien chih,* 10:51.

27. Ibid., 9:23. Where the sources cited in notes 21–27 differ, I have chosen to follow the text which gives what appears to me to be the most reasonable or likely account of the event in question.

28. *Ch'in-ting p'ing-ting Kuei-chou Miao-fei chi lüeh,* 7:20b–22. See also *Ch'ing wen-tsung hsien huang-ti shih-lu* (Tokyo, 1937–1938), 270:31.

29. *Lo-shan hsien chih,* 8:66b and 9:23. This title is untranslatable. It was the eighth of nine hereditary ranks and was inheritable for one generation only. See H. S. Brunnert and V. V. Hagelstrom,

Present Day Political Organization of China, tr. from the Russian by
A. Beltchenko and E. E. Moran (Taipei, n.d.), p. 492.

30. *SYC,* p. 110; Kuo Mo-jo, "Pa-chiao hua," originally completed
in 1924, in his *Pao-chien chi* (Shanghai, 1955), p. 79; *WTYN,* p. 14.
There are certain discrepancies between these three accounts, written
by Kuo Mo-jo in 1920, 1924, and 1928.

31. *WTYN,* p. 14. Tu-chia ch'ang means Tu Family Village. For
a map showing Tu-chia ch'ang in relationship to Chia-ting, see the
first map at the front of the *Lo-shan hsien chih.* For a more detailed
map showing the location of Tu-chia ch'ang in An-ku hsiang, the
rural district in which it was situated, see the seventh map in the
same work. See also ibid., 1:29b.

32. *SYC,* p. 111; Kuo Mo-jo, "Pa-chiao hua," p. 79; *WTYN,* pp.
14–15.

33. *WTYN,* p. 15.

34. *SYC,* p. 109; *WTYN,* p. 13.

35. Kuo Mo-jo, "Ting," originally completed on April 13, 1936, in
MJWC, XI, 119.

36. *WTYN,* p. 13.

37. See Shih Chien (pen name of Ma Pin), *Kuo Mo-jo p'i-p'an*
(Hong Kong, 1954), p. 21.

38. For the date, see Kuo Mo-jo, "Wo ti hsüeh-sheng sheng-huo,"
originally completed on April 19, 1942, reprinted as "Hsüeh-sheng
shih-tai," in his *Ko-ming ch'un-ch'iu* (Shanghai, 1956), p. 3.

39. *WTYN,* p. 31; Kuo Mo-jo, "Wo ti hsüeh-sheng sheng-huo,"
p. 3.

40. *WTYN,* pp. 28–33.

41. The *San tzu ching* is of disputed authorship, but definitely
dates from the Southern Sung dynasty (1127–1279). For a more detailed description, see Samuel Wells Williams, *The Middle Kingdom*
(New York, 1901), I, 526–530.

42. See Richard Wilhelm, tr., *The I Ching or Book of Changes,*
tr. from the German by Cary F. Baynes, 2nd ed. (Bollingen Series
XIX; New York, 1961).

43. See James Legge, tr., *The Shoo King or The Book of Historical
Documents,* vol. III in James Legge, *The Chinese Classics,* 5 vols.
(Hong Kong, 1960).

44. See James Legge, tr., *The She King or The Book of Poetry,*
vol. IV in Legge, *The Chinese Classics;* Arthur Waley, tr., *The Book
of Songs* (London, 1954); and Bernhard Karlgren, tr., *The Book of
Odes* (Stockholm, 1950).

45. See James Legge, tr., *The Ch'un Ts'ew with the Tso Chuen,*
vol. V in Legge, *The Chinese Classics.*

46. See Édouard Biot, tr., *Le Tcheou-li; ou, Rites des Tcheou*, 3 vols. (Paris, 1851).

47. See John Steele, tr., *The I-li; or, Book of Etiquette and Ceremonial* (London, 1917). For the list of the classics which he read, see *WTYN*, p. 38 and Kuo Mo-jo, "Wo ti hsüeh-sheng sheng-huo," p. 3.

48. This anthology was compiled in the late seventeenth century by Wu Ch'u-ts'ai and Wu T'iao-hou. The preface is dated 1695.

49. Most, but by no means all, of the selections included in this anthology are in the *ku-wen* style, for a brief description of which, see James Robert Hightower, *Topics in Chinese Literature* (Cambridge, Mass., 1962), pp. 72–74.

50. Compiled by Liu K'o-chuang (1187–1269) of the Southern Sung dynasty.

51. Compiled by Sun Chu in the eighteenth century. The preface is dated 1763. For an English translation of this anthology, see Witter Bynner and Kiang Kang-hu, tr., *The Jade Mountain* (New York, 1951).

52. Compiled by Kao Ping (1350–1423) in the early years of the Ming dynasty.

53. This work has been translated into English by Yang Hsien-yi and Gladys Yang under the title "The twenty-four modes of poetry," *Chinese Literature* (no. 7, 1963), pp. 65–77.

54. For the list of Kuo Mo-jo's first readings in Chinese poetry, see *WTYN*, p. 38; Kuo Mo-jo, "Wo ti tso-shih ti ching-kuo," originally completed on September 4, 1936, in *MJWC*, XI, 138; and Kuo Mo-jo, "Wo ti hsüeh-sheng sheng-huo," p. 3.

55. *WTYN*, p. 38.

56. Ibid., p. 34.

57. Ibid., pp. 34–36.

58. See the description of this work and some translated excerpts in Arthur Waley, *Yuan Mei, Eighteenth Century Chinese Poet* (New York, 1956), pp. 120–140.

59. See the biography of Chi Yün in Arthur W. Hummel, ed., *Eminent Chinese of the Ch'ing Period* (Washington D.C., 1943, 1944), I, 37–38.

60. *WTYN*, pp. 26–27.

61. Wolfgang Franke, *The Reform and Abolition of the Traditional Chinese Examination System* (Cambridge, Mass., 1960), pp. 52–53.

62. *WTYN*, p. 40. The first of these works was devoted to world geography. It was written in 1897 by Chang Shih-ying and published in Nanking. See "Chiao-k'o-shu i-ch'ien ti t'ung-meng tu-wu," comp. library of the Chung-hua shu-chü, in Chang Ching-lu, comp., *Chung-kuo chin-tai ch'u-pan shih-liao* (Shanghai, 1953–1954), I, 218; and

"Chiao-k'o-shu chih fa-k'an kai-k'uang, i-pa-liu-pa — i-chiu-i-pa nien," comp. Ministry of Education in Chang Ching-lu, comp., *Chung-kuo chin-tai ch'u-pan shih-liao,* I, 223. The second of these works was by Pao Tung-li and was also published in Nanking. See "Chiao-k'o-shu i-ch'ien ti t'ung-meng tu-wu," I, 217.

63. *WTYN*, p. 42; Kuo Mo-jo, "Wo it hsüeh-sheng sheng-huo," p. 3. The name of this textbook was *Pi-suan shu-hsüeh.* It was translated by Tsou Li-wen from a book in English by an American whose name is transliterated as Ti-k'ao-wen. See "Chiao-k'o-shu chih fa-k'an kai-k'uang," I, 230.

64. Kuo Mo-jo, "Wo ti hsüeh-sheng sheng-huo," p. 4.

65. See Legge, *The Ch'un Ts'ew with the Tso Chuen.*

66. *WTYN,* p. 43.

67. For a brief description of this school and its accomplishments, see Liang Ch'i-ch'ao, *Intellectual Trends in the Ch'ing Period,* tr. Immanuel C. Y. Hsü (Cambridge, Mass., 1959), pp. 51-75.

68. Kuo Mo-jo, "Wo ti hsüeh-sheng sheng-huo," p. 4. For a short biography of Kuo Chao-hsiu, see *Lo-shan hsien chih,* 9:39. For the title of his collected works, see ibid., 11:31b. For the location of Liu-hua ch'i, see the first map in ibid.; and for further details, see ibid., 1:30b. In both the latter places the name of the village is given as Niu-hua ch'i. For an account by Chang Chih-tung (1837–1909) of the famous Tsun-ching shu-yüan, see Chang Chih-tung, *Ssu-ch'uan sheng-ch'eng Tsun-ching shu-yüan chi,* in Lu Ching, comp., *Shen shih chi chai ts'ung-shu* (n.p., 1923), ts'e 1, item 4, pp. 1–11.

69. For a biography of Tuan Yü-ts'ai see Hummel, *Eminent Chinese of the Ch'ing Period,* II 782–784.

70. Kuo Mo-jo, "Wo ti hsüeh-sheng sheng-huo," p. 4.

71. A primitive version of this novel, which deals with the turbulent period of the breakup of the Han empire in the second and third centuries A.D., was printed as early as the last decade of the thirteenth century, but the version which is read today dates from the mid-seventeenth century. It has been translated into English by C. H. Brewitt-Taylor, *Romance of the Three Kingdoms,* 2 vols. (Rutland, Vt., 1959).

72. Kuo Mo-jo, "Wu-shih nien chien-p'u," p. 319.

73. Franke, *The Reform and Abolition of the Traditional Chinese Examination System,* p. 54.

74. *WTYN,* pp. 40, 43.

75. This periodical was founded in 1903. See Chang Ching-lu, comp., "Ch'ing-mo Min-ch'u Ching Hu hua-k'an lu," in Chang Ching-lu, comp., *Chung-kuo chin-tai ch'u-pan shih-liao,* II, 298. Two illustrations from this journal are reproduced in the plate facing ibid., II, 300. It is also described in A Ying (pen name of Ch'ien

Hsing-ts'un), *Wan-Ch'ing wen-i pao-k'an shu-lüeh* (Shanghai, 1958), p. 95, where it is erroneously described as a monthly periodical.

76. For a description of this periodical and a listing of some of its more significant contents, see A Ying, *Wan-Ch'ing wen-i pao-k'an shu-lüeh*, pp. 13–16. A Ying gives the date of the periodical's founding as 1903, when it should be 1902. For the correct date, see Ting Wen-chiang, comp., *Liang Jen-kung hsien-sheng nien-p'u ch'ang-pien ch'u-kao* (Taipei, 1958), I, 163. A Ying also gives the place of publication as Tokyo, when it should be Yokohama. For the correct place, see Chang Ching-lu, comp., *Chung-kuo ch'u-pan shih-liao pu-pien* (Shanghai, 1957), caption under the plate on p. 23 of the illustrative material preceding the text. This plate is a photographic reproduction of the front cover of the first issue of the magazine.

77. This periodical was founded in January 1903. See Feng Tzu-yu, "Hsin-hai ch'ien hai nei-wai ko-ming shu-pao i-lan," in Chang Ching-lu, comp., *Chung-kuo chin-tai ch'u-pan shih-liao*, II, 284. See also A Ying, *Wan-Ch'ing wen-i pao-k'an shu-lüeh*, p. 144.

78. *WTYN*, pp. 40–41.

79. On the Japanese novel, see G. B. Sansom, *The Western World and Japan* (New York, 1951), pp. 400–401, 409. There is a theatrical poster depicting a scene from the dramatic version of this novel reproduced in ibid., facing p. 399.

80. The first translation was made by Chou Hung-yeh and was originally published in 1900, when it appeared serially in Liang Ch'i-ch'ao's periodical, the *Ch'ing-i pao* (Journal of pure criticism), which was published at ten-day intervals in Yokohama. It was later republished in an independent volume. See Feng Tzu-yu, "Hsin-hai ch'ien hai nei-wai ko-ming shu-pao i-lan," p. 288. The second translation was made by someone who used the pen name Yü-ch'en tzu and was published in Shanghai in 1902. See A Ying, comp., *Wan-Ch'ing hsi-ch'ü hsiao-shuo mu* (Shanghai, 1957), p. 156.

81. This drama appeared serially in 1903–1904 in the periodical *Hsiu-hsiang hsiao-shuo* (Illustrated fiction), which was edited by Li Pao-chia. For the attribution of authorship, see A Ying, comp., *Wan-Ch'ing hsi-ch'ü hsiao-shuo mu*, p. 48.

82. For this novel and the other works discussed in the preceding two paragraphs, see *WTYN*, pp. 40–41.

83. Ibid., pp. 43–44. For Mr. Liu's name, see Kuo Mo-jo, "Wu-shih nien chien-p'u," p. 319.

84. *WTYN*, pp. 44–46.

85. See Mai-mai Sze, tr., *The Tao of Painting, a Study of the Ritual Disposition of Chinese Painting; with a Translation of the Chieh tzu yüan hua chuan*, 2 vols. (Bollingen Series, XLIX; New York, 1956).

86. Kuo Mo-jo, "Ch'u ch'u K'uei-men," originally published in 1936, in his *Shao-nien shih-tai* (Shanghai, 1956), p. 384. See also *Lo-shan hsien chih*, 8:67.

87. On the influence of his eldest brother, see *WTYN*, pp. 48–49.

88. The authorship of this play is usually attributed to Wang Shih-fu. For a translation, see S. I. Hsiung, tr., *The Romance of the Western Chamber* (London, 1935).

89. The anonymous author of this collection wrote under the pen name Mo Lang-tzu. The preface is dated 1673. See Cheng Chen-to, *Chung-kuo wen-hsüeh yen-chiu* (Peking, 1957), I, 454–456. For a translation of the fifteenth of these stories, a version of the famous "Legend of the White Snake," see Arthur Waley, *The Real Tripitaka and Other Pieces* (London, 1952), pp. 183–213. The Tokugawa (1600–1868) author, Ueda Akinari (1734–1809), included a version of this story in his *Ugetsu monogatari* (Tales of rain and moon). See Aoki Masaru, *Chung-kuo chin-shih hsi-ch'ü shih*, tr. Wang Ku-lu (Peking, 1958), I, 430. The contemporary Japanese movie *Ugetsu* is based on this story.

90. The author's preface is dated 1858, but it was not published until 1888. For a description of this novel, including some excerpts and a brief biography of the author, see Lu Hsun, *A Brief History of Chinese Fiction*, tr. Yang Hsien-yi and Gladys Yang (Peking, 1959), pp. 340–345.

91. *WTYN*, p. 53. It is interesting to note that the first two works of Chinese fiction read by Yü Ta-fu (1895–1945), who joined Kuo Mo-jo in founding the Creation Society in 1921, were *Hsi-hu chia-hua* and *Hua-yüeh hen*. See Yü Ta-fu, *Ta-fu ch'üan-chi* (Shanghai, 1927–1933), III, 6. Kuo Mo-jo did not discover the masterpiece of all Chinese novels of love, the *Hung-lou meng*, or *Dream of the Red Chamber*, until the winter of 1909, when he devoured it in one night, reading only those parts having to do with the heroine, Lin Tai-yü. See Kuo Mo-jo, "Wu-shih nien chien-p'u," p. 321.

2. THE NEW SCHOOL SYSTEM IN CHIA-TING,1906–1909

1. Franke, *The Reform and Abolition of the Traditional Chinese Examination System*, pp. 70–71.

2. For the location of the school, see the second map at the front of *Lo-shan hsien chih*.

3. *WTYN*, p. 55.

4. These were later made over into the new Chia-ting middle school. For their location, see the second map at the front of *Lo-shan hsien chih*.

5. Franke, *The Reform and Abolition of the Traditional Chinese Examination System*, p. 66.

6. *WTYN,* p. 63. For the number of competitors from Sha-wan, see Kuo Mo-jo, "Wu-shih nien chien-p'u," p. 320.

7. *WTYN,* p. 68.

8. For a brief biography of Ch'en Jun-hai, see *Lo-shan hsien chih,* 9:40.

9. For a brief biography of I Shu-hui, see *Lo-shan hsien chih,* 9:40a–b.

10. *WTYN,* pp. 69–71, 77, 98.

11. On the New Text school of the Ch'ing dynasty, see Fung Yu-lan, *A History of Chinese Philosophy,* tr. Derk Bodde (Princeton, 1953), II, 673–675.

12. On Liao P'ing, see Fung Yu-lan, *A History of Chinese Philosophy,* II, 705–721. On K'ang Yu-wei, see ibid., II, 676–691.

13. See Derk Bodde, "Harmony and Conflict in Chinese Philosophy," in A. F. Wright, ed., *Studies in Chinese Thought* (Chicago, 1953), p. 71. For a more recent appraisal of Liao P'ing, see Joseph R. Levenson, "Liao P'ing and the Confucian Departure from History," in Arthur F. Wright and Denis Twitchett, eds., *Confucian Personalities* (Stanford, 1962), pp. 317–325.

14. See Lyon Sharman, *Sun Yat-sen, His Life and Its Meaning* (New York, 1934), pp. 16–19.

15. *WTYN,* p. 72.

16. Kuo Mo-jo, "Wei-yang," originally written in January 1921, revised on September 18, 1922, *CTCK,* 1.3, sec. 1, pp. 10–12. See also *WTYN,* pp. 78–79.

17. Kuo Mo-jo, "Wei-yang," p. 12; *WTYN,* pp. 80–81, 85–89.

18. *WTYN,* pp. 82–83.

19. For a succinct description of this controversy, see Fung Yu-lan, *A History of Chinese Philosophy,* II, 7.

20. For a brief biography of Wang Ping-chi, see *Lo-shan hsien chih,* 9:25.

21. *WTYN,* pp. 81–85.

22. On Ssu-ma Ch'ien, see Burton Watson, *Ssu-ma Ch'ien, Grand Historian of China* (New York, 1958). About half of the *Shih-chi,* the part dealing with the first century of the Han dynasty and its founding, is available in English translation; see Ssu-ma Ch'ien, *Records of the Grand Historian of China,* tr. Burton Watson, 2 vols. (New York, 1961).

23. *WTYN,* pp. 91–93; and Kuo-Mo-jo, "Wu-shih nien chien-p'u," p. 321.

24. *WTYN,* pp. 94–99.

25. Ibid., pp. 102, 105, 107.

26. Ibid., pp. 106–118. For a description of the prevalence of

homosexuality in Szechwan at the turn of the century, see Li Chieh-jen, *Ssu-shui wei-lan* (Shanghai, 1936), pp. 148–149.

27. See Shih Chien, *Kuo Mo-jo p'i-p'an*, pp. 23–25.

28. For a brief biography of Huang Jung, see *Lo-shan hsien chih*, 9:40b. For a list of his works, see ibid., 11:32b–33.

29. *WTYN*, pp. 124–125.

30. For a brief biography of Lin Shu in English, see Chow Tse-tsung, "Lin Shu," in Howard L. Boorman, ed., *Men and Politics in Modern China, Preliminary 50 Biographies* (New York, 1960), pp. 88–95. Also see Leo Ou-fan Lee, "Lin Shu and His Translations: Western Fiction in Chinese Perspective," *Papers on China*, 19:159–193 (December 1965).

31. This was first published in Shanghai in 1905. See Chu Hsi-chou, comp., *Ch'un-chüeh chai chu-shu chi*, in Chu Hsi-chou, comp., *Lin Ch'in-nan hsien-sheng hsüeh hsing p'u chi ssu chung* (Taipei, 1961), 3:40. There was also an earlier translation of the second half of this novel made by Yang Tzu-lin and Pao T'ien-hsiao and published in 1901. See A Ying, comp., *Wan-Ch'ing hsi-ch'ü hsiao-shuo mu*, p. 129. Kuo Mo-jo read both of these versions but does not indicate which one he read first. See *WTYN*, p. 127. For Lin Shu's preface to his translation and other material bearing on both versions of this novel, see A Ying, comp., *Hsiao-shuo hsi-ch'ü yen-chiu chüan* (Peking, 1960), in A Ying, comp., *Wan-Ch'ing wen-hsüeh ts'ung-ch'ao* (Shanghai and Peking, 1960–), pp. 210, 283–287, 532, 597–598.

32. This was first published in Shanghai in 1905. See Chu Hsi-chou, comp., *Ch'un-chüeh chai chu-shu chi*, 3:18. For Lin Shu's preface to his translation, see A Ying, comp., *Hsiao-shuo hsi-ch'ü yen-chiu chüan*, pp. 218–220. For a reproduction of the front cover of the original edition, see A Ying, comp., *Yü-wai wen-hsüeh i-wen chüan* (Peking, 1961), in A Ying, comp., *Wan-Ch'ing wen-hsüeh ts'ung-ch'ao*, plate no. 2 at the front of vol. I. For a reprint of the text of the translation see ibid., II, 447–653.

33. *WTYN*, p. 127.

34. This was first published in Shanghai in 1904. See Chu Hsi-chou, comp., *Ch'un-chüeh chai chu-shu chi*, 3:32. For Lin Shu's preface to his translation, see A Ying, comp., *Hsiao-shuo hsi-ch'ü yen-chiu chüan*, pp. 207–209. For a reproduction of the front cover of the original edition, see A Ying, comp., *Yü-wai wen-hsüeh i-wen chüan*, plate no. 2 at the front of vol. I. For a reprint of the text of the translation, see ibid., I, 31–136.

35. *WTYN*, pp. 126–127. See also Kuo Mo-jo, "Wei-yang," p. 13.

36. This periodical was published monthly in Shanghai from 1905

to 1911. See *Chung-kuo shih-hsüeh lun-wen so-yin*, comp. First and Second Offices of the Institute of Historical Research, Chinese Academy of Sciences, and the Department of History, Peking University (Peking, 1957), I, 31. The principles for which this periodical stood are enunciated in the opening editorial statement of the first issue, which is reprinted in Ko Kung-chen, *Chung-kuo pao-hsüeh shih* (Peking, 1955), pp. 138–139.

37. This periodical was published every ten days in Yokohama from 1898 to 1901. See Ting Wen-chiang, *Liang Jen-kung hsien-sheng nien-p'u ch'ang-pien ch'u-kao*, I, 84, 145.

38. On Liang Ch'i-ch'ao, see Joseph R. Levenson, *Liang Ch'i-ch'ao and the Mind of Modern China* (Cambridge, Mass., 1953). For the influence which Liang Ch'i-ch'ao exerted at about the same time on Hu Shih (1891–1962), Kuo Mo-jo's famous contemporary, see Hu Shih, *Ssu-shih tzu-shu* (Taipei, 1962), pp. 46–47, 50–54.

39. *WTYN*, pp. 125–126.

40. Ibid., pp. 128–142.

41. See Shih Chien, *Kuo Mo-jo p'i-p'an*, pp. 30–31.

42. See Herbert A. Giles, tr., *Chuang Tzu, Mystic, Moralist, and Social Reformer* (London, 1926); and Burton Watson, tr., *Chuang Tzu: Basic Writings* (New York, 1964).

43. See A. C. Graham, tr., *The Book of Lieh-tzu* (London, 1961).

44. See Kuo Mo-jo, "Wu-shih nien chien-p'u," p. 321.

45. Kuo Mo-jo, *Hei mao*, originally published in 1930, in his *Shao-nien shih-tai*, p. 324.

46. *WTYN*, pp. 151–153.

47. Ibid., pp. 158–165. See also Kuo Mo-jo, "Wei-yang," pp. 13–14.

48. *WTYN*, pp. 166–169.

3. MIDDLE SCHOOL, REVOLUTION, AND MARRIAGE: CHENGTU, 1910–1913

1. *FCCH*, pp. 179–192.

2. Ibid., pp. 220–221; *CTHP*, p. 224.

3. *FCCH*, pp. 194–199.

4. On Huang Hsing, see Hsüeh Chün-tu, *Huang Hsing and the Chinese Revolution* (Stanford, 1961).

5. *FCCH*, pp. 219–220. For a study of Chinese fictional treatment of the Russian terrorists, see Don Price, "The Russian Revolutionaries in Chinese Fiction," mimeographed typescript (Cambridge, Mass., 1965).

6. See Li Chien-nung, *The Political History of China, 1840–1928*, tr. and ed. Ssu-yü Teng and Jeremy Ingalls (Princeton, 1956), pp. 233–234.

7. For contemporary accounts of this student agitation in Chengtu, see the *North China Herald*, January 6, 1911, p. 43, and February 10, 1911, p. 305.

8. See *Lo-shan hsien chih*, 8:62.

9. *FCCH*, pp. 223–244; 252–254.

10. See Li Chien-nung, *The Political History of China, 1840–1928*, p. 242. See also Albert Feuerwerker, *China's Early Industrialization, Sheng Hsuan-huai (1844–1916) and Mandarin Enterprise* (Cambridge, Mass., 1958), pp. 80–82.

11. For the name, see *Lo-shan hsien chih*, 8:68.

12. See *WTYN*, p. 51.

13. See *Hsin-hai ko-ming*, ed. Chung-kuo shih-hsüeh hui (Shanghai, 1957), IV, 449–452.

14. *FCCH*, pp. 254–260. For other references to this event and its correct date, see: P'eng Fen, *Hsin-hai sun-Ch'ing cheng-pien fa-yüan chi*, in *Hsin-hai ko-ming*, IV, 350, 375, 378; San-yü shu-she chu-jen, comp., *Ssu-ch'uan hsüeh*, in *Hsin-hai ko-ming*, IV, 403; Wang Jen-wen, *Hsin-hai Ssu-ch'uan lu-shih tsui-yen*, in *Hsin-hai ko-ming*, IV, 415, 418, 422; Chou Shan-p'ei, *Hsin-hai Ssu-ch'uan shih-pien chih wo*, in *Hsin-hai ko-ming*, IV, 440–442; Tai Chih-li, comp., *Ssu-ch'uan pao-lu yün-tung shih-liao* (Peking, 1959), pp. 190–191, 266; and Chou Shan-p'ei, *Hsin-hai Ssu-ch'uan cheng-lu ch'in-li chi* (Chungking, 1957), pp. 10–11. For a thinly fictionalized account of this meeting in an historical novel by a classmate of Kuo Mo-jo's, see Li Chieh-jen, *Ta-po* (Peking, 1958), pp. 26–34, 45–47, 49.

15. Kuo Mo-jo, *Hei mao*, p. 308.

16. For the date of this event, see Tai Chih-li, *Ssu-ch'uan pao-lu yün-tung shih-liao*, p. 435.

17. For a contemporary picture of this event, see the third page of plates at the front of *Hsin-hai ko-ming*, IV. For an account of the events in Chengtu from August 24 to September 7 by a participant, see Chou Shan-p'ei, *Hsin-hai Ssu-ch'uan cheng-lu ch'in-li chi*, pp. 23–38. For Kuo Mo-jo's account of these events, see *FCCH*, pp. 261–269.

18. *FCCH*, p. 249.

19. For the date, see Chou Shan-p'ei, *Hsin-hai Ssu-ch'uan cheng-lu ch'in-li chi*, p. 57.

20. *FCCH*, p. 278.

21. For the date and an eyewitness account of this event, see Chou Shan-p'ei, *Hsin-hai Ssu-ch'uan cheng-lu ch'in-li chi*, pp. 58–60.

22. *FCCH*, pp. 292–293.

23. Kuo Mo-jo, *Hei mao*, pp. 313–320.

24. Ibid., pp. 307–312, 321–338. For an earlier account of the wedding which differs in certain details, see Kuo Mo-jo, "Wei-yang," pp. 16–19. In *SYC*, p. 42, the wedding is said to have taken place in 1913.

25. Kuo Mo-jo, "Shih-tzu chia," originally completed on March 18, 1924, *CTCP*, 47:10–11 (April 5, 1924).
26. Kuo Mo-jo, *Hei mao*, p. 321.
27. *FCCH*, p. 296.
28. Kuo Mo-jo, *Hei mao*, pp. 339–344.
29. Ibid., p. 341.
30. Ibid., pp. 345–346.
31. See David Hawkes, tr., *Ch'u Tz'u: the Songs of the South* (Oxford, 1959).
32. See Erwin von Zach, tr., *Die Chinesische Anthologie: Ubersetzungen aus dem Wen hsüan,* 2 vols. (Cambridge, Mass., 1958).
33. This was published under the title *T'ien-yen lun* in 1898. See Wang Ch'ü-ch'ang, *Yen Chi-tao nien-p'u* (Shanghai, 1936), p. 41.
34. This was published under the title *Ch'ün-hsüeh i-yen* in 1903. See Wang Ch'ü-ch'ang, *Yen Chi-tao nien-p'u,* p. 69. For a study of Yen Fu's thought and his interpretations of Huxley and Spencer, see Benjamin Schwartz, *In Search of Wealth and Power: Yen Fu and the West* (Cambridge, Mass., 1964), especially pp. 91–112.
35. Kuo Mo-jo, *Hei mao*, p. 324.
36. Kuo Mo-jo, "Wu-shih nien chien-p'u," p. 322.
37. Kuo Mo-jo, "Ch'u ch'u K'uei-men," pp. 358, 368, 385. For a description of this school by a classmate of Kuo Mo-jo's, see Li Chieh-jen, *Pao feng-yü ch'ien* (Shanghai, 1940), pp. 72, 78–81.
38. Kuo Mo-jo, "Ch'u ch'u K'uei-men," pp. 355, 368.
39. This has been translated into German by Erwin von Zach in *Sinologische Beiträge,* 3:150–156 (1935).
40. For these lines, see Ni Fan, *Yü Tzu-shan chi chu* (Taipei, 1959), II, 9.
41. See Kao Yin-tsu, comp., *Chung-hua min-kuo ta-shih chi* (Taipei, 1957), p. 14.
42. The date is derived by calculating backwards from that given in Kuo Mo-jo, "Ch'u ch'u K'uei-men," p. 370.
43. For Wang Ling-chi, see *Lo-shan hsien chih,* 8:67.
44. For descriptions of this curious vessel, see Wu Yü-chang, *Hsin-hai ko-ming* (Peking, 1961), p. 119; and Li Chieh-jen, *Ta-po,* pp. 1–2.
45. Yen Fu used these words in the preface to his translation. See Wang Ch'ü-ch'ang, *Yen Chi-tao nien-p'u,* p. 65.
46. For Yin Ch'ao-chen, see *Lo-shan hsien chih,* 8:62 and 8:67.
47. The above narrative from June to November 1913 is derived from Kuo Mo-jo, "Ch'u ch'u K'uei-men," pp. 355–373.
48. Ibid., pp. 384–402.
49. Kuo Mo-jo, "Wo ti hsüeh-sheng sheng-huo," p. 10.

4. HIGHER SCHOOL IN TOKYO AND OKAYAMA, 1914–1918

1. Kuo Mo-jo, "Tzu-jan chih chui-huai," originally written in 1934, *Hsien-tai*, 4.6:954 (April 1, 1934). This work is translated from the Japanese. It was originally published in the February 1934 issue of *Bungei* (Literary arts).

2. Ibid., p. 954. See also *CTSN*, p. 107.

3. Kuo Mo-jo, "Tzu-jan chih chui-huai," p. 954. See also Kuo Mo-jo, "Wo ti hsüeh-sheng sheng-huo," p. 10.

4. *WTYN*, p. 124.

5. Kuo Mo-jo, "Wo ti hsüeh-sheng sheng-huo," pp. 10–11.

6. See Shih Chien, *Kuo Mo-jo p'i-p'an*, p. 50.

7. Kuo Mo-jo, "Tzu-jan chih chui-huai," pp. 954–955.

8. Kuo Mo-jo, "Wo ti hsüeh-sheng sheng-huo," p. 11.

9. Kuo Mo-jo, "T'ai-ko-erh lai Hua ti wo-chien," originally completed on October 11, 1923, *CTCP*, 23:3 (October 14, 1923).

10. *CTSN*, pp. 36, 39. The Japanese yen was worth approximately $.50 in American currency between 1914 and 1923. See *Nihon kindaishi jiten* (Cyclopedia of modern Japanese history), compiled by the Japanese History Research Center of the Liberal Arts Department of Kyoto University (Tokyo, 1958), p. 899, table no. 49.

11. *CTSN*, pp. 34–35, 42.

12. See Kuo Mo-jo's preface to Tu Kuo-hsiang, *Tu Kuo-hsiang wen-chi* (Peking, 1962), pp. 1–2. See also Yü Li-ch'ün, "Ping chung ti Kuo Mo-jo hsien-sheng," originally written in January 1938, in Ting San, ed., *K'ang-chan chung ti Kuo Mo-jo* (Canton, n.d.), p. 103.

13. As Benjamin Schwartz has pointed out, there was a strong interest in Buddhism among leading Chinese intellectuals in the late nineteenth and early twentieth centuries. See Schwartz, *In Search of Wealth and Power*, p. 106.

14. See Chow Tse-tsung, *The May Fourth Movement* (Cambridge, Mass., 1960), pp. 19–20.

15. Ibid., pp. 20–21. See also Kao Yin-tsu, *Chung-hua min-kuo ta-shih chi*, p. 28.

16. *CTSN*, pp. 36–37.

17. Ibid., p. 35.

18. Ibid., p. 46.

19. Kuo Mo-jo, "Wang Yang-ming," originally completed on June 17, 1924, in Kuo Mo-jo, *Li-shih jen-wu* (Shanghai, 1947), p. 76. See also Kuo Mo-jo, "T'ai-ko-erh lai Hua ti wo-chien," p. 3.

20. Kuo Mo-jo, "Wang Yang-ming," pp. 76–77.

21. Fung Yu-lan, *A History of Chinese Philosophy*, II, 608.
22. Ibid., II, 609.
23. Ibid., II, 603.
24. Ibid., II, 600.
25. Ibid., II, 603–604.
26. See Arthur Waley, *The Way and Its Power; a Study of the Tao Te Ching and Its Place in Chinese Thought* (London, 1956).
27. Kuo Mo-jo, "Wang Yang-ming," p. 77.
28. *CTSN*, p. 194. It is interesting to note that Tu Kuo-hsiang also began his intellectual career as an adherent of Wang Yang-ming's philosophy and became a Marxist-Leninist at about the same time that Kuo Mo-jo did. See *Tu Kuo-hsiang wen-chi*, p. 603.
29. Kuo Mo-jo, "T'ai-ko-erh lai Hua ti wo-chien," p. 3.
30. See Fung Yu-lan, *A History of Chinese Philosophy*, I, 221–245.
31. *WTYN*, p. 107.
32. Kuo Mo-jo, "Wo ti hsüeh-sheng sheng-huo," p. 11.
33. Kuo Mo-jo, "Tzu-jan chih chui-huai," pp. 956–957.
34. *SYC*, pp. 36–42. See also Kuo Mo-jo, "K'ua-che tung-hai," originally written in 1947, in Kuo Mo-jo, *Hai-t'ao* (Shanghai, 1956), p. 78. In 1924 Kuo Mo-jo wrote an epistolary novel entitled *Lo-yeh* in which he vividly recreates, in forty-one letters, the development of his relationship with Satō Tomiko from the time of his departure from Tokyo in early September 1916 until her arrival in Okayama in late December. For his conversion to Christianity, see Kuo Mo-jo, *Lo-yeh* (Shanghai, 1928), pp. 135, 140, 145, 148.
35. Kuo Mo-jo, "Shih-tzu chia," pp. 10–11.
36. For some early examples of Kuo Mo-jo's traditional poetry, see Kuo Mo-jo, *Hei mao*, pp. 341–342; "Ch'u ch'u K'uei-men," p. 378; *CTSN*, pp. 36–37, 58–59; "Tzu-jan chih chui-huai," pp. 954–958; *SYC*, pp. 9–10; and "Li Hu chih ch'ien," originally completed on February 23, 1928, *Hsien-tai*, 4.3:466–467 (January 1, 1934).
37. For the title, see Kuo Mo-jo, *Lo-yeh*, p. 146. This poem has been preserved, translated into Chinese by Kuo Mo-jo himself, at the beginning of *Hsin-i chi* (Magnolia), an anthology of prose and poetry by members of the Creation Society, published in 1923, but I have been unable to locate a copy of this work. See *CTSN*, p. 62.
38. Kuo Mo-jo has singled out the following poems as falling into this category: "Venus," "Pieh-li" (Parting), "Hsin-yüeh yü pai-yün (New moon and white clouds), "Ssu ti yu-huo" (The temptation of death), and the songs of the shepherdess in "Mu-yang ai-hua" (The sad tale of a shepherdess). See Kuo Mo-jo, "Wo ti tso-shih ti ching-kuo," p. 140. The texts of these poems can be found in *MJWC*, I, 112, 113–115, 118, 119; and V, 2–4. The first three have been translated into English in Kuo Mo-jo, *Selected Poems from The God-*

desses, tr. John Lester and A. C. Barnes (Peking, 1958), pp. 48–51.

39. See Krishna Kripalani, *Rabindranath Tagore: A Biography* (New York, 1962), pp. 254–257.

40. For the preceding account of Tagore's influence on Kuo Mo-jo, see Kuo Mo-jo, "T'ai-ko-erh lai Hua ti wo-chien," pp. 3–5; "Wo ti tso-shih ti ching-kuo," pp. 138–141; and *CTSN,* pp. 62–63.

41. *CTSN,* p. 63.

42. See Kuo Mo-jo, "Mai-shu," originally written in 1924, in Kuo Mo-jo, *Pao-chien chi,* p. 102; and "Wu-shih nien chien-p'u," pp. 322–323.

43. *CTSN,* pp. 62–63.

44. For the date, see *SYC,* p. 40.

45. See Chow Tse-tsung, *The May Fourth Movement,* pp. 372–373; Kao Yin-tsu, *Chung-hua min-kuo ta-shih chi,* pp. 51–52; and Saneto Keishū, "Kaku Matsu-jaku no Nihon ryūgaku jidai," autographed offprint from a volume entitled *Ajia bunka no sai-ninshiki,* apparently a symposium volume of unidentified editorship (n.p., n.d.), pp. 272–273.

46. See Ting Chih-p'ing, comp., *Chung-kuo chin ch'i-shih nien lai chiao-yü chi-shih* (Taipei, 1961), p. 32.

47. See, for example, Morris R. Wills, as told to J. Robert Moskin, "An American Defector Comes Home. Part Two: Why I Quit China," *Look,* 30.4:85–86 (February 22, 1966).

48. See Chow Tse-tsung, *The May Fourth Movement,* pp. 33, 35, 373.

49. *CTSN,* pp. 35–36.

50. Ibid., p. 33.

51. Kuo Mo-jo, "Wo ti tso-shih ti ching-kuo," p. 141.

5. THE MEDICAL STUDENT AS ROMANTIC ARTIST: FUKUOKA, 1918–1921

1. *CTSN,* pp. 33–34, 48–49.

2. Ibid., pp. 34–45. See also Chang Tzu-p'ing, "Tung-ching jih-chi," originally completed on October 30, 1928, in Chün-sheng, comp., *Hsien-tai jih-chi wen-hsüan* (Shanghai, 1937), pp. 215–216.

3. *CTSN,* pp. 46–58, 80.

4. Ibid., pp. 54–56.

5. See ibid., pp. 59–60, and Kuo Mo-jo, "Mu-yang ai-hua," pp. 1–12.

6. For a comprehensive study of this movement, see Chow Tse-tsung, *The May Fourth Movement.*

7. *CTSN,* p. 46.

8. Ibid., p. 61; and *Wu-ssu shih-ch'i ch'i-k'an chieh-shao,* comp.,

Research Section of the Bureau of Translation of the Works of Marx, Engels, Lenin, and Stalin, Central Committee of the CCP (Peking, 1958–1959), III, 758.

9. See Wang Yao, *Chung-kuo hsin wen-hsüeh shih kao* (Shanghai, 1953), I, 59.

10. See *MJWC*, I, 119.

11. Kuo Mo-jo has singled out the following poems as falling into this category: "Lu-ssu" (Egret), "Ch'un-ch'ou" (Spring sadness), and "Hsin-yüeh yü ch'ing-hai" (New moon and clear sea). See Kuo Mo-jo, "Wo ti tso-shih ti ching-kuo," p. 141. The texts of these poems can be found in *MJWC*, I, 121, 116, and 291. The first two have been translated into English in Kuo Mo-jo, *Selected Poems from The Goddesses*, pp. 53 and 51.

12. For "Lu-ssu," see the preceding note. "Pao erh yü Po-to wan" is not included in any of the published collections of his poetry. For a Japanese translation of this poem, see *SYC*, pp. 79–80.

13. See *CTSN*, p. 61, and Kuo Mo-jo, "Wo ti tso-shih ti ching-kuo," pp. 141–142. There are some minor discrepancies between these two accounts. For the date of publication, see *Wu-ssu shih-ch'i ch'i-k'an chieh-shao*, III, 761.

14. See Kuo Mo-jo, "Ting," p. 119.

15. See *WTYN*, pp. 3–4. For the location of these rivers, see the first map at the front of *Lo-shan hsien chih*.

16. The "Nan Shu fu-lao" is included in the biography of Ssu-ma Hsiang-ju in the *Shih-chi*. See Takikawa Kametarō, *Shiki kaichū kōshō* (Tokyo, 1934), vol. IX, chüan 117, p. 73. The same passage is translated by Burton Watson in *Records of the Grand Historian of China*, II, 328, where, however, he erroneously transliterates Mei as Mo.

17. *CTHP*, pp. 184–185.

18. As late as the summer of 1921 he was still writing his name as Mei-jo. See the photographic reproduction of the cover of *Nü-shen* (Goddesses) at the front of *MJWC*, I.

19. The texts of these poems can be found in *MJWC*, I, 62, 68–72, 55–57, 32–44, 49–50, 98–100, 45–46, 47–48, and 94–97. The first five have been translated into English in Kuo Mo-jo, *Selected Poems from The Goddesses*, pp. 24, 29–32, 21–22, 10–18, and 19. "T'ien-kou" has been translated in William R. Schultz, "Kuo Mo-jo and the Romantic Aesthetic: 1918–1925," *Journal of Oriental Literature*, 6.2:58 (April 1955).

20. *CTSN*, pp. 63–64; Kuo Mo-jo, "Wo ti tso-shih ti ching-kuo," p. 143.

21. Achilles Fang, "From Imagism to Whitmanism in Recent Chinese Poetry: a Search for Poetics that Failed," in Horst Frenz and

G. L. Anderson, eds., *Indiana University Conference on Oriental-Western Literary Relations* (Chapel Hill, 1955), pp. 186–188.

22. Walt Whitman, *Leaves of Grass* (London, Everyman's Library, 1949), p. 309.

23. See *MJWC*, I, 98–100.

24. Walt Whitman, *Leaves of Grass*, p. 401.

25. Ibid., p. xxvii.

26. Ibid., pp. 23, 39, 45.

27. Quoted by Emory Holloway in his introduction to ibid., p. x.

28. Kuo Mo-jo, "Wo ti tso-shih ti ching-kuo," pp. 143–144. See also Kuo Mo-jo, "Hsieh tsai *San-ko p'an-ni ti nü-hsing* hou-mien," in his *San-ko p'an-ni ti nü-hsing* (Shanghai, 1929), pp. 24–25.

29. *CTSN*, pp. 68–69.

30. See Karl Viëtor, *Goethe the Poet* (Cambridge, Mass., 1949), p. 294.

31. *CTSN*, p. 69.

32. See Mei Yi-pao, tr., *The Ethical and Political Works of Motse* (London, 1929).

33. Kuo Mo-jo, "Wo ti tso-shih ti ching-kuo," pp. 142–143. Between January 22 and February 7, 1920, for example, Kuo Mo-jo's name appeared eleven times in seventeen days. See *Wu-ssu shih-ch'i ch'i-k'an chieh-shao*, III, 773, 775.

34. *CTSN*, p. 64.

35. See *SYC*, pp. 3–4, 28–43.

36. Ibid., p. 108.

37. Ibid., p. 120. For the name, see Kuo Mo-jo's preface to *Mo-jo tzu-hsüan chi*, originally completed on August 26, 1933 (Hong Kong, 1962), p. 4. This son of Kuo Mo-jo's has returned to mainland China with his Japanese wife and is now working in Shanghai as an architectural engineer. See T'ang Jen, "Strive for Greater Achievements Through Collective Wisdom and Collective Strength," *Selections from China Mainland Magazines*, 322:35 (July 16, 1962), translated from *Ch'iao-wu pao*, no. 2 (April 1962).

38. *SYC*, p. 137.

39. Ibid., pp. 135–137.

40. For a detailed description of T'ien Han's visit, see *SYC*, pp. 120–166. See also *CTSN*, pp. 65–66; and T'ien Han, "Ying Mo-jo," originally completed on February 7, 1938, in Ting San, ed., *K'ang-chan chung ti Kuo Mo-jo*, p. 40.

41. *SYC*, p. 167.

42. Ibid., p. 44.

43. Ibid., pp. 6–8.

44. On the characteristics of the *chüeh-chü*, or quatrain, see Hightower, *Topics in Chinese Literature*, pp. 69–70.

45. *SYC*, pp. 15–16.
46. Ibid., pp. 45–49.
47. Ibid., pp. 138, 157.
48. Kuo Mo-jo, "Wo ti tso-shih ti ching-kuo," pp. 144–145.
49. For the name, see *CTCK*, 1.3: sec. 3, p. 53.
50. *CTSN*, p. 70.
51. Ibid., pp. 71–72. See also Kuo Mo-jo, tr., *Fu-shih-te* (Shanghai, 1947), pp. 367–368.
52. *CTSN*, p. 73.
53. Karl Viëtor, *Goethe the Poet*, p. 47.
54. Ibid., p. 193.
55. See Kuo Mo-jo, "Li Hu chih ch'ien," p. 466.
56. *CTSN*, p. 73.
57. Kuo Mo-jo, "Wo tsen-yang hsieh *T'ang-ti chih hua*," originally completed on December 9, 1941, in his *T'ang-ti chih hua* (Shanghai, 1946), pp. 128–129.
58. *CTSN*, p. 75.
59. Ibid., pp. 74–75. "The rebirth of the goddesses" has been translated into English in Kuo Mo-jo, *Selected Poems from The Goddesses*, pp. 1–9.
60. S. H. Steinberg, ed., *Cassell's Encyclopedia of Literature* (London, 1953), II, 1853.
61. Kuo Mo-jo, "T'ang-ti chih hua," originally completed on September 23, 1920, in *MJWC*, I, 25.
62. Kuo Mo-jo, "*T'ang-ti chih hua* ti erh mu," originally published on May 1, 1922, *CTCK*, 1.1: sec. 1, p. 14.
63. *MJWC*, I, 55.
64. Ibid., I, 94–97.
65. Kuo Mo-jo, "Wei-yang," p. 6.
66. *MJWC*, I, 73. This poem has been translated into English in Kuo Mo-jo, *Selected Poems from The Goddesses*, p. 33.
67. See *CTCK*, 1.3: sec. 1, p. 69, and T'ao Ching-sun, *Yin-yüeh hui hsiao-ch'ü* (Shanghai, 1927), pp. 198–201.
68. *CTSN*, pp. 76–79.
69. Among the founders of this organization were Ch'en Ch'i-hsiu, Wang Chao-jung, Wu Yung-ch'üan, Chou Ch'ang-shou, and Cheng Chen-wen. For a description of its founding and its history through May 1923, see "Ping-ch'en hsüeh-she chih hui-ku," in *Hsüeh-i*, 5.2:1–5 (June 1, 1923).
70. See the back cover of *Hsüeh-i*, 5.2 (June 1, 1923).
71. See Kuo Mo-jo's letter to Chang Tzu-p'ing in *Hsüeh-i*, 2.10 (April 1, 1921).
72. For the debate on the historicity and significance of the well-field system which raged in Chinese intellectual circles in the early

1920's, see Joseph R. Levenson, "Ill Wind in the Well-field: The Erosion of the Confucian Ground of Controversy," in Arthur F. Wright, ed., *The Confucian Persuasion* (Stanford, 1960), pp. 268–287.

73. Kuo Mo-jo, "Wo-kuo ssu-hsiang-shih shang chih P'eng-p'ai ch'eng," originally published on May 30, 1921, in *Hsüeh-i*, 3.1:1–17 (May 30, 1921). See especially pp. 12–13.

74. On this organization, see Chow Tse-tsung, *The May Fourth Movement*, pp. 80, 188–189, 251–253, 322–323; Tso Shun-sheng, *Chin san-shih nien chien-wen tsa-chi* (Hong Kong, 1952), pp. 3–10; and I Chün-tso, *Hui-meng san-shih nien* (Hong Kong, 1954), pp. 25–28.

75. See Tseng Ch'i, "Wu-wu jih-chi," in his *Tseng Mu-han hsien-sheng i-chu* (Taipei, 1954), pp. 391–394.

76. See Tso Shun-sheng, *Chin san-shih nien chien-wen tsa-chi*, p. 5. It is probably no coincidence that this number corresponds with that of the heroes in the famous novel *Shui-hu chuan* (Water margin; translated by Pearl Buck under the title *All Men Are Brothers*; 2 vols., New York, 1933).

77. See Wang Tu-ch'ing, *Wo tsai Ou-chou ti sheng-huo* (Shanghai, 1932), pp. 93–94.

78. *CTSN*, p. 77.

79. See Satō Tomiko, *Wo-ti chang-fu Kuo Mo-jo* (Shanghai, 1938), pp. 2–3. This work is translated from the Japanese. It was originally published in the April 22, 1938, issue of *Shin-jo-en* (Modern woman's world).

80. *CTSN*, p. 79.

81. Ibid., pp. 79–80.

82. Kuo Mo-jo, "Lien-yü," originally completed on March 7, 1924, *CTCP*, 44:4 (March 16, 1924).

83. *CTSN*, pp. 80–81.

84. Ibid., p. 100.

85. *MJWC*, I, 138. This poem has been translated into English in Kuo Mo-jo, *Selected Poems from The Goddesses*, p. 64.

86. *MJWC*, I, 139. This poem has been translated into English in Kai-yu Hsu, *Twentieth Century Chinese Poetry* (New York, 1963), p. 33.

87. *CTSN*, pp. 81–83.

6. THE HEYDAY OF THE CREATION SOCIETY: SHANGHAI AND FUKUOKA, 1921–1924

1. *CTSN*, pp. 83–84.

2. On Chao Nan-kung and the T'ai-tung Book Company, see Chang Ching-lu, *Tsai ch'u-pan chieh erh-shih nien* (Hankow, 1938), pp. 91–96; and I Chün-tso, *Hui-meng san-shih nien*, pp. 10–11, 22–25.

On the nature of the Political Science Clique, see Hsieh Pin, *Min-kuo cheng-tang shih* (Taipei, 1962), pp. 80–81, and especially pp. 182–185.

3. *CTSN*, p. 88.

4. *MJWC*, I, 141.

5. Ibid., I, 142.

6. Ibid., I, 140–147; *CTSN*, pp. 84–87. This excursion is also described in a poem by Ch'eng Fang-wu entitled "Ch'ang-sha chi Mo-jo" (To Kuo Mo-jo from Changsha), *CTCK*, 1.2: sec. 1, pp. 43–50.

7. *CTSN*, pp. 88–89. On Wang Ching, see Chang Ching-lu, *Tsai ch'u-pan chieh erh-shih nien*, pp. 56–57, 94–98.

8. See *CTSN*, pp. 88–90, 117; *CTHP*, p. 222; Chang Ching-lu, *Tsai ch'u-pan chieh erh-shih nien*, pp. 93–99; I Chün-tso, *Hui-meng san-shih nien*, pp. 22–25; and Lo Tun-wei, *Wu-shih nien hui-i lu* (Taipei, 1952), p. 26.

9. I Chün-tso, *Hui-meng san-shih nien*, pp. 23–24.

10. See *CTCK*, 2.2: sec. 3, pp. 8–16.

11. *CTSN*, pp. 90–91; and *CTHP*, p. 200.

12. See Chow Tse-tsung, *The May Fourth Movement*, pp. 283–285.

13. *CTSN*, pp. 91–95. See also Ch'eng Fang-wu, "Ch'uang-tsao she yü Wen-hsüeh yen-chiu hui," originally completed on November 12, 1922, *CTCK*, 1.4: sec. 4, pp. 12–13 (1923).

14. *CTSN*, pp. 98–99.

15. Ibid.. pp. 100–101. The dates for this and the following sequence of events are established from those in Yü Ta-fu's story "Wei-ping," which was written immediately after the events described. Kuo Mo-jo states that these events occurred in early July, but he was writing eleven years later and his memory may have played tricks on him. See Yü Ta-fu, "Wei-ping," in *Ta-fu ch'üan-chi*, II, 1–21. For confirmation that these events took place in June, see Kuo Mo-jo, "Wo ti tso-shih ti ching-kuo," p. 147.

16. *CTSN*, pp. 101–105.

17. Ibid., pp. 105–107. Yü Ta-fu, "Wei-ping," pp. 15–18.

18. *CTSN*, pp. 107–113. Chang Tzu-p'ing's version of this meeting differs slightly from Kuo Mo-jo's. He states that those present were Kuo Mo-jo, Yü Ta-fu, T'ien Han, an outsider named Yang Cheng-yü, and himself, and that they discussed the publication of the *Ch'uang-tsao she ts'ung-shu* (Creation Collectanea) as well as the *Ch'uang-tsao chi-k'an*. See Chang Tzu-p'ing, "Tu 'Ch'uang-tsao she,'" in Shih Ping-hui, ed., *Chang Tzu-p'ing p'ing-chuan* (Shanghai, 1932), p. 142, and note 1 on p. 153.

19. *CTSN*, pp. 114–116.

20. On Yeh Sheng-t'ao, see C. T. Hsia, *A History of Modern Chinese Fiction* (New Haven, 1961), pp. 57–71.
21. *CTSN*, pp. 95–96.
22. Ibid., p. 123.
23. For the date, see Chu Tzu-ch'ing, ed., *Shih-chi*, in Chao Chia-pi, ed., *Chung-kuo hsin wen-hsüeh ta-hsi* (Hong Kong, n.d.), VIII, 12.
24. *CTSN*, pp. 120–123.
25. On Kao Meng-tan, see Hu Shih, "Kao Meng-tan hsien-sheng hsiao-chuan," in Chang Yüeh-jui, ed., *Chin-jen chuan-chi wen-hsüan* (Changsha, 1938), pp. 106–110.
26. *CTSN*, pp. 124–127.
27. Ibid., p. 128.
28. *CTHP*, p. 209.
29. For the date, see *CTCK*, 1.1: sec. 3, pp. 5–6.
30. *CTSN*, p. 129.
31. Ibid., pp. 129–130, 134.
32. Ibid., p. 130.
33. See *CTCK*, 1.2: sec. 1, p. 51; and 1.3: sec. 2, p. 11.
34. For the address, see *CTCK*, 1.3: sec. 3, p. 58.
35. *CTSN*, p. 132.
36. For the composition of this poem, see Wang Tu-ch'ing, *Wo tsai Ou-chou ti sheng-huo*, pp. 106–107.
37. *CTSN*, p. 116. Kuo Mo-jo states that this took place in the summer of 1921, but it must have been the summer of 1922 because Wang Tu-ch'ing did not mail his manuscripts to Cheng Po-ch'i until December 13, 1921. See his letter to Cheng Po-ch'i, *CTCK*, 1.2: sec. 3, pp. 15–16.
38. *CTSN*, pp. 137–139. The song is in *MJWC*, I, 318–319 under the title "Ch'ien-chin ch'ü" (Forward march), where the date of composition is erroneously given as 1923. For the original title, see the advertisement in *Hsüeh-i*, 4.4 (October 1, 1922).
39. *CTSN*, p. 132.
40. The date is calculated on the basis of the fact that Yü Ta-fu's ship left Moji for Shanghai on July 21, 1922. It was normally a two-day crossing. See Yü Ta-fu, "Chung-t'u," *Ta-fu ch'üan-chi*, III, 95.
41. *CTSN*, pp. 132–133.
42. Ibid., pp. 135–136.
43. For the date of publication, see the last page of Kuo Mo-jo, *Chüan-erh chi* (Shanghai, 1929).
44. *CTSN*, pp. 140–141.
45. See A Ying, comp., *Shih-liao so-yin*, in Chao Chia-pi, *Chung-kuo hsin wen-hsüeh ta-hsi*, X, 307.

46. See Ts'ao Chü-jen, ed., *Chüan-erh t'ao-lun chi* (Shanghai, 1925).
47. *MJWC*, I, 183.
48. See *CTCK*, 1.3: sec. 3, pp. 55–56.
49. *CTSN*, pp. 141–147.
50. *CTCK*, 1.3: sec. 1, pp. 1–20.
51. *MJWC*, I, 173–184, 326–329. See also *CTSN*, pp. 142–147.
52. *CTCK*, 1.3: sec. 3, pp. 1–41. See also *CTSN*, p. 142.
53. *CTSN*, p. 135.
54. Ibid., pp. 156, 159. He arrived in Shanghai sometime before October 13, 1922. See Ch'eng Fang-wu, "Hsüeh-che ti t'ai-tu," *CTCK*, 1.3: sec. 2, pp. 14, 27.
55. *CTSN*, pp. 156–157.
56. *MJWC*, I, 195–213. See also *CTSN*, pp. 73, 141–143, 147.
57. *CTCK*, 1.4: sec. 3, pp. 19–57. The introduction to the selection of Shelley's poetry is dated December 4, 1922.
58. *MJWC*, I, 185–194.
59. See Kuo Mo-jo, tr., *I-tuan* (Shanghai, 1947), pp. 2–3.
60. *MJWC*, III, 1–42. See also *CTSN*, pp. 162, 166.
61. For the original story, see Watson, *Records of the Grand Historian of China*, II, 298–300.
62. *CTSN*, p. 159. In the preface to Kuo Mo-jo, *Mo-jo tzu-hsüan chi*, p. 4, he says that his third son was born in 1922, and he gives his name as Fo-sheng. I do not know which version is correct.
63. *CTSN*, p. 159.
64. Ibid., p. 158.
65. Ibid., p. 158.
66. See *CTCP*, 52:15–16.
67. For the name of the ship, see Yü Ta-fu, "Kei Mo-jo," in *Ta-fu ch'üan-chi*, III, 229.
68. *MJWC*, I, 302–304, where the date is erroneously given as April 1, 1929.
69. *CTSN*, p. 158.
70. For the date, see *CTCK*, 2.1: sec. 3, p. 45.
71. *CTSN*, p. 160.
72. Kuo Mo-jo gives the date as May 1, 1923, but see *CTCP*, 1:16 (May 13, 1923).
73. See *CTCK*, 2.1: sec. 2, p. 24.
74. See Chow Tse-tsung, "Wen I-to," in Boorman, *Men and Politics in Modern China*, p. 146; and Shih Ching, *Wen I-to ti tao-lu* (Shanghai, 1947), p. 19.
75. He translated only the first book of *Also Sprach Zarathustra*, which was published in installments between May 1923 and January 1924. See *CTCP*, nos. 1–39.

76. See Hsieh Pin, *Min-kuo cheng-tang shih*, p. 185.
77. *CTSN*, pp. 164–165. Kuo Mo-jo states that his first meeting with Chang Chi-luan took place in early September 1923, but this cannot be correct, since the first issue of the *Creation Daily* was published on July 26, 1923. See *CTCP*, 26:13 (November 4, 1923).
78. *CTSN*, pp. 168–169.
79. See Yü Ta-fu, "Li-san chih ch'ien," *Ta-fu ch'üan-chi*, III, 187–190.
80. Yü Ta-fu, "Hai-shang t'ung-hsin," in *Ta-fu ch'üan-chi*, III, 199–200.
81. See Lu Hsiao-man, ed., *Chih-mo jih-chi* (Hong Kong, 1961), p. 31. The editor has erroneously dated this part of the diary in 1918, but internal evidence proves conclusively that it must be 1923.
82. Ibid., p. 32.
83. Ibid., p. 36.
84. Kuo Mo-jo, "Shih-tzu chia," p. 10.
85. *CTCP*, 32:15 (December 16, 1923).
86. Kuo Mo-jo, "Shih-tzu chia," pp. 9–14.
87. See *CTSN*, pp. 170–171. Kuo Mo-jo states that Yin Chu-fu's visit took place in mid-December 1923, but this is impossible, since the last issue of the *Creation Daily* appeared on November 2, 1923. See *CTCP*, 26:13 (November 4, 1923).
88. See the back cover of *Hsüeh-i*, 5.2 (June 1, 1923).
89. In *Hsüeh-i*, 5.7 (November 1, 1923), Kuo Mo-jo is listed on the masthead as one of the two editors for the first time. See also "She-pao" (News of the association), p. 1, in the same issue. *Hsüeh-i*, 8.6 (April 15, 1927), is the first issue after that of November 1, 1923, in which Kuo Mo-jo's name does not appear on the masthead.
90. See "She-pao," p. 1, in *Hsüeh-i*, 5.9 (February 29, 1924).
91. See "She-pao," pp. 1–4, in *Hsüeh-i*, 6.1 (May 31, 1924).
92. On this speech and the circumstances under which it was given, see *CTHP*, pp. 179–188.
93. Kuo Mo-jo's postface to the last issue of the *Creation Quarterly* is dated January 4, 1924. See *CTCK*, 2.2: sec. 3, p. 26.
94. See Kuo Mo-jo, "Ch'i-lu," originally completed on February 17, 1924, *CTCP*, 41:6 (February 24, 1924); and Kuo Mo-jo, "Shih-tzu chia," pp. 9–10.
95. *CTSN*, pp. 173–174; and Kuo Mo-jo, "Ch'i-lu," pp. 5–10.
96. Kuo Mo-jo, "Shih-tzu chia," p. 4.
97. Ibid., pp. 9–14.
98. *CTHP*, p. 190.
99. See Yü Ta-fu, "Kei Mo-jo," p. 229.
100. See *CTCP*, 52:15. For further information on Huang Hui-ch'üan, see *CTCK*, 1.3: sec. 3, pp. 52–55.

101. See Kuo Mo-jo, "Tao I-hsing ch'ü," in Kuo Mo-jo, *Hou-hui* (Shanghai, 1931), p. 3. This sentence has been omitted from the recent edition of his collected works. See *MJWC*, VII, 325.

102. See *CTCP*, 51:16 (April 27, 1924).

103. See Yü Ta-fu, "Kei Mo-jo," pp. 230–234.

104. On this periodical, see Chow Tse-tsung, *Research Guide to the May Fourth Movement* (Cambridge, Mass., 1963), p. 37.

105. See Yü Ta-fu, "Kei Mo-jo," pp. 234, 239.

106. *CTSN*, pp. 172–173. See also *CTHP*, pp. 197–198.

107. See Yü Ta-fu, "Kei Mo-jo," p. 239.

108. See *CTSN*, p. 159.

109. *CTHP*, p. 202. On the founding of the Whampoa Military Academy, see Li Chien-nung, *The Political History of China, 1840–1928*, pp. 461–462.

110. See *CTHP*, pp. 189–194.

7. FROM ROMANTICISM TO MARXISM-LENINISM, 1918–1924

1. See Kuo Mo-jo, "*Shao-nien Wei-t'e chih fan-nao* hsü-yin," originally completed on January 23, 1922, *CTCK*, 1.1: sec. 2, pp. 1–9. For a vivid picture of the way in which Kuo Mo-jo's translation of this book affected young Chinese at the time, see Mao Tun, *Midnight*, tr. Hsu Meng-hsiung and A. C. Barnes (Peking, 1957), pp. 83–87.

2. Kuo Mo-jo, "*Shao-nien Wei-t'e chih fan-nao* hsü-yin," p. 2.

3. Ibid., p. 3.

4. Ibid., pp. 3–4.

5. Ibid., p. 4.

6. Ibid., p. 5.

7. *CTSN*, p. 44.

8. Arthur O. Lovejoy, *Essays in the History of Ideas* (New York, 1955), p. 232.

9. Iredell Jenkins, "Romanticism," in Dagobert D. Runes, ed., *The Dictionary of Philosophy* (New York, 1942), pp. 272–273.

10. *CTSN*, p. 74.

11. *SYC*, pp. 44–45.

12. Kuo Mo-jo, "*Shao-nien Wei-t'e chih fan-nao* hsü-yin," p. 7.

13. *SYC*, p. 47.

14. *MJWC*, I, 98–100.

15. Ibid., I, 3.

16. *CTSN*, p. 141.

17. Ibid., pp. 101–102.

18. *CTCK*, 1.1: sec. 3, p. 18.

19. *CTSN*, p. 157.

20. Ibid., p. 140.

21. *CTCK*, 1.2: sec. 3, p. 12.

22. Kuo Mo-jo, "Ku-chu chün chih erh tzu," originally completed on November 23, 1922, *CTCK*, 1.4: sec. 1, p. 12.

23. *CTSN*, p. 147.

24. Kuo Mo-jo, "I-shu chih she-hui-ti shih-ming," originally completed on May 2, 1923, *MJWC*, X, 84–85.

25. Kuo Mo-jo, "Wo-men ti wen-hsüeh hsin yün-tung," originally completed on May 18, 1923, *CTCP*, 3:13–15 (May 27, 1923).

26. Kuo Mo-jo, "Lun Chung-Te wen-hua shu," originally completed on May 20, 1923, *CTCP*, 5:11–16 (June 16, 1923).

27. For these controversies, see Chow Tse-tsung, *The May Fourth Movement*, pp. 327–337.

28. *CTCP*, 3:10–11 (May 27, 1923).

29. Ibid., 8:15 (June 30, 1923).

30. *MJWC*, I, 312.

31. Ibid., I, 311.

32. *CTCP*, 4:12–13 (June 3, 1923). This poem has been translated into English in Kai-yu Hsu, *Twentieth Century Chinese Poetry*, pp. 36–37.

33. Kuo Mo-jo, "I-shu chia yü ko-ming chia," originally completed on September 4, 1923, *CTCP*, 18:1–2 (September 9, 1923).

34. Kuo Mo-jo, "Chung-hua ch'üan-kuo i-shu hsieh-hui hsüan-yen," *CTCP*, 22:15 (October 7, 1923).

35. Kuo Mo-jo, "T'ai-ko-erh lai Hua ti wo-chien," p. 5.

36. Kuo Mo-jo, "Ch'i-lu," pp. 5–14.

37. Kuo Mo-jo, "Sheng-che," originally completed on February 22, 1924, *CTCP*, 42:1–6 (March 2, 1924).

38. Kuo Mo-jo, "Lien-yü," pp. 1–8.

39. Kuo Mo-jo, "Shih-tzu chia," pp. 4–14.

40. Kuo Mo-jo, "Sheng-che," p. 6.

41. Kuo Mo-jo, "Shih-tzu chia," pp. 4–14.

42. *CTSN*, p. 174.

43. On January 25, 1924, he wrote a poem on the death of Lenin, entitled "The sun has set," in which he compared Lenin to Prometheus. See *CTCP*, 38:7–8.

44. *CTSN*, p. 174.

45. On the beginnings of Marxist influence in China, see Chow Tse-tsung, *The May Fourth Movement*, pp. 297–299.

46. Kuo Mo-jo, "An-wu-t'ien-jih ti shih-chieh," originally completed on June 16, 1923, *CTCP*, 7:14 (June 23, 1923).

47. *CTHP*, p. 191.

48. *CTCP*, 52:16.

49. For the date, see *MJWC*, X, 301.

199

50. The word "Trotsky" has been deleted from the current edition of Kuo Mo-jo's collected works. See *MJWC*, X, 290.
51. *Kuo Mo-jo shu-hsin chi* (Shanghai, 1937), pp. 157–160.
52. Ibid., pp. 175–176.

EPILOGUE

1. *CTHP*, p. 190.
2. Kuo Mo-jo, "Hsing-lu nan," originally completed on October 15, 1924, in his *Kan-lan* (Shanghai, 1932), p. 66.
3. *Kuo Mo-jo shu-hsin chi*, pp. 154–155.
4. *CTCP*, 52:16.
5. Kuo Mo-jo, "Wang Yang-ming," p. 90; and *Kuo Mo-jo shu-hsin chi*, p. 164.
6. *CTHP*, p. 195.
7. *Kuo Mo-jo shu-hsin chi*, pp. 161–164.
8. *CTHP*, p. 195.
9. Kuo Mo-jo, "Hsing-lu nan," p. 66; and *Kuo Mo-jo shu-hsin chi*, pp. 164–165.
10. *Kuo Mo-jo shu-hsin chi*, pp. 171–172.
11. Ibid., pp. 156–159.
12. Ibid., pp. 171–172.
13. Ibid., pp. 173–175.
14. Ibid., pp. 175–177.
15. Kuo Mo-jo, "Hsing-lu nan," p. 127. This passage has been deleted from the current edition of Kuo Mo-jo's collected works. See *MJWC*, V, 205.
16. Kuo Mo-jo, "Tao I-hsing ch'ü," p. 27.
17. *CTHP*, pp. 262–263.
18. Ibid., pp. 278–283.
19. See Kuo Mo-jo, "Chi-nien Teng Tse-sheng hsien-sheng," originally completed on November 24, 1946, in his *T'ien-ti hsüan-huang* (Shanghai, 1947), pp. 466–468; and Kuo Mo-jo, "T'o-li Chiang Chieh-shih i-hou," originally completed in July 1927, in *MJWC*, VIII, pp. 147–148.
20. See Kuo Mo-jo, "T'u-chia pu," originally completed on June 5, 1948, in his *Hai-t'ao*, pp. 1–18; and Kuo Mo-jo, "Nan-ch'ang chih i yeh," originally completed on June 21, 1948, in his *Hai-t'ao*, pp. 19–20, 27–34.
21. According to Chou I-ch'ün, who commanded the third division of Ho Lung's Twentieth Army on the Southern Expedition to Swatow in the wake of the Nanchang Uprising, Kuo Mo-jo joined the Chinese Communist Party at that time, along with Ho Lung.

See Chou I-ch'ün, "Chou I-ch'ün pao-kao," *Chung-yang t'ung-hsün,* no. 7, p. 59 (October 30, 1927). I owe this information to Professor C. Martin Wilbur, of Columbia University, who was kind enough to send me a xerox reproduction of his own handwritten copy of this rare document.

BIBLIOGRAPHY

A Ying 阿英 (pen name of Ch'ien Hsing-ts'un 錢杏邨), comp. *Hsiao-shuo hsi-ch'ü yen-chiu chüan* 小說戲曲研究卷 (Materials for the study of fiction and drama). Peking, 1960; in A Ying, comp., *Wan-Ch'ing wen-hsüeh ts'ung-ch'ao.*

————comp. *Shih-liao so-yin* 史料索引 (Source material and indices), in Chao Chia-pi, comp., *Chung-kuo hsin wen-hsüeh ta-hsi*, vol. 10.

————comp. *Wan-Ch'ing hsi-ch'ü hsiao-shuo mu* 晚清戲曲小說目 (Bibliography of late Ch'ing drama and fiction). Shanghai, 1957.

————comp. *Wan-Ch'ing wen-hsüeh ts'ung-ch'ao* 晚清文學叢鈔 (Collectanea of late Ch'ing literature). Shanghai and Peking, 1960–

————*Wan-Ch'ing wen-i pao-k'an shu-lüeh* 晚清文藝報刊述略 (Brief descriptions of literary newspapers and periodicals in the late Ch'ing period). Shanghai, 1958.

————comp. *Yü-wai wen-hsüeh i-wen chüan* 域外文學譯文卷 (Translations of foreign literature). 4 vols.; Peking, 1961; in A Ying, comp., *Wan-Ch'ing wen-hsüeh ts'ung-ch'ao.*

Aoki Masaru 青木正兒. *Chung-kuo chin-shih hsi-ch'ü shih* 中國近世戲曲史 (A history of Chinese drama during the Ming and Ch'ing periods), tr. Wang Ku-lu 王古魯. 2 vols.; Peking, 1958.

Bodde, Derk. "Harmony and Conflict in Chinese Philosophy," in Arthur

F. Wright, ed., *Studies in Chinese Thought*, pp. 19–80.

Boorman, Howard L., ed. *Men and Politics in Modern China, Preliminary 50 Biographies*. New York: Modern China Project, Columbia University, 1960.

Brunnert, H. S., and V. V. Hagelstrom. *Present Day Political Organization of China*, tr. A. Beltchenko and E. E. Moran. Taipei: Book World Co., n.d.

Chang Chih-tung 張之洞. *Ssu-ch'uan sheng-ch'eng Tsun-ching shu-yüan chi* 四川省城尊經書院記 (An account of the Tsun-ching Academy in the capital of Szechwan), in Lu Ching, comp., *Shen shih chi chai ts'ung-shu*, ts'e 1, item 4, pp. 1–11.

Chang Ching-lu 張靜廬, comp. "Ch'ing-mo Min-ch'u Ching Hu hua-k'an lu" 清末民初京滬畫刊録 (Catalogue of illustrated periodicals published in Peking and Shanghai during the late Ch'ing and early Republican periods), in Chang Ching-lu, comp. *Chung-kuo chin-tai ch'u-pan shih-liao*, II, 297–301.

————comp. *Chung-kuo chin-tai ch'u-pan shih-liao* 中國近代出版史料 (Historical materials on publishing in modern China). 2 vols.; Shanghai, 1953–1954.

————comp. *Chung-kuo ch'u-pan shih-liao pu-pien* 中國出版史料補編 (A supplementary collection of historical materials on publishing in China). Shanghai, 1957.

————comp. *Chung-kuo hsien-tai ch'u-pan shih-liao* 中國現代出版史料 (Historical materials on publishing in contemporary China). 4 vols.; Peking, 1954–1959.

————*Tsai ch'u-pan chieh erh-shih nien* 在出版界二十年 (Twenty years in the publishing world). Hankow, 1938.

Chang Tzu-p'ing 張資平. "Tu 'Ch'uang-tsao she' " 讀創造社 (On reading "The Creation Society"), in Shih Ping-hui, ed., *Chang Tzu-p'ing p'ing-chuan*, pp. 141–178.

————"Tung-ching jih-chi" 東京日記 (Tokyo diary). Completed on October 30, 1928; in Chün-sheng, comp., *Hsien-tai jih-chi wen-hsüan*, pp. 208–260.

Chang Yüeh-jui 張越瑞, ed. *Chin-jen chuan-chi wen-hsüan* 近人傳記文選 (An anthology of modern biography). Changsha, 1938.

Chao Chia-pi 趙家璧, ed. *Chung-kuo hsin wen-hsüeh ta-hsi* 中國新文學大系 (A corpus of China's new literature). 10 vols.; Hong Kong, n.d.

Cheng Chen-to 鄭振鐸. *Chung-kuo wen-hsüeh yen-chiu* 中國文學研究 (Studies in Chinese literature). 3 vols.; Peking, 1957.

Ch'eng Fang-wu 成仿吾. "Ch'uang-tsao she yü Wen-hsüeh yen-chiu

hui" 創造社與文學研究會 (The Creation Society and the Literary Research Society). Completed on November 12, 1922; in *Ch'uang-tsao chi-k'an*, vol. 1, no. 4, sec. 4, pp. 12–18.

———"Hsüeh-che ti t'ai-tu" 學者的態度 (The attitude of a scholar). Completed on October 13, 1922; in *Ch'uang-tsao chi-k'an*, vol. 1, no. 3, sec. 2, pp. 13–27.

"Chiao-k'o shu chih fa-k'an kai-k'uang, i-pa-liu-pa—i-chiu-i-pa nien" 教科書之發刊概況，一八六八——一九一八年 (An outline of textbook publication between 1868 and 1918), comp. Ministry of Education, in Chang Ching-lu, comp. *Chung-kuo chin-tai ch'u-pan shih-liao*, I, 219–253.

"Chiao-k'o shu i-ch'ien ti t'ung-meng tu-wu" 教科書以前的童蒙讀物 (Children's readers in use before the introduction of modern textbooks), comp. Library of the Chung-hua shu-chü, in Chang Ching-lu, comp., *Chung-kuo chin-tai ch'u-pan shih-liao*, I, 215–219.

Ch'in-ting p'ing-ting Kuei-chou Miao-fei chi-lüeh 欽定平定貴州苗匪紀畧 (The imperially commissioned account of the pacification of the Miao rebels in Kweichow), comp. Ch'en Pang-jui 陳邦瑞 et al. 40 chüan; Peking, 1896.

Chinese Literature. Peking: Foreign Languages Press, 1951–

Ch'ing wen-tsung hsien huang-ti shih-lu 清文宗顯皇帝實錄 (Veritable records of the Hsien-feng Emperor of the Ch'ing dynasty). 356 chüan; Tokyo, 1937–1938.

Chou I-ch'ün 周逸羣. "Chou I-ch'ün pao-kao" 周逸羣報告 (The report of Chou I-ch'ün), in *Chung-yang t'ung-hsün*, 7:52, 59 (October 30, 1927).

Chou Shan-p'ei 周善培. *Hsin-hai Ssu-ch'uan cheng-lu ch'in-li chi* 辛亥四川爭路親歷記 (A record of my personal experiences in the Szechwan railway strife of 1911). Chungking, 1957.

———"Hsin-hai Ssu-ch'uan shih-pien chih wo" 辛亥四川事變之我 (My role in the disturbances in Szechwan in 1911), in *Hsin-hai ko-ming*, IV, 424–448.

Chow Tse-tsung. "Lin Shu," in Howard L. Boorman, ed., *Men and Politics in Modern China, Preliminary 50 Biographies*, pp. 88–95.

———*The May Fourth Movement*. Cambridge, Mass.: Harvard University Press, 1960.

———*Research Guide to the May Fourth Movement*. Cambridge, Mass.: Harvard University Press, 1963.

———"Wen I-to," in Howard L. Boorman, ed., *Men and Politics in Modern China, Preliminary 50 Biographies*, pp. 144–150.

———"Yen Fu," in Howard L. Boorman, ed., *Men and Politics in Modern China, Preliminary 50 Biographies*, pp. 161–166.

Chu Hsi-chou 朱羲冑, comp. *Ch'un-chüeh chai chu-shu chi* 春覺齋著述記 (A bibliography of the works of Lin Shu). 3 chüan; in his *Lin Ch'in-nan hsien-sheng hsüeh hsing p'u chi ssu chung* 林琴南先生學行譜記四種 (Four studies of the life and works of Lin Shu). Taipei, 1961.

Chu Tzu-ch'ing 朱自清, ed. *Shih chi* 詩集 (Poetry), in Chao Chia-pi, ed., *Chung-kuo hsin wen-hsüeh ta-hsi*, vol. 8.

Ch'uang-tsao chi-k'an 創造季刊 (Creation quarterly). Shanghai, 1922–1924.

Ch'uang-tsao chou-pao 創造周報 (Creation weekly). Shanghai, 1923–1924.

Chung-kuo shih-hsüeh lun-wen so-yin 中國史學論文索引 (An index to articles on Chinese history), comp. First and Second Offices of the Institute of Historical Research, Chinese Academy of Sciences, and the Department of History, Peking University. 2 vols.; Peking, 1957.

Chung-yang t'ung-hsün 中央通訊 (Central intelligence). N.p., 1927.

Chün-sheng 俊生, comp. *Hsien-tai jih-chi wen-hsüan* 現代日記文選 (An anthology of contemporary diary literature). Shanghai, 1937.

Fang, Achilles. "From Imagism to Whitmanism in Recent Chinese Poetry: a Search for Poetics that Failed," in Horst Frenz and G. L. Anderson, eds., *Indiana University Conference on Oriental-Western Literary Relations*, pp. 177–189.

Feng Tzu-yu 馮自由. "Hsin-hai ch'ien hai nei-wai ko-ming shu-pao i-lan" 辛亥前海內外革命書報一覽 (A list of the revolutionary books and periodicals published in China and abroad before the 1911 revolution), in Chang Ching-lu, comp. *Chung-kuo chin-tai ch'u-pan shih-liao*, II, 276–297.

Feuerwerker, Albert. *China's Early Industrialization, Sheng Hsüan-huai (1844–1916) and Mandarin Enterprise*. Cambridge, Mass.: Harvard University Press, 1958.

Franke, Wolfgang. *The Reform and Abolition of the Traditional Chinese Examination System*. Cambridge, Mass.: Harvard University Press, 1960.

Frenz, Horst, and G. L. Anderson, eds. *Indiana University Conference on Oriental-Western Literary Relations*. Chapel Hill: University of North Carolina Press, 1955.

Fu Lien-chang 傅連暲. *Tsai Mao chu-hsi chiao-tao hsia* 在毛主席教導下 (Under the guidance of Chairman Mao). Peking, 1959.

Fung Yu-lan. *A History of Chinese Philosophy*, tr. Derk Bodde. 2 vols.;

205

Princeton: Princeton University Press, 1953.

Hightower, James Robert. *Topics in Chinese Literature*. Cambridge, Mass.: Harvard University Press, 1962.

Ho Ping-ti. *Studies on the Population of China, 1368–1953*. Cambridge, Mass.: Harvard University Press, 1959.

Hsia, C. T. *A History of Modern Chinese Fiction*. New Haven: Yale University Press, 1961.

Hsieh Pin 謝彬. *Min-kuo cheng-tang shih* 民國政黨史 (A history of the political parties under the Republic). Taipei, 1962.

Hsien-tai 現代 (Les contemporains). Shanghai, 1932–1935.

Hsin-hai ko-ming 辛亥革命 (The revolution of 1911), ed. Chung-kuo shih-hsüeh hui 中國史學會 (Chinese historical society). 8 vols.; Shanghai, 1957.

Hsu Kai-yu. *Twentieth Century Chinese Poetry*. New York: Doubleday, 1963.

Hsüeh-i 學藝 (Wissen und Wissenschaft). Tokyo, Peking, Shanghai, 1917–1937.

Hu Shih 胡適. "Kao Meng-tan hsien-shēng hsiao-chuan" 高夢且先生小傳 (A brief biography of Kao Meng-tan). Completed on November 26, 1936; in Chang Yüeh-jui, ed. *Chin-jen chuan-chi wen-hsüan*, pp. 106–110.

————*Ssu-shih tzu-shu* 四十自述 (Autobiography at forty). Taipei, 1962.

Hummel, Arthur W., ed. *Eminent Chinese of the Ch'ing Period (1644–1912)*. 2 vols.; Washington, D.C.: Government Printing Office, 1943–1944.

I Chün-tso 易君左. *Hui-meng san-shih nien* 迴夢三十年 (Thirty years of dream memories). Hong Kong, 1954.

Jenkins, Iredell. "Romanticism," in Dagobert D. Runes, ed., *The Dictionary of Philosophy*, pp. 272–273.

The Journal of Asian Studies. Ann Arbor, Mich.: Association for Asian Studies, 1957–

Journal of Oriental Literature. Honolulu: Oriental Literature Society, University of Hawaii, 1947–1955.

Kao Yin-tsu 高蔭祖, comp. *Chung-hua min-kuo ta-shih chi* 中華民國大事記 (A chronology of major events under the Chinese Republic). Taipei, 1957.

Ko Kung-chen 戈公振. *Chung-kuo pao-hsüeh shih* 中國報學史 (A history of journalism in China). Peking, 1955.

Kripalani, Krishna. *Rabindranath Tagore: A Biography*. New York: Grove Press, 1962.

Kuo Mo-jo 郭沫若. "An-wu-t'ien-jih ti shih-chieh" 暗無天日的世界 (This dark and sunless world). Completed on June 16, 1923; in *Ch'uang-tsao chou-pao*, 7:12–16 (June 23, 1923).

———"Chi-nien Teng Tse-sheng hsien-sheng" 紀念鄧擇生先生 (In memory of Teng Yen-ta). Completed on November 24, 1946; in his *T'ien-ti hsüan-huang*, pp. 465–470.

———"Ch'i-lu" 歧路 (The crossroads). Completed on February 17, 1924; in *Ch'uang-tsao chou-pao*, 41:5–14 (February 24, 1924).

———"Ch'u ch'u K'uei-men" 初出夔門 (My first trip out of Szechwan). Originally published in 1936; in his *Shao-nien shih-tai*, pp. 353–402.

———*Chüan-erh chi* 卷耳集 (Cockleburs). Shanghai, 1929.

———*Ch'uang-tsao shih-nien* 創造十年 (Ten years of creation). Originally published in 1932; in his *Ko-ming ch'un-ch'iu*, pp. 15–176.

———*Ch'uang-tsao shih-nien hsü-pien* 創造十年續編 (Ten years of creation continued). Originally published in 1938; reprinted under the title *Ch'uang-tsao shih-nien hsü-p'ien* 創造十年續篇 in his *Ko-ming ch'un-ch'iu*, pp. 177–283.

———"Chung-hua ch'üan-kuo i-shu hsieh-hui hsüan-yen" 中華全國藝術協會宣言 (The manifesto of the All-China Arts Association). Written in 1923; in *Ch'uang-tsao chou-pao*, 22:14–16 (October 7, 1923).

———*Fan-cheng ch'ien-hou* 反正前後 (Before and after the 1911 revolution). Originally published in 1929; in his *Shao-nien shih-tai*, pp. 171–303.

———tr. *Fu-shih-te* 浮士德 (*Faust*). Shanghai, 1947.

———*Hai-t'ao* 海濤 (Ocean waves). Shanghai, 1956.

———*Hei mao* 黑貓 (The black cat). Originally published in 1930; in his *Shao-nien shih-tai*, pp. 305–351.

———*Hou-hui* 後悔 (Repentance). Shanghai, 1931.

———"Hsieh tsai *San-ko p'an-ni ti nü-hsing* hou-mien" 寫在三個叛逆的女性後面 (A postface to *Three Rebellious Women*). Completed on March 7, 1926; in his *San-ko p'an-ni ti nü-hsing*, pp. 1–35.

———"Hsing-lu nan" 行路難 (Hard going). Completed on October 15, 1924; in his *Kan-lan*, pp. 61–151.

———"I-shu-chia yü ko-ming-chia" 藝術家與革命家 (The artist and the revolutionary). Completed on September 4, 1923; in *Ch'uang-tsao chou-pao*, 18:1–2 (September 9, 1923).

———"I-shu chih she-hui-ti shih-ming" 藝術之社會的使命 (The social mission of art). Completed on May 2, 1923; in his *Mo-jo wen-chi*, X, 83–88.

————tr. *I-tuan* 異端 (*Der Ketzer von Soana*). Shanghai, 1947.

————*Kan-lan* 橄欖 (Olives). Shanghai, 1932.

————*Ko-ming ch'un-ch'iu* 革命春秋 (The revolutionary years). Shanghai, 1956.

————"Ku-chu chün chih erh tzu" 孤竹君之二子 (The two princes of Ku-chu). Completed on November 23, 1922; in *Ch'uang-tsao chi-k'an*, vol. 1, no. 4, sec. 1, pp. 1–25.

————"K'ua-che tung-hai" 跨着東海 (Crossing the eastern sea). Written in 1947; in his *Hai-t'ao*, pp. 66–102.

————"Li Hu chih ch'ien" 離滬之前 (Before leaving Shanghai). Completed on February 23, 1928; in *Hsien-tai*, 4.1:32–39 (November 1, 1933); 4.2:301–307 (December 1, 1933); 4.3:462–468 (January 1, 1934).

————*Li-shih jen-wu* 歷史人物 (Historical personalities). Shanghai, 1947.

————"Lien-yü" 煉獄 (Purgatory). Completed on March 7, 1924; in *Ch'uang-tsao chou-pao*, 44:1–8 (March 16, 1924).

————*Lo-yeh* 落葉 (Fallen leaves). Shanghai, 1928.

————"Lun Chung-Te wen-hua shu" 論中德文化書 (A letter on Chinese and German culture). Completed on May 20, 1923; in *Ch'uang-tsao chou-pao*, 5:11–16 (June 16, 1923).

————"Mai-shu" 賣書 (Selling books). Written in 1924; in his *Pao-chien chi*, pp. 101–104.

————*Mo-jo tzu-hsüan chi* 沫若自選集 (A Kuo Mo-jo anthology selected by the author). Hong Kong, 1962.

————*Mo-jo wen-chi* 沫若文集 (Collected literary works of Kuo Mo-jo). 17 vols.; Peking, 1957–1963.

————"Mu-yang ai-hua" 牧羊哀話 (The sad tale of a shepherdess). Written in February-March 1919; in his *Mo-jo wen-chi*, V, 1–12.

————"Nan-ch'ang chih i yeh" 南昌之一夜 (A night in Nanchang). Completed on June 21, 1948; in his *Hai-t'ao*, pp. 19–34.

————"Pa-chiao hua" 芭蕉花 (The banana blossom). Written in 1924; in his *Pao-chien chi*, pp. 79–82.

————*Pao-chien chi* 抱箭集 (A sheaf of arrows). Shanghai 1955.

————*San-ko p'an-ni ti nü-hsing* 三個叛逆的女性 (Three rebellious women). Shanghai, 1926.

————*San yeh chi. See* T'ien Shou-ch'ang.

————*Selected Poems from The Goddesses*, tr. John Lester and A. C. Barnes. Peking: Foreign Languages Press, 1958.

————*Shao-nien shih-tai* 少年時代 (The period of my youth). Shanghai, 1956.

———"Shao-nien Wei-t'e chih fan-nao hsü-yin" 少年維特之煩惱序引 (A preface to *The Sorrows of Young Werther*). Completed on January 23, 1922; in *Ch'uang-tsao chi-k'an*, vol. 1, no. 1, sec. 2, pp. 1–9.

———"Sheng-che" 聖者 (The saints). Completed on February 22, 1924; in *Ch'uang-tsao chou-pao*, 42:1–6.

———"Shih-tzu chia" 十字架 (The cross). Completed on March 18, 1924; in *Ch'uang-tsao chou-pao*, 47:4–14 (April 5, 1924).

———"T'ai-ko-erh lai Hua ti wo-chien" 太戈兒來華之我見 (My views on Tagore's visit to China). Completed on October 11, 1923; in *Ch'uang-tsao chou-pao*, 23:1–6 (October 14, 1923).

———"T'ang-ti chih hua" 棠棣之花 (Wild cherry blossoms). Completed on September 23, 1920; in his *Mo-jo wen-chi*, I, 24–29.

———*T'ang-ti chih hua* 棠棣之花 (Wild cherry blossoms). Shanghai, 1946.

———"*T'ang-ti chih hua* ti-erh mu" 棠棣之花第二幕 (The second act of *T'ang-ti chih hua*). Originally published on May 1, 1922; in *Ch'uang-tsao chi-k'an*, vol. 1, no. 1, sec. 1, pp. 5–21.

———"Tao I-hsing ch'ü" 到宜興去 (An expedition to I-hsing). Completed on December 3, 1924; in his *Hou-hui*, pp. 2–86.

———*T'ien-ti hsüan-huang* 天地玄黃 (Black heaven and yellow earth). Shanghai, 1947.

———"Ting" 鼎 (Cauldron). Completed on April 13, 1936; in his *Mo-jo wen-chi*, XI, 118–123.

———"T'o-li Chiang Chieh-shih i-hou" 脫離蔣介石以後 (After breaking with Chiang Kai-shek). Written in July 1927; in his *Mo-jo wen-chi*, VIII, 145–194.

———"T'u-chia Pu" 涂家埠 (T'u-chia Pu). Completed on June 5, 1948; in his *Hai-t'ao*, pp. 1–18.

———"Tzu-jan chih chui-huai" 自然之追懷 (Recollections of nature). Written in 1934; in *Hsien-tai*, 4.6:953–958 (April 1, 1934).

———"Wang Yang-ming" 王陽明 (Wang Yang-ming). Completed on June 17, 1924; in his *Li-shih jen-wu*, pp. 75–90.

———"Wei-yang" 未央 (Unfinished). Written in January 1921; revised on September 18, 1922; in *Ch'uang-tsao chi-k'an*, vol. 1, no. 3, sec. 1, pp. 1–20.

———"Wo-kuo ssu-hsiang shih shang chih P'eng-p'ai ch'eng" 我國思想史上之澎湃城 (The Pompeii of Chinese intellectual history). Written in 1921; in *Hsüeh-i*, 3.1:1–17 (May 30, 1921).

———"Wo-men ti wen-hsüeh hsin yün-tung" 我們的文學新運動 (Our new literary movement). Completed on May 18, 1923; in *Ch'uang-*

209

tsao chou-pao, 3:13–15 (May 27, 1923).

——"Wo ti hsüeh-sheng sheng-huo" 我的學生生活 (My life as a student). Completed on April 19, 1942; reprinted under the title "Hsüeh-sheng shih-tai" 學生時代 (My student years); in his *Ko-ming ch'un-ch'iu*, pp. 1–13.

——"Wo ti tso-shih ti ching-kuo" 我的作詩的經過 (My experience in writing poetry). Completed on September 4, 1936; in his *Mo-jo wen-chi*, XI, 137–148.

——*Wo ti yu-nien* 我的幼年 (The years of my youth). Originally published in 1929; reprinted under the title *Wo ti t'ung-nien* 我的童年 (The years of my boyhood); in his *Shao-nien shih-tai*, pp. 1–170.

——"Wo tsen-yang hsieh *T'ang-ti chih hua*" 我怎樣寫棠棣之花 (How I wrote *Wild Cherry Blossoms*). Completed on December 9, 1941; in his *T'ang-ti chih hua*, pp. 127–137.

——"Wu-shih nien chien-p'u" 五十年簡譜 (A concise chronology of my first fifty years). Completed on September 25, 1941; in Chang Ching-lu, *Chung-kuo hsien-tai ch'u-pan shih-liao*, III, 318–327.

Kuo Mo-jo shu-hsin chi 郭沫若書信集 (The letters of Kuo Mo-jo). Shanghai, 1937.

Kuo Shou-hua 郭壽華. *K'o-tsu yüan-liu hsin-chih* 客族原流新志 (A new record of the origins and movements of the Hakka). Taipei, 1964.

Lee, Leo Ou-fan. "Lin Shu and His Translations: Western Fiction in Chinese Perspective," in *Papers on China*, 19:159–193 (December 1965).

Levenson, Joseph R. "Ill Wind in the Well-field: The Erosion of the Confucian Ground of Controversy," in Arthur F. Wright, ed., *The Confucian Persuasion*, pp. 268–287.

——"Liao P'ing and the Confucian Departure from History," in Arthur F. Wright and Denis Twitchett, eds., *Confucian Personalities*, pp. 317–325.

Li Chieh-jen 李劼人. *Pao feng-yü ch'ien* 暴風雨前 (Before the storm). Shanghai, 1940.

——*Ssu-shui wei-lan* 死水微瀾 (Ripples on a still surface). Shanghai, 1936.

——*Ta-po* 大波 (The great wave). Peking, 1958.

Li Chien-nung. *The Political History of China, 1840–1928*, tr. and ed. Ssu-yü Teng and Jeremy Ingalls. Princeton: Van Nostrand, 1956.

Liang Ch'i-ch'ao. *Intellectual Trends in the Ch'ing Period*, tr. Immanuel C. Y. Hsü. Cambridge, Mass.: Harvard University Press, 1959.

Lo Hsiang-lin 羅香林. *K'o-chia shih-liao hui-p'ien* 客家史料匯篇 (His-

BIBLIOGRAPHY

torical sources for the study of the Hakkas). Hong Kong, 1965.

Lo-shan hsien chih 樂山縣志 (Gazetteer of Lo-shan hsien), comp. Huang Jung et al. 12 chüan; Chengtu, 1934.

Lo Tun-wei 羅敦偉. *Wu-shih nien hui-i lu* 五十年回憶錄 (Reminiscences of fifty years). Taipei, 1952.

Look. New York: Cowles, 1936–

Lovejoy, Arthur O. *Essays in the History of Ideas.* New York: George Braziller, 1955.

Lu Ching 盧靖, comp. *Shen shih chi chai ts'ung-shu* 慎始基齋叢書 (Shen shih chi chai collectanea). 8 ts'e; n.p., 1923.

Lu Hsiao-man 陸小曼, ed. *Chih-mo jih-chi* 志摩日記 (Hsü Chih-mo's diaries). Hong Kong, 1961.

Lu Hsun. *A Brief History of Chinese Fiction,* tr. Yang Hsien-yi and Gladys Yang. Peking: Foreign Languages Press, 1959.

Mao Tun. *Midnight,* tr. Hsu Meng-hsiung and A. C. Barnes. Peking: Foreign Languages Press, 1957.

Ni Fan 倪璠. *Yü Tzu-shan chi chu* 庾子山集注 (Commentary on the collected works of Yü Hsin). 2 vols.; Taipei, 1959.

Nihon kindai-shi jiten 日本近代史辭典 (Cyclopedia of modern Japanese history), comp. Japanese History Research Center of the Liberal Arts Department of Kyoto University. Tokyo, 1958.

North China Herald. Shanghai, 1870– .

Papers on China. Cambridge, Mass.: East Asian Research Center, Harvard University, 1947– .

Parsons, James B. "The Culmination of a Chinese Peasant Rebellion: Chang Hsien-chung in Szechwan, 1644–46," in *Journal of Asian Studies,* 16.3:387–400 (May 1957).

P'eng Fen 彭芬. *Hsin-hai sun-Ch'ing cheng-pien fa-yüan chi* 辛亥遜清政變發源記 (An account of the origins of the revolution of 1911 and the Manchu abdication), in *Hsin-hai ko-ming,* IV, 331–389.

"Ping-ch'en hsüeh-she chih hui-ku" 丙辰學社之回顧 (A retrospective look at the 1916 Society), in *Hsüeh-i,* 5.2:1–5 (June 1, 1923).

Price, Don. "The Russian Revolutionaries in Chinese Fiction." Cambridge, Mass.: mimeographed typescript, 1965.

Runes, Dagobert D., ed. *The Dictionary of Philosophy.* New York: Philosophical Library, 1942.

San-yü shu-she chu-jen 三餘書社主人, comp. *Ssu-ch'uan hsüeh* 四川血 (The blood of Szechwan), in *Hsin-hai ko-ming,* IV, 390–414.

Sanetō Keishū 實藤惠秀. "Kaku Matsu-jaku no Nihon ryūgaku jidai" 郭沫若の日本留學時代 (Kuo Mo-jo's student days in Japan),

211

autographed offprint from a volume entitled *Ajia bunka no sai-ninshiki* アジア文化の再認識 (A new understanding of Asian culture), apparently a symposium volume of unidentified editorship, pp. 265–303.

Sansom, G. B. *The Western World and Japan.* New York: Alfred A. Knopf, 1951.

Satō Tomiko 佐藤富子. *Wo ti chang-fu Kuo Mo-jo* 我的丈夫郭沫若 (My husband Kuo Mo-jo). Shanghai, 1938.

Schultz, William R. "Kuo Mo-jo and the Romantic Aesthetic: 1918–1925," in *Journal of Oriental Literature*, 6.2:49–81 (April 1955).

Schwartz, Benjamin. *In Search of Wealth and Power: Yen Fu and the West.* Cambridge, Mass.: Harvard University Press, 1964.

Selections from China Mainland Magazines. Hong Kong: American Consulate General, 1960–

Sharman, Lyon. *Sun Yat-sen, His Life and Its Meaning.* New York: John Day, 1934.

Shih Chien 史劍 (pen name of Ma Pin 馬彬). *Kuo Mo-jo p'i-p'an* 郭沫若批判 (A critique of Kuo Mo-jo). Hong Kong, 1954.

Shih Ching 史靖. *Wen I-to ti tao-lu* 聞一多的道路 (The road of Wen I-to). Shanghai, 1947.

Shih Ping-hui 史秉慧, ed. *Chang Tzu-p'ing p'ing-chuan* 張資平評傳 (Critical appraisals of Chang Tzu-p'ing). Shanghai, 1932.

Steinberg, S. H., ed. *Cassell's Encyclopedia of Literature.* 2 vols.; London: Cassell, 1953.

Tai Chih-li 戴執禮, comp. *Ssu-ch'uan pao-lu yün-tung shih-liao* 四川保路運動史料 (Historical materials on the railway protection movement in Szechwan). Peking, 1959.

Takikawa Kametarō 瀧川龜太郎. *Shiki kaichū kōshō* 史記會注考證 (The *Shih-chi* with collected commentaries and critical notes). 10 vols.; Tokyo, 1934.

T'ang Jen 唐人. "Strive for Greater Achievements through Collective Wisdom and Collective Strength," in *Selections from China Mainland Magazines*, 322:34–36 (July 16, 1962); tr. from *Ch'iao-wu pao* 僑務報 (Overseas Chinese affairs bulletin). Peking, 1956– ; no. 2 (April 1962).

T'ao Ching-sun 陶晶孫. *Yin-yüeh hui hsiao-ch'ü* 音樂會小曲 (Concert song). Shanghai, 1927.

T'ien Han 田漢. "Ying Mo-jo" 迎沫若 (Welcoming Kuo Mo-jo). Completed on February 7, 1938; in Ting San, ed., *K'ang-chan chung ti Kuo Mo-jo*, pp. 38–40.

T'ien Shou-ch'ang 田壽昌 (tzu of T'ien Han), Tsung Po-hua 宗白華, and Kuo Mo-jo. *San yeh chi* 三葉集 (Cloverleaf). Shanghai, 1927.

Ting Chih-p'ing 丁致聘, comp. *Chung-kuo chin ch'i-shih nien lai chiao-yü chi-shih* 中國近七十年來教育記事 (Chinese education in the last seventy years). Taipei, 1961.

Ting San 丁三, ed. *K'ang-chan chung ti Kuo Mo-jo* 抗戰中的郭沫若 (Kuo Mo-jo during the Sino-Japanese war). Canton, n.d.

Ting Wen-chiang 丁文江, comp. *Liang Jen-kung hsien-sheng nien-p'u ch'ang-pien ch'u-kao* 梁任公先生年譜長編初稿 (First draft of an unabridged chronological biography of Liang Ch'i-ch'ao). 3 vols.; Taipei, 1958.

Ts'ao Chü-jen 曹聚仁, ed. *Chüan-erh t'ao-lun chi* 卷耳討論集 (Discussions on *Cockleburs*). Shanghai, 1925.

Tseng Ch'i 曾琦. "Wu-wu jih-chi" 戊午日記 (Diary for 1918), in *Tseng Mu-han hsien-sheng i-chu* 曾慕韓先生遺著 (Posthumously published works of Tseng Ch'i), pp. 371–402. Taipei, 1954.

Tseng chiao Ch'ing-ch'ao chin-shih t'i-ming pei lu, fu yin-te 增校清朝進士題名碑錄附引得 (An enlarged, revised, and indexed record of the names of Ch'ing dynasty *chin-shih*), comp. Fang Chao-ying 房兆楹 and Tu Lien-che 杜聯喆. Harvard-Yenching Institute Sinological Index Series, Supplement no. 19. Peiping, 1941.

Tso Shun-sheng 左舜生. *Chin san-shih nien chien-wen tsa-chi* 近三十年見聞雜記 (Recollections of the last thirty years). Hong Kong, 1952.

Tsung Po-hua 宗白華. *San yeh chi*. See T'ien Shou-ch'ang.

Tu Kuo-hsiang wen-chi 杜國庠文集 (The works of Tu Kuo-hsiang). Peking, 1962.

Viëtor, Karl. *Goethe the Poet*. Cambridge, Mass.: Harvard University Press, 1949.

Waley, Arthur. *The Real Tripitaka and Other Pieces*. London: Allen and Unwin, 1952.

———*Yuan Mei, Eighteenth Century Chinese Poet*. London: Allen and Unwin, 1956.

Wang Ch'ü-ch'ang 王蘧常. *Yen Chi-tao nien-p'u* 嚴幾道年譜 (A chronological biography of Yen Fu). Shanghai, 1936.

Wang Jen-wen 王人文. *Hsin-hai Ssu-ch'uan lu-shih tsui-yen* 辛亥四川路事罪言 (Recriminations in connection with the railway affair in Szechwan in 1911), in *Hsin-hai ko-ming*, IV, 415–423.

Wang Tu-ch'ing 王獨清. *Wo tsai Ou-chou ti sheng-huo* 我在歐洲的生活 (My life in Europe). Shanghai, 1932.

Wang Yao 王瑤. *Chung-kuo hsin wen-hsüeh shih kao* 中國新文學史稿 (Draft history of China's new literature). 2 vols.; Shanghai, 1953.

Watson, Burton, tr. *Records of the Grand Historian of China*. 2 vols.; New York: Columbia University Press, 1961.

Whitman, Walt. *Leaves of Grass*. London: Everyman's Library, 1949.

Williams, Samuel Wells. *The Middle Kingdom*. 2 vols.; New York: Scribner, 1901.

Wills, Morris R., as told to J. Robert Moskin. "An American Defector Comes Home. Part Two: Why I Quit China," in *Look*, 30.4:84–88, 90–94 (February 22, 1966).

Wright, Arthur F., ed. *The Confucian Persuasion*. Stanford: Stanford University Press, 1960.

———ed. *Studies in Chinese Thought*. Chicago: University of Chicago Press, 1953.

———and Denis Twitchett, eds. *Confucian Personalities*. Stanford: Stanford University Press, 1962.

Wu-ssu shih-ch'i ch'i-k'an chieh-shao 五四時期期刊介紹 (An introduction to the periodicals of the May Fourth period), comp. Research Section of the Bureau of Translation of the Works of Marx, Engels, Lenin, and Stalin, Central Committee of the Chinese Communist Party. 3 vols.; Peking, 1958–1959.

Wu Yü-chang 吳玉章. *Hsin-hai ko-ming* 辛亥革命 (The revolution of 1911). Peking, 1961.

Yü Li-ch'ün 于立羣. "Ping chung ti Kuo Mo-jo hsien-sheng" 病中的郭沫若先生 (Kuo Mo-jo during his illness). Written in January 1938; in Ting San, ed., *K'ang-chan chung ti Kuo Mo-jo*, pp. 102–108.

Yü Ta-fu 郁達夫. "Chung-t'u" 中途 (En route). Completed on July 26, 1922; in his *Ta-fu ch'üan-chi*, III, 91–105.

———"Hai-shang t'ung-hsin" 海上通信 (Letters written at sea). Completed on October 8, 1923; in his *Ta-fu ch'üan-chi*, III, 197–208.

———"Kei Mo-jo" 給沫若 (To Kuo Mo-jo). Completed on July 29, 1924; in his *Ta-fu ch'üan-chi*, III, 229–239.

———"Li-san chih ch'ien" 離散之前 (Before dispersion). Written in September 1923; in his *Ta-fu ch'üan-chi*, III, 181–196.

———*Ta-fu ch'üan-chi* 達夫全集 (Complete works of Yü Ta-fu). 7 vols.; Shanghai, 1927–1933.

———"Wei-ping" 胃病 (Stomach trouble). Written in June 1921; in his *Ta-fu ch'üan-chi*, II, 1–21.

GLOSSARY

"Ai chiang-nan fu" 哀江南賦
"Ai-shih ku-tiao chiu-shou" 哀世
古調九首
An-ch'ing fa-cheng hsüeh-hsiao
安慶法政學校
An-ku hsiang 安谷鄉
An-tung 安東
Arishima Takeo 有島武郎
Bashō 芭蕉
Biwa 琵琶
Bungei 文藝
bun-ka 文科
Bunkyō-ku 文京區
Chang Chi-luan 張季鸞
Chang Feng-chü 張鳳擧
Chang Hsien-chung 張獻忠
Chang Ping-lin 章炳麟
Chang Shih-chao 章士釗
Chang Shih-ying 張士瀛
Chang Tung-sun 張東蓀
Chang Tz'u-yü 張次瑜
Chang Wen-t'ien 張聞天

"Ch'ang-sha chi Mo-jo" 長沙寄
沫若
Chapei 閘北
Chao Erh-feng 趙爾豐
Chao Erh-sun 趙爾巽
Chao Nan-kung 趙南公
Che-chiang ch'ao 浙江潮
Ch'en 陳
"Ch'en-an" 晨安
Ch'en Ch'i-hsiu 陳啓修
Ch'en Chün-che 陳君哲
Ch'en Jun-hai 陳潤海
Ch'en Lung-chi 陳龍驥
Ch'en Shen-hou 陳慎侯
Cheng Chen-wen 鄭貞文
Cheng-hsüeh hsi 政學系
Cheng Po-ch'i 鄭伯奇
Ch'eng Shao-wu 成劭吾
Chi Yün 紀昀
Ch'i-meng hua-pao 啓蒙畫報
Ch'i Shu-fen 漆樹芬
Chia-ting 嘉定

215

Chia-t'ing yen-chiu 家庭研究
Chiang Kai-shek 蔣介石
Chiba-ken 千葉縣
Chieh-kuang 潔光
Chieh-tzu-yüan hua-chuan 芥子園畫
　傳
Ch'ien chia shih 千家詩
"Ch'ien-chin ch'ü" 前進曲
Ch'ien Chün-hsü 錢君胥
Ch'ien-lung 乾隆
Chin-kang Fo 金剛佛
chin-shih 進士
Ch'in 秦
Ch'in P'i-chi 奉丕基
Ch'in Shih Huang-ti 秦始皇帝
Ching-kuo mei-t'an 經國美談
ching-tso 靜坐
Ch'ing-i pao 清議報
Ch'iu 邱
Cho Wen-chün 卓文君
Chou 周
Chou Ch'ang-shou 周昌壽
Chou Ch'üan-p'ing 周全平
Chou Hung-yeh 周宏業
Chou li 周禮
Chou Tso-jen 周作人
Chou Wu 周無
Chu Ch'ien-chih 朱謙之
Chu Ching-nung 朱經農
Chu han-chien hui 誅漢奸會
Chu-tzu chi 猪子記
ch'u-shih 處士
Ch'u-tz'u 楚辭
Chuan Hsü 顓頊
Chuang-tzu 莊子
Ch'uang-tsao 創造
Ch'uang-tsao jih 創造日
Ch'uang-tsao she ts'ung-shu 創造社
　叢書
Ch'un-ch'iu 春秋

"Ch'un-ch'ou" 春愁
chung-hsüeh 中學
Chung-hua hsin-pao 中華新報
Chung-hua Hsüeh-i She 中華學
　藝社
Chung-hua shu-chü 中華書局
Chung-kuo ch'ing-nien tang 中國
　青年黨
Chung Ying-mei 鍾應梅
chü-jen 舉人
"Chü-p'ao chih chiao-hsün" 巨砲
　之教訓
Ch'ü Yüan 屈原
chüeh-chü 絕句
Ch'ün-ching yün-p'u 羣經韻譜
Ch'ün-hsüeh i-yen 羣學肄言
Daini Kaiseikan 第二改盛館
Dazaifu 太宰府
fa-k'o chü-jen 法科舉人
Fan Shou-k'ang 范壽康
Fei Che-min 費哲民
"Fei-t'u sung" 匪徒頌
fen-she chung-hsüeh 分設中學
"Feng-huang nieh-p'an" 鳳凰涅
　槃
Fo-sheng 佛生
Fo-sun 佛孫
Fu 涪
Fukuda Tokuzō 福田德三
Fukuoka 福岡
Getsuin Shōja 月印精舍
Hai-shang ming-jen hua kao 海上名
　人書稿
haiku 俳句
Hakata Bay 博多灣
Hakka 客家
Hakozaki 箱崎
Han Yü 韓愈
Hangyakusha 反逆者
Hiroshima 廣島

Ho-ch'uan 合川
Ho Kung-kan 何公敢
Ho Kung-tu 何公度
Ho Lung 賀龍
Ho-sheng 和生
Ho Wei 何畏
Hōjō 北條
Hongō 本鄉
Hōyōkaku 抱洋閣
Hsi-hsiang chi 西廂記
Hsi-hu chia-hua 西湖佳話
Hsia-she 夏社
"Hsiang lei" 湘累
hsiao-hsüeh 小學
Hsiao-shuo yüeh-pao 小說月報
Hsieh Liu-i 謝六逸
Hsien-feng 咸豐
Hsien-tai 現代
Hsin ch'ing-nien 新青年
Hsin hsiao-shuo 新小說
Hsin-i 辛夷
Hsin-i chi 辛夷集
"Hsin-teng" 心燈
"Hsin-yüeh yü ch'ing-hai" 新月與晴海
"Hsin-yüeh yü pai-yün" 新月與白雲
hsing-tsou 行走
Hsiu-hsiang hsiao-shuo 繡像小說
hsiu-ts'ai 秀才
Hsiung K'o-wu 熊克武
Hsiung-nu 匈奴
Hsü Chih-mo 徐志摩
Hsü Shen 許慎
Hsü Tsu-cheng 徐祖正
"Hsüeh-chao" 雪朝
hsüeh-fei 學匪
Hsüeh-i ta-hsüeh 學藝大學
Hsüeh-teng 學燈
"Hu-chia shih-pa p'ai" 胡笳十八拍

Hua-yüeh hen 花月痕
Huang-Ch'ing ching-chieh 皇清經解
Huang Hsing 黃興
Huang Hui-ch'üan 黃恢權
Huang Jung 黃鎔
Huang Lu-yin 黃盧隱
Huang-p'ing chou 黃平州
Huang-p'u 黃浦
"Huang-p'u chiang k'ou" 黃浦江口
Hung-lou meng 紅樓夢
I-ch'ang 宜昌
I ching 易經
I-chou shuang-chi 藝舟雙楫
I-li 儀禮
I-pin 宜賓
I-p'in Hsiang 一品香
I Shu-hui 易曙煇
I Sou-yü 易漱瑜
Ichigaya 市谷
Jo-shui 若水
Juan Yüan 阮元
Jung-ch'ang 榮昌
Kagami-ga-ura 鏡ガ浦
Kameyama 龜山
Kanda 神田
K'ang Po-ch'ing 康白情
K'ang Yu-wei 康有為
Kao Meng-tan 高夢旦
Kao Ping 高楩
kao-teng hsiao-hsüeh 高等小學
kao-teng hsüeh-t'ang 高等學堂
Kasuga-maru 春日丸
Kawakami Hajime 河上肇
K'o I-ts'en 柯一岑
K'o Jung-chieh 柯榮階
Kōbun 宏文
Koishikawa 小石川
kōtō gakkō 高等學校

217

Kōtō shihan gakkō 高等師範學校

"Ku-chu chün chih erh tzu" 孤竹君之二子

Ku-chün 孤軍

"Ku-chün hsing" 孤軍行

Ku-chün She 孤軍社

Ku-liang chuan 穀梁傳

ku-wen 古文

Ku-wen kuan-chih 古文觀止

Ku-wen shang-shu shu-cheng 古文尚書疏證

"K'u-lou" 骷髏

"kuan Mei Jo" 關沫若

Kuan-O hsiang 觀嶽鄉

Kuang-hsü 光緒

Kuang Ming-fu 光明甫

Kuang-tung ta-hsüeh 廣東大學

Kuei Hsing-ku 桂馨谷

Kumamoto 熊本

Kung-hsüeh She 共學社

Kung Kung 共工

Kung-yang chuan 公羊傳

K'ung-tzu kai-chih k'ao 孔子改制考

Kuo Chao-hsiu 郭肇修

"Kuo-feng" 國風

Kuo Hsien-lin 郭賢林

Kuo K'ai-chen 郭開貞

Kuo K'ai-chen *nü-shih* 郭開貞女士

Kuo K'ai-ch'eng 郭開成

Kuo K'ai-tso 郭開佐

Kuo K'ai-wen 郭開文

Kuomintang 國民黨

Kuo Ming-hsing 郭鳴興

Kuo P'u 郭璞

Kuo Shao-yü 郭紹虞

Kuo-ts'ui hsüeh-pao 國粹學報

Kuo Tzu-i 郭子儀

Kuriyagawa Hakuson 厨川白村

Kyōbashi 京橋

Kyōun 杏雲

Lao-tzu 老子

Lei-feng t'a 雷峰塔

Li Feng-t'ing 李鳳亭

Li-hsüeh yüan 理學院

Li Pao-chia 李寶嘉

Li Po 李白

"Li-sao" 離騷

Li Shan-t'ing 李閃亭

Li Shih-ts'en 李石岑

"Li tsai ti-ch'iu pien shang fang-hao" 立在地球邊上放號

Liang Ch'i-ch'ao 梁啓超

Liang Shih-ch'iu 梁實秋

Liao P'ing 廖平

Lieh-tzu 列子

Lin Shu 林紓

Lin Tai-yü 林黛玉

Liu 劉

Liu-hua ch'i 流華溪

Liu-Jih hsüeh-sheng chiu-kuo t'uan 留日學生救國團

Liu K'ai-yüan 劉愷元

Liu K'o-chuang 劉克莊

"Liu-pieh Jih-pen" 留別日本

Liu Shu-lin 劉書林

Liu Tsung-yüan 柳宗元

Liu Tzu-t'ung 劉子通

Liu Yü-pin 劉虞賓

Lu-chou 瀘州

"Lu chung mei" 爐中煤

"Lu-ssu" 鷺鷥

Lü Tsu-ch'ien 呂祖謙

Ma-huo Lu 馬霍路

Ma Su 馬驌

Maeda Eun 前田慧雲

"Mang-mang yeh" 茫茫夜

Mao Tun 茅盾

Mei-jo 沫若

Mei-li Ch'uan 美麗川

Mei-shui 沫水

218

Mei Tse 梅賾
Meng Hao-jan 孟浩然
Miao 苗
Min 岷
Min-hou Nan Li 民厚南里
Min-hou Pei Li 民厚北里
Min-to 民鐸
Miyajima 宮島
Mo Lang-tzu 墨浪子
Mo Ti 墨翟
Moji 門司
Mu Hua 木華
Mu Mu-t'ien 穆木天
Nagasaki-maru 長崎丸
"Nan Shu fu-lao" 難蜀父老
Ni I-te 倪貽德
Nichiren 日蓮
Nieh Cheng 聶政
Nieh Ying 聶嫈
Ning-hua hsien 寧華縣
Nippon Yūsen Kaisha 日本郵船
會社
Niu-hua ch'i 牛華溪
Nü-shen 女神
"Nü-shen chih tsai-sheng" 女神之
再生
O-mei 峨眉
Okada Torajirō 岡田虎次郎
Okayama 岡山
Ōtsu 大津
Ōtsuka 大塚
Pan-sung Yüan 半淞園
"Pao erh yü Po-to wan" 抱兒浴
博多灣
Pao-lu t'ung-chih hui 保路同志會
Pao Shih-ch'en 包世臣
Pao T'ien-hsiao 包天笑
Pao-ting 保定
Pao Tung-li 鮑東里
Pi Jui-sheng 畢瑞生

Pi-suan shu-hsüeh 筆算數學
"Pieh-li" 別離
Ping-ch'en Hsüeh-she 丙辰學社
Po I 伯夷
Po-sheng 博生
Ritsurin Park 栗林公園
Saigyō 西行
San-kuo yen-i 三國演義
San tzu ching 三字經
Seisoku 正則
Sendai 仙臺
Sha-wan 沙灣
Shakai mondai kenkyū 社會問題研究
Shang 商
"Shang-hai yin-hsiang" 上海印象
Shang-shu chin ku wen chu-shu 尚書
今古文注疏
Shang-wu yin-shu kuan 商務印
書館
Shao-nien Chung-kuo hsüeh-hui
少年中國學會
She-hui tsu-chih yü she-hui ko-ming
社會組織與社會革命
She-pao 社報
Shen Huan-chang 沈煥章
Shen Sung-ch'üan 沈松泉
Shen Te-ch'ien 沈德潛
Shen Yen-ping 沈雁冰
Shen Yin-mo 沈尹默
Sheng Hsüan-huai 盛宣懷
Shih 史
Shih-chi 史記
Shih chien chieh-yao 史鑑節要
Shih ching 詩經
Shih-liu kuo ch'un-ch'iu 十六國春秋
Shih p'in 詩品
Shih-shih hsin-pao 時事新報
shih-yeh chiu-kuo 實業救國
Shikoku 四國
Shin-jo-en 新女苑

Shina 支那
Shu Ch'i 叔齊
Shu ching 書經
Shu-t'ung 蜀通
shu-yüan 書院
Shuai P'ing-chün 帥平均
Shui-hu chuan 水滸傳
Shuo-wen chieh-tzu 說文解字
Ssu-k'ung T'u 司空圖
Ssu-ma Ch'ien 司馬遷
Ssu-ma Hsiang-ju 司馬相如
"Ssu-ti yu-huo" 死的誘惑
Su Tung-p'o 蘇東坡
Su Wu 蘇武
Sun Chu 孫洙
Sun Hsiang-lin 孫項琳
Sun Hsing-yen 孫星衍
Sun Yat-sen 孫逸仙
Surugadai 駿河臺
Ta-chien-lu 打箭爐
ta-hsüeh 大學
Ta-ch'eng ch'i hsin lun 大乘起信論
Ta-tu 大渡
T'ai-p'ing Yang 太平洋
T'ai-tung t'u-shu-chü 泰東圖書局
Takamatsu 高松
T'an Yen-k'ai 譚延闓
T'ang shih cheng sheng 唐詩正聲
T'ang shih san-pai shou 唐詩三百首
T'ang Sung pa ta chia wen tu-pen
  唐宋八大家文讀本
tanka 短歌
tao 道
Tao-te ching 道德經
T'ao Ch'ien 陶潛
Te-fu Li 德福里
Teng Chün-wu 鄧均吾
"Ti-ch'iu, wo ti mu-ch'in" 地球，
  我的母親
Ti-ch'iu yün-yen 地球韻言

Ti-k'ao-wen 狄考文
T'ieh-tao hsüeh-t'ang 鐵道學堂
t'ien 天
T'ien Han 田漢
"T'ien-kou" 天狗
T'ien-yen lun 天演論
Ting P'ing-tzu 丁平子
T'ing-chou fu 汀州府
Tōkyō kōtō shihan gakkō 東京高
  等師範學校
"t'o-tou yü yao-ni" 拓都與么匿
Ts'ai Yen 蔡琰
Ts'ao-t'ang Ssu 草堂寺
Tso-chuan 左傳
Tso-chuan shih-wei 左傳事緯
Tsou Li-wen 鄒立文
Ts'ui Hung 崔鴻
Tsun-ching shu-yüan 尊經書院
Ts'un-ku Hsüeh-t'ang 存古學堂
Tu-chia ch'ang 杜家場
Tu Ching-chieh 杜靜皆
Tu Cho-chang 杜琢章
Tu Fu 杜甫
Tu K'ai-ch'eng 杜開誠
Tu Mu 杜牧
Tu Shao-shang 杜少裳
T'u Ch'iao 屠喬
T'u Mo 屠模
Tuan Ch'i-jui 段祺瑞
Tuan Fang 端方
Tuan Yü-ts'ai 段玉裁
Tung-fang tsa-chih 東方雜誌
Tung-lai Tso-shih po-i 東萊左氏
  博議
Tung-wen Hsüeh-t'ang 東文學堂
"T'ung hsün" 通訊
T'ung-meng Hui 同盟會
Tzu pu yü 子不語
Ueda Akinari 上田秋成
Ugetsu Monogatari 雨月物語

Wang Chao-jung 王兆榮

Wang-chih 王制

Wang Ching 王靖

Wang Fu-ch'üan 汪馥泉

Wang Kai 王槩

Wang K'ai-yün 王闓運

Wang Kuang-ch'i 王光祈

Wang Ling-chi 王陵基

Wang Ping-chi 王秉基

Wang Shih-fu 王實甫

Wang Wei 王維

Wang Wei-yen 王畏巖

Wang Yang-ming 王陽明

Wei Hsiu-jen 魏秀仁

Wei Ssu-luan 魏嗣鑾

Wen-hsüan 文選

Wen-hsüeh yen-chiu hui 文學研究會

Wen I-to 聞一多

Wen-pao 文豹

Whampoa 黃浦

Wu-ch'ang kao-teng shih-fan hsüeh-hsiao 武昌高等師範學校

Wu Ch'u-ts'ai 吳楚材

Wu Ming 吳明

Wu-pei Hsüeh-t'ang 武備學堂

Wu T'iao-hou 吳調侯

Wu Yung-ch'üan 吳永權

Ya-ho 雅河

Ya-tung t'u-shu kuan 亞東圖書館

Yang Cheng-yü 楊正宇

Yang Lang-sheng 楊朗生

Yang Tzu-lin 楊紫麟

Yano Fumio 矢野文雄

Yeh Sheng-t'ao 葉聖陶

Yen Fu 嚴復

Yen Jo-chü 閻若璩

Yin Ch'ang-heng 尹昌衡

Yin Ch'ao-chen 尹朝楨

Yin Chu-fu 尹柱夫

Yü 禹

Yü-ch'en tzu 雨塵子

Yü Hsin 庾信

Yü-p'i t'ung-chien chi-lan 御批通鑑輯覽

yüan 圓

Yüan Mei 袁枚

Yüan Shih-k'ai 袁世凱

Yüeh-wei ts'ao-t'ang pi-chi 閱微草堂筆記

yün ch'i wei 雲騎尉

zōhei-ka 造兵科

Index

INDEX

Fukuoka, Kuo Mo-jo in, 72–107, 113, 116–119, 121–124, 130, 158–170

Galsworthy, John, 104
Gambling, by Kuo Mo-jo, 28, 50
Garibaldi, Giuseppe, 31
General Political Department of Northern Expeditionary Army, 171
Geography, study of, 23, 25–26, 33, 51, 178n62
German (language), 102, 106, 162; Kuo Mo-jo's study of, 3, 62, 68–69
Germany, 75, 92–93, 95, 139, 149; medical education in, 62
Getsuin Shōja, 114
Ghost stories, 14–15
Globe in Rhyme, The. See *Ti-ch'iu yün-yen*
God, 135–136, 140. *See also* Absolute; Brahma; *Tao;* Ultimate reality
Goddesses, The (Nü-shen), 171; editing of, 111; fame from publication of, 116; anniversary of, 121; admired by Hsü Chih-mo, 126; quoted, 142–143
Goethe, Johann Wolfgang von, 3–4, 86, 88, 92, 162, 166; *Dichtung und Wahrheit,* 69–70; parts of *Faust* translated, 84–85, 93–94, 123; Kuo Mo-jo influenced by, 94–97, 146; translation of *The Sorrows of Young Werther,* 86, 115, 118, 134–142; *Wilhelm Meister,* 124; influence of replaced by Marx and Lenin, 139, 157
Golden age, China's, 103, 141, 147. *See also* Classless society; Ideal society; "Primitive communism"; Utopia
Goldsmith, Oliver, 92
"Good Morning" (Ch'en an): influenced by Whitman, 79; quoted, 98

Gorky, Maxim, 92
Grandfather, Kuo Mo-jo's: paternal, 8–9; maternal, 9–11
Grandmother, Kuo Mo-jo's maternal, 10
"Grapes of Wrath, The" (Ts'ang-nao ti p'u-t'ao), quoted, 152
Gray, Thomas, 92; "Elegy Written in a Country Churchyard" translated, 111
Great-grandfather, Kuo Mo-jo's. *See* Kuo Hsien-lin
Great-grandmother, Kuo Mo-jo's, 8
Great-uncle, Kuo Mo-jo's, 8
Green, 100
Grosse, Ernst, 129
Guilt feelings, Kuo Mo-jo's, 87, 156; over adolescent experiences, 21, 29; over first marriage, 45–46, 59; over seduction of Satō Tomiko, 65
Guyau, Jean-Marie, 129

Haggard, H. Rider, 30
Hai-nieh shih hsüan. See *Selection of Heine's Poetry, A*
Hai-shang ming-jen hua kao, 20–21
Haiku, 88
Hakata Bay, 72, 78, 122
Hakka, 7, 175n3, 175n4
Hakozaki (Fukuoka), 72, 74, 105
Hakozaki Shintō Shrine, 72, 74
Haldane, J. B. S., 48
Hamsun, Knut, 104
Han dynasty, 78, 123
Han Yü, 14, 92
Hangchow, 21, 108–109, 112, 129
Hankow, 40–42, 52
Hauptmann, Gerhart, 92, 104; *Der Ketzer von Soana* translated, 123
Heine, Heinrich, 69, 92; *A Selection of Heine's Poetry,* 71; Kuo Mo-jo's early poetry influenced by, 78
Hero worship, 37, 98–100, 139
Higher schools, Chinese (*kao-teng hsüeh-t'ang*). *See* Chengtu Higher School; Ts'un-ku Hsüeh-t'ang (Chengtu)

229

Kuriyagawa Hakuson, 92
Kwangtung, 132
Kwangtung University (Kuang-tung
ta-hsüeh), 132
Kweichow, 9–10
Kweiyang, 10
Kyōbashi (Tokyo), 63
Kyoto, 100–101, 113–114, 143
Kyoto Imperial University, 104,
113–114, 143
Kyōun Hospital (Tokyo), 114–115
Kyushu, 72–73, 105
Kyushu Imperial University: Kuo
Mo-jo in medical school of, 32,
71–105, 116–119, 121–123, 128,
164; in physiology department
of, 162–163

Lamb, Charles and Mary, 30–31
Lamp of Learning. See *Hsüeh-teng*
"Lamp of the Mind, The" (Hsin-
teng), 79
Lao-tzu, 92, 98. See also *Tao-te
ching*
Latin (language), Kuo Mo-jo's
study of, 62
Lavater, Johann Kasper, 92
Law, 21, 39, 53, 105, 108, 120, 131
Lei-feng t'a (Thunder peak pagoda;
Hangchow), 109
Lenin, 4, 159; Kuo Mo-jo's
admiration for, 80–81, 98, 142,
149, 157; in Kuo Mo-jo's writings,
98–99, 157; Kuo Mo-jo a convert
to theories of, 168–170. See also
Marxism-Leninism
Leninist theory of imperialism,
145, 147
"Lesson of the Cannons, The"
(Chü-p'ao chih chiao-hsün):
influenced by Whitman, 79;
contents described, 98–99; quoted,
99
Lewis, Matthew Gregory, 74
Li chi (Book of rites), 23
Li Chieh-jen, 36, 103
Li Feng-t'ing, 105, 108, 116
Li Pao-chia, 19

Li Po, 14, 88, 92
"Li-sao" (Ch'ü Yüan), 88
Li Shan-t'ing, 113–114, 143–144,
158
Li Shih-ts'en, 92–93, 105, 108, 112,
115
"Li shih-yeh ti yu-jen." *See* "To
Encourage My Friends the
Unemployed"
"Li ti chui-ch'iu-che." *See* "Seeker
after Strength, A"
"Li tsai ti-ch'iu pien shang
fang-hao." *See* "Shouting on
the Rim of the World"
Liang Ch'i-ch'ao, 18, 31, 37
Liang Shih-ch'iu, 124, 128
Liao P'ing, 3, 23–24, 29, 147
Liberal arts, 57, 84, 103
Liberalism, 131–132
Lieh-tzu, 32
"Lien-yü." *See* "Purgatory"
Liliencron, Detlev von, 92
Lin Shu, 30
Lin Tai-yü, 181n91
Literary criticism, Chinese, 14, 78
Literary Research Society
(Wen-hsüeh yen-chiu hui),
111–112, 115, 118, 121
Liu-hua ch'i (Szechwan), 16, 23.
See also Niu-hua ch'i
Liu-Jih Hsüeh-sheng Chiu-kuo
T'uan. *See* Corps of Chinese
Students in Japan for National
Salvation
Liu K'ai-yüan, 100
Liu K'o-chuang, 178n50
"Liu-pieh Jih-pen." *See* "Farewell
to Japan"
Liu Shu-lin, 23, 25
Liu Tsung-yüan, 14
Liu Tzu-t'ung, 38
Liu Yü-pin, 19–20
Living accommodations, Kuo
Mo-jo's: in Fukuoka, 72, 74, 105,
130, 164–165; in Shanghai,
109–110, 119, 124, 126
Lo Hsiang-lin, 175n3
Lo Tun-wei, 110

INDEX

Lo-yeh. See *Fallen Leaves*
Longfellow, Henry Wadsworth, 67
Love, gospel of, 68, 86, 98, 136, 155
Lovejoy, Arthur O., 137
Lu-chou (Szechwan), 49
"Lu chung mei." See "Coal in the Grate"
"Lu-ssu." See "Egret"
Lü Tsu-ch'ien, 16
"Lumpen-proletariat," 146
Luther, Martin, 81
Lyricism, 90–91

Ma-huo Lu (Shanghai), 110, 116, 119, 124
Ma Su, 36
Maeda Eun, 92
Maeterlinck, Maurice, 92
Magnolia. See *Hsin-i* and *Hsin-i chi*
Malthus, Thomas Robert, 92
Manchuria, 70
Manchus, 31, 37, 43, 169
"Mang-mang yeh." See "Endless Night"
"Manifesto of the All-China Arts Association" (Chung-hua ch'üan-kuo i-shu hsieh-hui hsüan-yen), 154–155
Mao Tun. See Shen Yen-ping
Maps, 175n1, 175n3, 177n31, 179n68, 181n2, 181n4, 190n15
Mariana, 169
Markelov, 168–169
Marriages: Kuo Mo-jo's first, 44–46, 59, 64–65; Kuo Mo-jo's common-law, 63–65, 86; between Chinese and foreigners, 70–71; Kuo Mo-jo on, 86
Marx, Karl, 4, 92; Kuo Mo-jo's admiration for, 80–81, 98, 142, 149, 157, 159; Goethe compared with, 139
Marxism, Kuo Mo-jo's conversion to, 48, 97–98, 103, 113, 133, 139–171. *See also* Communism; Marxism-Leninism; Leninist theory of imperialism

Marxism-Leninism, Kuo Mo-jo's conversion to, 2, 4–5, 82, 97–99, 107, 133, 139–171. *See also* Communism; Marxism; Leninist theory of imperialism
Masturbation, 21
Materialism, 141, 144, 149, 155
Mathematics, 15, 23, 26, 35, 37, 57
Maturin, Charles Robert, 74
Maupassant, Guy de, 104
May Fourth Movement, 3, 75–77, 80–81, 94, 111
May Thirtieth Movement, 171
Mazzini, Giuseppe, 31
Medical schools, Chinese. See Army Medical School
Medical schools, Japanese. See Ichigaya Women's Medical School; Kyushu Imperial University Medical School
Medicine, modern: Kuo Mo-jo's attitude toward, 48, 53, 57, 84, 93, 103–104, 127–128, 130–131
Medicine, traditional Chinese, 9, 31–32
Mei-jo (Kuo Mo-jo's pen name), 78–79, 190n18
Mei River (Mei-shui; Szechwan), 78–79
Mei Tse, 26
Memorization, 12–13, 15, 66–67, 84
Mencius, 92
Meng Hao-jan, 14
Metaphysics, 138, 149
Miao tribes, 9–10
Michelangelo, 92
Middle schools (*chung-hsüeh*). *See* Annexed Middle School; Chengtu Prefectural Middle School; Chia-ting middle school
Military academies. See Wu-pei Hsüeh-t'ang; Whampoa Military Academy
Militia, local, 9–10, 42
Millet, Jean Francois, 79, 92
Milton, John, 88, 92
Min-hou Nan Li (Shanghai), 119–120, 122–124, 126, 157

234

Phonology, 16–17
Physical education, 19, 21, 23
Physiology, 162–163, 167
Pi Jui-sheng, 117
Pi-suan shu-hsüeh, 15–16
"Pieh-li." *See* "Parting"
Ping-ch'en Hsüeh-she. See *1916*
Society
Plutarch, 18, 27
Po I, 146. *See also* "Two Princes
of Ku-chu, The"
Po-sheng (Kuo Mo-jo's second son),
84, 86, 104. *See also* Children
of Kuo Mo-jo
Poetry: Kuo Mo-jo's, 1, 3, 59, 62,
67, 77–85, 89, 93, 98–101, 106,
109, 111, 116, 120–124, 126, 138,
142–143, 146, 150–153, 171; Kuo
Mo-jo on, 65–69, 78, 87–95, 136,
141–142; embryology of, 91
Political parties. *See* Chinese
Communist Party; Chinese
Youth Party; Kuomintang;
Political Science Clique
Political Science Clique (Cheng-
hsüeh hsi), 108, 124, 128
Political thought, Kuo Mo-jo's,
119–120, 139–171
"Pompeii of Chinese Intellectual
History, The" (Wo-kuo ssu-hsiang
shih shang chih P'eng-p'ai
ch'eng), 102–103
"Preface to *The Sorrows of Young
Werther,* A" (*Shao-nien Wei-t'e
chih fan-nao* hsü-yin), 134,
135–142
Premedical education, Japanese,
57, 62, 68–69, 84
Preparatory class, First Higher
School (Tokyo), 57–59, 65, 72–73
Primary schools (hsiao-hsüeh),
17, 19. *See also* Chia-ting
upper-level primary school
"Primitive communism," 103, 141,
146–147. *See also* Classless
society; Golden age; Ideal society;
Utopia

Primitive man, 90, 136, 141–142,
155. *See also* Peasants; People;
Proletariat
Private property, system of, 97–98,
102, 141, 143, 154–155
Progress, 3, 24, 47–48, 82, 149
Proletarian literature, 19, 148
Proletariat, 19, 99–100, 142–144,
148, 150, 155. *See also* Peasants;
People; Primitive man
Prometheus, 122, 199n43
Propaganda, 1, 31, 37; Kuo Mo-jo
on, 154–155, 165, 168, 170
Prose poetry, 67, 90
Prosody, traditional Chinese, 14,
67, 76
Provincial Assembly, Szechwan, 42
Publishers. *See* China Book
Company; Commercial Press;
Oriental Book Company;
T'ai-tung Book Company
Punish the Traitors Club (Chu
han-chien hui), 70
Pure Light (Chieh-kuang), 162. See
also *Fallen Leaves*
"Purgatory" (Lien-yü), 156
Pusan, 55

Quietude, 135, 140. *See also*
Tranquility

Railroad Academy (T'ieh-tao
hsüeh-t'ang), 38
Railroads, 38–42
Railway Protection Club (Pao-lu
t'ung-chih hui), 40–42
"Railway Protection" movement,
39–42
Reason, 89, 135, 138–140, 159
"Rebirth of the Goddesses, The"
(Nü-shen chih tsai-sheng), 96–97
"Rebuttal to the Elders of Shu."
See "Nan Shu fu-lao"
Records of the Grand Historian.
See *Shih-chi*
Red Cross Hospital (Chungking),
127–128, 130–131
Reform movement of *1898,* 15, 31

INDEX

INDEX

Harvard East Asian Series